The humanities and the Irish university

MANCHESTER
1824

Manchester University Press

The humanities and the Irish university

Anomalies and opportunities

Michael O'Sullivan

Manchester University Press

Manchester and New York

distributed in the United States exclusively by Palgrave Macmillan

The right of Michael O'Sullivan to be identified as the author of this work has been asserted by him in accordance with the Copyright, Designs and Patents Act 1988.

Published by Manchester University Press
Oxford Road, Manchester M13 9NR, UK
and Room 400, 175 Fifth Avenue, New York, NY 10010, USA
www.manchesteruniversitypress.co.uk

Distributed in the United States exclusively by
Palgrave Macmillan, 175 Fifth Avenue, New York,
NY 10010, USA

Distributed in Canada exclusively by
UBC Press, University of British Columbia, 2029 West Mall,
Vancouver, BC, Canada V6T 1Z2

British Library Cataloguing-in-Publication Data
A catalogue record for this book is available from the British Library

Library of Congress Cataloging-in-Publication Data applied for

ISBN 978 0 7190 8873 5 hardback

First published 2014

The publisher has no responsibility for the persistence or accuracy of URLs for any external or third-party internet websites referred to in this book, and does not guarantee that any content on such websites is, or will remain, accurate or appropriate.

Typeset
by SPi Publisher Services, Pondicherry, India
Printed in Great Britain
by CPI Antony Rowe Ltd, Chippenham, Wiltshire

Contents

Acknowledgements

I wish to thank the Faculty of Arts and the Research Institute for the Humanities of the Chinese University of Hong Kong for granting me a research fellowship to pursue research for this book. I thank the Department of English of the Chinese University of Hong Kong, and in particular, Simon Haines, Chair of English there, for granting me occasional research leave during the writing up of the different chapters. I thank the following friends, colleagues and educationalists for sharing their expertise and insights on the humanities and education in our conversations over the last number of years: Tim Kelleher, Cian O'Sullivan, Tomás Mulcahy, Billy Ramsell, Francis O'Sullivan, Graham Allen, Roy Sellars, Eddie Tay, Julian Lamb, Matthew DeCoursey, Grant Hamilton, David Huddart, Longxi Zhang, Yangsheng Guo, Li Ou, Leo Ou-Fan Lee, David Parker, Ve-Yin Tee, Elizabeth Richards, Jason Gleckman, Daniel Short, James Carney, Pádraig Kirwan, Peter Crisp, James P. Byrne, Nancy Bourques and Leonard Madden. Thanks also to Tony Mason and Ms. Uma Shankar. Irene has been a constant support throughout the project, and my parents, Mary and Jeremiah, have always kept me in touch with the real value of enquiry and education. This book is dedicated to Irene and to my parents, Jeremiah and Mary.

Preface

The largest university body in Ireland is the National University of Ireland (NUI). However, pinning down the precise dimensions of the word 'National' in its title is fraught with the same difficulties that accompany any assessment of Ireland's emergence into, and evolution within, nation-state identity. According to the Universities Act of 1997, the title the '"National University of Ireland" refers to the university by that name in Dublin, constituted and founded by charter in pursuance of the Irish Universities Act, 1908'.[1] However, this was a designation of 'National' that was drawn up, passed into law and disseminated by Edward VII's Parliament. If we have learned anything from the relatively recent 'turn' to the postcolonial in Irish Studies, it is that such externally assigned markers of national identity must be deconstructed and re-imagined by the newly emergent postcolonial states. The Senate of the NUI defines the institution as a 'federal university comprising the largest element of the Irish university system at the present time'. The obvious 'element' that is not incorporated into this body is the University of Dublin with its single constituent college, Trinity College. The 'National University of Ireland', which was first created in the 1908 Act, was ultimately 'redefined' by the 1997 Universities Act. The other universities in the Republic of Ireland are the University of Limerick and Dublin City University and both were established as universities in 1989. Since this book examines the emergence of a humanities ethos in Ireland in the period from Newman to Bologna, it will chiefly focus on the NUI.

Perhaps the biggest change brought about by the 1997 Universities Act was that the three 'constituent colleges' became 'constituent universities' with, despite the federal arrangement, a greater degree of autonomy through governing bodies and academic councils. Officially, then, Ireland had only two universities until 1989: the National University with its four large colleges and the University of Dublin. However, this system of nomenclature was made even more complex by the fact that each of the four 'constituent colleges' of the National University had the title 'University College' at least until 1997. The NUI currently comprises four constituent universities, five recognized colleges and one college of a constituent university. The two acts have therefore sought to construct educational institutions around the political tensions and divisions the island of Ireland experienced both before and after independence and before and after the Troubles. The loose confederacy of institutions under the NUI banner has always had to define itself against those universities on the island that were more independent, namely, Queen's University[2] Belfast and Trinity College Dublin.

The institutional history and structure of the National University mirrors the traumatic political history of the island of Ireland since the nineteenth century. In examining how the humanities subjects – those subjects in a university curriculum that speak most profoundly for how a people employ and understand notions of identity – have been structured and organized, one is always running up against this history. However, it is these same humanities subjects that also enable a people to realize that identity is not only history; it is aspiration, both imagined and reasoned, and it is, for many, grounded on spiritual and ethical enquiry. This book argues that the examination and practice of the humanities in the Irish universities was constrained by political realities that necessitated that the institutions of learning follow dictates laid down before independence was gained. Because it was painful and politically divisive to implement policy at university level to address the implications for education of the religion and language questions, successive governments were slow to tamper with the university system in place.

Brief histories of the universities that are key to the discussion that follows

The names Trinity College Dublin and University of Dublin are regarded as synonymous for practical purposes. Trinity College achieved its charter in 1592. Until well into the nineteenth century, it was generally regarded as the university of the Protestant ascendancy. The Catholic Relief Act of 1793 finally opened Trinity's doors to catholics and dissenters. The sacramental test and other oaths were removed, and the act stated that 'it shall be lawful for papists' to take degrees 'without taking and subscribing the oaths of allegiance, supremacy, or adjuration' (in Parkes, 2010:541).[3] However, even though general religious tests were abolished in 1873, catholics were slow to attend.[4] Trinity College was largely unaffected by the Universities Acts of 1908 and 1997. It remains outside the NUI confederacy, and many of the principal clauses of the 1997 Act relating to university governance do not apply to Trinity College (the Act makes clear that 'Sections 16(1) to (7), 21(6), 22, 23, 32 and 33 shall not apply to or in relation to Trinity College' – Section 16 (1) to (7) relates to the structure of a university's governing authority).[5] As the NUI has educated the majority of students in the humanities in Ireland since independence and as Trinity College is often regarded as following an Oxbridge model (J. J. Lee refers to it as their 'silent sister'), a model whose structure is well researched, this book focuses on the humanities in the National University. In saying this, Trinity College will be referred to frequently as an example of an Irish university that has a more traditional humanities structure.

The Irish Universities Association's *Irish Universities Study* of 2009 reveals that there were 92,668 undergraduate and taught postgraduate students in the Irish higher education system in 2009 and that 84,248 of these attended the seven universities. There were 16,807 students enrolled in Trinity College for the 2009/10 academic year.[6] This represents approximately 18% of the total number of students in higher education in universities in Ireland in that year. Trinity College has three faculties: a Faculty of Arts, Humanities and Social Sciences; a Faculty of Engineering, Mathematics and Science; and a Faculty of Health Sciences. The Faculty of Arts, Humanities and Social

Sciences includes Schools of Business Drama, Film and Music Education English Histories and Humanities Languages, Literatures and Cultural Studies Law Linguistics, Speech and Communication Studies Psychology Social Sciences and Philosophy Social Work and Social Policy and Religions Theology and Ecumenics. It is noteworthy that the School of Histories and Humanities includes the Departments of Classics, History and History of Art as well as the Centre for Gender and Women's Studies. Whether Trinity regards the humanities as finding its core ethos in these disciplines is unclear; however, the humanities, as we will see in reading Newman, Bourdieu and others in later chapters, are frequently regarded as being grounded in the study of Classics. One notable feature of Trinity College's humanities curriculum is the Irish School of Ecumenics, a 'postgraduate institute' that was established in 1970.

University College Dublin (UCD) is the largest university in Ireland. For the 2010/11 academic year, it had 24,625 students enrolled. This represents approximately 26% of the total university student body in Ireland. The university was established in 1854, and John Henry Newman was its first rector. The university website informs us that his 'classic work' *The Idea of a University* is 'a source of inspiration for UCD's current educational philosophy'.[7] Given that Newman privileged the place and role of the humanities subjects in the university curriculum, chapter 2 will examine how the structure of the humanities in the National University departed from Newman's model. UCD was originally known as the Catholic University and later as the Royal University. The Catholic University was renamed University College Dublin in 1882, and in 1883, it was placed under the management of the Society of Jesus. In 1908, it became a constituent college of the NUI. With the 1997 Universities Act, UCD became an 'autonomous university within the loose federal structure of the NUI'. UCD has colleges instead of faculties. There is no Faculty or College of Humanities. The College of Arts and Celtic Studies includes Schools of Archaeology; Art History and Cultural Policy; Classics; English, Drama and Film; History and Archives; Languages and Literatures; Irish, Celtic Studies, Irish Folklore and Linguistics; and Music. Other subjects that might be regarded as humanities subjects, subjects Newman would have included in his humanities curriculum, are found in the College of Human Sciences. This college includes Schools of Philosophy, Psychology and Sociology. There is no School of Divinity, Religious Studies or Comparative Religion. In 2002, the Humanities Institute of Ireland was established at UCD. It is open only to graduate students, and it has an intake of approximately thirty to forty students each year. It strives to showcase 'UCD's expertise and scholarship in the humanities to develop international distinction that enhances the vitality and richness of Ireland's cultural and intellectual experience'.[8]

University College Cork (UCC) was established in 1845 as one of the Queen's Colleges, but it did not open its doors to its first 115 students until 1849. The first president of the college, the industrial scientist Sir Robert Kane, 'passionately defended the "mixed education" non-denominational principle against the charge of "godlessness", emphasizing the built-in provisions for respecting religious beliefs and even for promoting religious practice'.[9] However, once the college was incorporated into the National University through the Irish Universities Act of 1908, any such 'built-in provisions for respecting religious beliefs' could not extend to including religious subjects on the university curriculum. The 1997 Universities Act made UCC a 'constituent university' of the NUI. This led to a 'transfer of powers' from the NUI to UCC in such areas as 'staff appointments, programme approval, conduct of examinations, and internal reorganization of universities (e.g. governing authorities)'.[10] This transfer of powers had an immediate effect and led to an opening up of the curriculum with subjects such as History of Art, Chinese Studies and Study of Religions being offered for the first time in the curriculum in 2001, 2007 and 2008, respectively. The student population for 2010/11 was 18,820 with almost 6,000 of these studying in the Faculty of Arts, Celtic Studies and Social Sciences.

National University of Ireland, Galway (NUI Galway), or University College Galway (UCG), was also established in 1845 as a Queen's College. The Queen's University Charter of 1850 provided that the Senate should have 'power to confer upon the students of the Queen's Colleges of Belfast, Cork and Galway such degrees and distinctions in the faculties of Arts, Law and Physics as are granted in other colleges of Great Britain and Ireland'.[11] The University Education (Ireland) Act, 1879, founded the Royal University and dissolved the Queen's University in 1882. UCG was also made a 'constituent college' of the NUI by the Irish Universities Act of 1908. UCG also has colleges instead of faculties. Its College of Arts, Social Sciences and Celtic Studies includes Schools of Political Science and Sociology, Psychology, Education, Geography and Archaeology, Humanities; Language, Literatures and Cultures, and Acadamh na hOllscolaíochta Gaeilge. The School of Humanities includes Departments of English, History, Film and Digital Media, Irish Studies, Journalism, Old and Middle Irish and Philosophy. Unlike Trinity, its Department of Classics is not in the School of Humanities but in the School of Languages, Literatures and Cultures. It does not have a Department of Religious Studies, Divinity, Theology or Comparative Religion.

National University of Ireland, Maynooth (NUI, Maynooth), emerged from a national seminary for the training of Catholic priests that was established in 1795 as St. Patrick's College, Maynooth. Theology and philosophy were the principal subjects, but languages, mathematics, classics and science were later added. It received its charter as a Pontifical University in 1896. The trustees of Maynooth applied for recognition of the College's non-theological courses in 1909 after the Irish Universities Act was passed in 1908. The following year, 1910, St. Patrick's College, Maynooth, became a Recognized College of the National University, with Faculties of Arts, Philosophy and Celtic Studies. The Faculty of Theology remained in 'splendid isolation' (Corish, 1995:264). Lay students were admitted in 1966. The constituent university of the National University at Maynooth offers degrees in many Arts subjects, including English, History and Philosophy, Politics and Economics. Its Faculty of Arts, Celtic Studies and Philosophy includes Departments and Schools of Ancient Classics, Celtic Studies, English, Media and Theatre Studies, History, Modern Languages, Literatures and Cultures, Music and Philosophy. The Department of Philosophy offers first year and third year courses on the philosophy of religion. There is no Department of Religious Studies, Divinity or Comparative Religion, and the historical roots lie in the fact that it was initially incorporated into the National University on the basis of its non-theological courses. Maynooth has long appealed to the Senate of the NUI to have the teaching of theology integrated into the Arts courses of the National University.

Notes

1 See www.irishstatutebook.ie/1997/en/act/pub/0024/index.html.
2 Founded by royal charter together with Queen's College Cork and Queen's College
   Galway in 1845 as one of the Queen's Colleges, Queen's University Belfast was
   granted 'autonomy' by the Irish Universities Act of 1908 and became an 'independent institution'. In being a UK institution that was never governed by the National
   University confederacy, it did not experience the same constraints in regard to the
   teaching of religion and theology. It has long offered courses in theology.
3 See Susan M. Parkes 'Higher Education, 1793–1908' in *A New History of Ireland
   VI: Ireland Under the Union 1870–1921*, pp. 539–70.
4 R. B. McDowell and D. A. Webb note in *Trinity College Dublin 1592–1952* that
   '[u]p to 1900 the proportion of Catholic entrants varied only between 5 per cent
   and 10 per cent but a rise then began, which carried the number up to well over
   20 per cent in the years from 1923 to 1930. The thirties, however, showed a sudden
   and most mysterious decline, the entry in two years in the middle of the decade
   falling as low as 8 per cent. Recovery began in 1938 and continued without inter-
   ruption, until by 1950 the figure once more stood at 23 per cent' (1982:504).
5 See www.irishstatutebook.ie/1997/en/act/pub/0024/index.html.
6 See www.tcd.ie.
7 www.ucd.ie.
8 *Ibid.*
9 www.ucc.ie.
10 See www.ucc.ie.
11 See www.nui.ie.

1

Introduction: defining the humanities

The phrase the 'crisis in the humanities' has been appearing in American academic circles at the very least since the founding of the Irish state in 1922. In that year, art historian Josef Strzygowski lectured in Boston on 'The Crisis in the Humanities as Exemplified in the History of Art', the same year James Joyce published *Ulysses* and changed the literary landscape of the humanities in Ireland forever (Bell, 2010:69). The humanities is, of course, a recognized disciplinary and institutional field in the Irish university system, but the humanities in the Irish context has not received anything like the critical interrogation or scholarly attention that the humanities enjoys in the American and British university systems.[1] This is despite the fact that Irish writers form an integral part of the literature curricula in these universities' humanities divisions and despite the fact that the mission statement for a modern education in the humanities had perhaps its most eloquent expression in John Henry Newman's founding series of talks for the Irish Catholic University. University College Dublin (UCD), Ireland's largest university, was established 'in direct succession from' Newman's Catholic University, and it regards Newman as its 'founder' (McCartney, 1999:145). On the centenary of Newman's university in 1954, Michael Tierney, the then president of UCD, described UCD as 'the harvest of Newman's sowing' (1955:146). However, despite this illustrious beginning, the nature and history of the humanities in the Irish university remains something of a mystery. Since speculation on the state of the university in general is very often sparked by reflection on the humanities subjects, there have been wider consequences. J. J. Lee argues that when the National University was founded in 1908, the 'same deficiencies that ensured so little thought about Irish society in the universities themselves ensured equally little thought about universities in that society'; he argues that the 'basic questions' 'remained not only unanswered, but largely unasked, at least until the 1950s' with the result that the 'higher education system is not in any real sense a system. It is bits and pieces of what might have been a system had the basic thinking been done in time' (1989:621). In 1983, on the seventy-fifth anniversary of the Irish Universities Act, John Coolahan makes a similar point in writing that the 1908 University Act 'left Ireland with three universities, each representing a different model. The University of Dublin had been modeled on the medieval Oxbridge tradition. Queen's Belfast, could be seen as representing the modern non-residential, non-denominational university, while the National University was designed on the federal plan' (1983:8). Despite government proposals to bring in new university legislation in 1968 and 1974, the 1908 Act was only revised in 1997.

Two of the key factors for the humanities subjects in the Irish university were the language and religion questions. Because the Irish education system at large and the early National University system struggled to find a place for religious enquiry and had to contend with a hostility towards the language of instruction by many leading educationalists, it is undeniable that key theological, philosophical and linguistic components of a general humanities education were omitted from the early humanities programmes in the National University. Since the foundations of any university system are important for what follows, this book argues that the humanities ethos in the Irish university in twentieth-century Ireland was slow to reflect on its educational scope and practices precisely because it was so painful to confront the residual political dimension of any institutional or philosophical change in regard to language and religion. As the century progressed, it was far easier to embrace new humanities and humanistic discourses such as the postcolonial and the post-structural – because these went against empire or gave the impression of cutting-edge research – than to confront key contradictions in educational policy and somewhat anomalous restrictions on practice and curricula in the humanities in the Irish university. This book will, therefore, examine some of the implications of these factors for a general humanities ethos as it was conceived in the Irish university and as it compares with the university education in the humanities subjects envisaged by writers and thinkers such as Immanuel Kant, John Henry Newman, Pádraig Pearse, Jacques Derrida and others.

Even though the focus of the book will be the National University because of the unique restrictions and conflicts at the heart of its humanities programmes, any such study is for many commentators by corollary a study of the influence of Trinity College on university life in Ireland. Following the second Presidents' and Bishops' Liaison Committee in 1952, Michael Tierney, the then president of UCD, sent a summary of what had been agreed at the committee meeting to the Archbishop of Armagh. He notes that 'the National University, historically speaking, owes its origin to the insistence of Trinity College on its exclusively Protestant character' (McCartney, 1999:190). R. F. Foster also describes the early Trinity College, a university that had

already established James Ussher as its first Professor of Divinity in 1607, as
the 'intellectual foundation' of the Church of Ireland (1989:49). Trinity College Dublin (TCD) was also largely unaffected by the 1908 Act which, I
argue, was responsible for many of the anomalies in Irish humanities education throughout the century. However, the response to the 1908 Act was often
fuelled by a sense that the resulting institution came up short when compared
to what Trinity already offered the Protestant community. The subsequent
'life' of the National University, as embodied by its largest institution UCD,
was also often measured against the performance of its illustrious neighbour,
Trinity. The protracted debate on the failed merger between TCD and UCD,
sparked by the establishment of the Commission on Higher Education in 1960
and only finally fizzling out in 1978 when UCD reluctantly accepted that
business studies and social studies should be taught at both TCD and UCD,
was in essence a debate that was 'on and off the agenda since Gladstone's
University Bill of 1873' (McCartney, 1999:343). Despite all the accusations
and recriminations, these two sectarian institutions made similar claims for
their Irish credentials. Hume Dudgeon, the then provost of Trinity College,
wrote to Tierney in 1953 reiterating that Trinity was an 'Irish institution' with
an 'Irish atmosphere' (McCartney, 1999:313), and the next year, Tierney
argued that UCD was 'one of Ireland's largest windows on the world'
(1955:147). These competing perspectives on Irishness from the Irish ivory
towers played out academically and in microcosm those recalcitrant sectarian
cues that would shape the state's future. Trinity loomed large in the background for the National University both as a template for how a modern
university should be structured and as a reminder of what the Oxbridge
tradition – a tradition it silently revered – embodied. Many Irish educationalists throughout the century such as Pearse and Hyde regarded the education
system in Ireland that Trinity epitomized as 'alien' and they called for the
education system to be 'intellectually nationalized' (in Kearney, 1987e:11).[2]
The different structure of Trinity College is therefore a constant benchmark
for this study even if it is at times a silent witness to the book's focus on the
humanities in the National University.

    Chapters 2 and 3 examine the history and development of the humanities in
the Irish university, focusing on key debates, constitutional questions and proposals on university education policy in Ireland that produced a somewhat
anomalous situation for the humanities for much of the twentieth century. The
work of Newman, the debate surrounding the 1908 University Act, and the
educational ideas of Pádraig Pearse will be central to this discussion. Chapter
4 examines how key critical and cultural movements in the humanities subjects (focusing on perspectives from literary studies, philosophy and history)[3]
in the Irish university system have served to address some of these constitutional anomalies in the Irish education system. It explores the nature of the

humanities in the Irish context since the 1930s by reading the work of leading international literary critics, cultural theorists, historians and philosophers who have described most clearly the cultural and political context of the humanities subjects they have studied and taught on in the Irish university. Chapters 5 and 6 contrast the humanities ethos in Ireland with leading cultural theorists' descriptions of the humanities programmes in other university systems, such as those in the UK, France, the United States and Asia. Chapter 6 also examines the opportunities that have arisen in the humanities in Ireland since the 1990s through the foundation of such research bodies as the IRCHSS.

At the outset, it is also important to acknowledge the rich educational heritage of the island of Ireland. Douglas Hyde's impassioned words of 1901 argue that 'during the sixth, seventh, eighth, and perhaps ninth centuries Ireland had caught and held aloft the torch of learning in the lampadia of mankind, and procured for herself the honourable title of the island of saints and scholars' (1901:214). Writing much later, Olaf Pedersen is less exuberant in noting that the 'influence of Irish monastic learning on England came to be very important for the development of culture in Europe' (1997:45). John Finnis reminds us that when Thomas Aquinas studied at the University of Naples, it was an 'Irish professor' who taught him Aristotle (1998:4), and Umberto Eco argues that the first 'allusion' to what he calls the 'dream of a perfect language' (1997:1) appears in an attempt made 'on the part of Irish grammarians, to defend spoken Gaelic over learned Latin'. He points to the Gaelic work *Auraicept na nÉces* that, in discussing the Tower of Babel, makes the argument that 'the Gaelic language constituted the first and only instance of a language that overcame the confusion of tongues' (1997:16). Given this rich heritage in learning, it is important that the subjects that pass on the spirit of these early schools, today's humanities subjects, be examined in the Irish context.

In a light-hearted article 'Crisis, What Crisis? Rhetoric and Reality in Higher Education', Malcolm Tight explains in 1994 that a 'crisis' culture has developed in post-war literature on higher education (1994:363–74). He lists ten books on British higher education and twenty books on American higher education that have crisis in the title that appeared between 1946 and 1994. However, rhetoric or no rhetoric, this clearly demonstrates that higher education and the humanities are under the spotlight in these countries in a way that is lacking in Ireland. Because the humanities is a branch of learning that evolves through self-questioning, such self-examination in terms of crisis is a vital part of its make-up. Geoffrey Galt Harpham has suggested that the 'humanities flourish in flux, the extreme form of which is crisis. Humanists should understand their work, not as a set of professional practices unfortunately afflicted with crises, but as part of the way we think of and in crisis' (2011:190). Louis Menand has also described this crisis in the humanities as a 'crisis of rationale' (in Harpham, 2011:22). This might lead one to believe that the Irish, in being quite adept at surviving crises, would have a privileged perspective on this vision of the humanities as the thinking of crisis. However, the way a community or a people survives and contemplates crisis is perhaps the most revealing marker of identity. Harpham's equating of the humanities with crisis thinking itself may only lead to further questions about different kinds of 'moral citizenship', 'national will' (2011:168) and 'national self-understanding' (2011:147). This book will explore some reasons why the humanities have received relatively little attention in the Irish context and why the Irish experience and contemplation of crisis has been somewhat removed from the philosophy of the humanities in the Irish university.

Before I go any further, it will be helpful to devise a working definition of the humanities. There are four perspectives on the humanities that I wish to outline briefly here so that they will underpin the discussion of the humanities in the Irish context that follows. The earliest of these is one that has recently been re-examined by Anthony Grafton and Lisa Jardine. Grafton and Jardine emphasize pedagogy, and in particular the pedagogical revolution inspired by the French humanist Petrus Ramus in the sixteenth century, in evaluating how the humanities emerged from humanism. They argue that in tracing the humanities back to Renaissance humanism, it is possible to point to a moment when humanism gave way to a modern notion of humanities. For Grafton and Jardine, the modern notion of the humanities was born when pedagogy in the Renaissance moved away from an 'emphasis' on 'formal logic and the Theology Faculty towards Agricolan dialectic and eloquence' (1986:163). What was known as the 'new philosophy' of the school of Agricola and Erasmus now makes *utility* its main criterion for success: 'utility being taken to mean, productive of the kind of competence which will make an individual a responsible, moral and active member of the civic community' (1986:163–4).[4] The pedagogue whom they credit with inciting this transformation is the sixteenth-century French arts educationalist Petrus Ramus. Ramus 'discarded the difficulty and rigour of high scholastic schooling and thereby attracted those who regarded education as a means to social position rather than as a preparation for a life of scholarship (or of theological debate)' (1986:168). One might argue that we begin to see here elements of the crisis of conscience that have haunted the humanities ever since in terms of the debate over social utility versus learning for learning's sake. However, if eloquence and the ability to 'engage in polemic in the public arena' have companion skills in the global university or in the 'knowledge industry', they are unlikely to be taught only in humanities departments. It is nevertheless clear that Ramus did raise the prospect that the 'purpose of education was to purvey information and skills, not to be morally improving' (1986:170). Newman's *Idea of a University*, which I examine in chapter 3, also regards the humanities subjects that he wished to incorporate into his Catholic University in Dublin, what Ireland's largest university UCD emerged

from, as offering his students both utilitarian value and universal knowledge.[5]
The return to pedagogy in studies on the humanities raises the question of how
important pedagogy has been for Irish academics in the humanities. Denis
Donoghue is one renowned, Irish-educated literature professor who has related
the 'spirit' of his discipline to teaching. I examine Donoghue's work in more
detail in chapter 4.

The second perspective on the humanities that is important for the discussion
that follows is the Kantian examination of the humanities subjects in terms of a
'conflict of the faculties'. I examine this more closely in relation to Jacques
Derrida's work on the university in chapter 5. However, it is an influential
description of the university and it is worth restating here. Kant's examination
of philosophy and theology in the university was made following a very public
reprimand and edict of censorship issued by King Frederick William II in 1794
in response to Kant's work on religion. In Kant's description of the university,
there are three higher faculties (Theology, Medicine and Law) and one lower
faculty (that of Philosophy that includes the humanities). Since the 'government is interested primarily in means for securing the strongest and most lasting
influence on the people', the higher faculties are higher precisely because the
'subjects which the higher faculties teach are just such means' (1979:27). However, it is this close connection between the government and these faculties that
necessitates that the faculty of philosophy, the lower faculty, be 'independent of
the government's command with regard to its teachings' so that it is 'free to
evaluate everything' (Kant, 1979:27) by way of reason and to 'speak out publicly' in regard to 'truth' (Kant, 1979:29). It is the conflict between the theology
and philosophy faculties, however, that is, for Kant, truly representative of the
most fundamental work of the university. Kant argues that if the 'source of
sanctioned teaching is *historical* (and the Church's espousal of doctrine in Irish
society might be an example here), then – no matter how highly it may be com-
mended as sacred to the unhesitating obedience of faith – the philosophy faculty is entitled and indeed obligated to investigate its origin with critical
scrupulosity' (1979:53–5). And this is because, as Kant argues, and as Garret
Fitzgerald has echoed in relation to the Church's teaching in Irish society, 'as
far as its matter or object is concerned, religion does not differ in any point from
morality, for it is concerned with duties as such. Its distinction from morality is
merely a formal one' (Kant, 1979:61). Kant therefore argues that the 'rational
theologian', the scholar '*versed in reason* with regard to *religious* faith' (Kant,
1979:61), must occupy a privileged place in the university alongside, even if in
conflict with, the philosopher. Irish society and the Irish university were denied
such a fundamental discourse and forum for public debate because there were
no religion or theology departments in the National University throughout the
twentieth century. Kant warns that the result for a society that does not allow for
such conflict in the university where philosophy must 'be on the lookout for a

moral meaning in scriptural texts' even to the extent of having 'to impose it on them' is that religious thought is never 'anchored to determinate concepts of reason, such as morality' and 'fantasy inevitably gets lost in the transcendent, where religious matters are concerned' (Kant, 1979:81). While it must be acknowledged that no discipline can truthfully claim to be independent of the government in the modern university, Kant's prophecy would prove true on a number of occasions for Irish society in the twentieth century.

Samuel Weber has made a more recent examination of the humanities that is important for work that seeks to compare and contrast different national humanities models. I return to Weber's argument in chapter 3. Weber demonstrates in *Institution and Interpretation* how different national university systems house the traditional humanities subjects under very different titles. Weber reminds us that despite terms such as *les belles lettres* or *Geisteswissenschaften* (the sciences of 'Spirit (or Mind)' (133)), 'there is nothing, in French or German academic discourse, that really corresponds to the English idea of the Humanities' (Weber, 1987:133). Weber's approach, therefore, raises the question of whether the different humanities traditions, as David R. Shumway[6] argues, should be regarded as representing different 'nationalities'. Whereas the humanities have traditionally defined themselves in opposition to the sciences, this opposition is impossible to sustain in the German university since subjects such as philosophy and literature are understood as belonging to the sciences of the 'Spirit' or of 'Man'. Weber points out that the 'English idea of the humanities is not centred on the Spirit' or on the 'life of the mind' but that it 'emphasizes the "more practical, social, and civic virtues felt to derive from the cultivation and mastery of certain "arts"' (1987:133). This account of the humanities points to a possible conflict at work in the humanities in the Irish university. Whereas the Irish universities and the humanities have always been formally 'steeped' (Lee, 1989:621) in the English university ethos, as J. J. Lee argues, Irish pedagogy in the humanities subjects, in often overlooking philology, rhetoric and the 'more practical, social, and civic virtues' of a humanities education, has in practice departed quite radically from this 'English' notion of the humanities. The humanities ethos in the Irish universities may in fact lie closer to the spirit of enquiry evident in continental universities where the rhetoric of crisis that consistently pitches the humanities against the sciences is perhaps less of an issue.

If we do, however, take 'the humanities' to be synonymous with 'the nationalities' (Shumway, 1998:371), as Shumway argues, then it obviously raises the question of whether the humanities as practised in Ireland should be prone to all the problems and conflicts nationalism has exhibited in Irish society. David Lloyd has given one of the most persuasive readings of Irish nationalism in terms of the cultural traditions the humanities must pass on. Lloyd argues that it is literature with its 'instrumental function as the medium of the spiritual nation' (1987:72) that truly embodies the 'spirit of the nation'. He argues that Irish literature, emerging as it did from a European nation that was also a colony, should be regarded as a minor literature. For Lloyd, a minor literature ideally embodies an opposition to the 'imperial hegemony' (1987:3) of the major, or colonialist, literature by challenging the chief characteristic of such literature, what Lloyd describes as its intention of producing 'an autonomous ethical identity for the subject' (1987:19). However, apart from this being too narrow a definition of major literature, the problem with minor literature in the Irish context is, Lloyd argues, that it became co-opted by a form of cultural nationalism that was buoyed up by a manufactured notion of national identity that 'obscures continuing exploitations of class and difference' (1987:x). If minor literature can somehow remain above these constricting nationalist tendencies, what proves exceedingly difficult in the Irish context even for writers as experimental as Joyce, then it can, as Lloyd argues for the work of James Clarence Mangan, be 'non-original and anaclitic' even in its 'parodic mimicry of the major work, and in doing so commence the questioning of the founding principles of canonical aesthetic judgments' (1987:23). However, there is a note of political essentialism in Lloyd's reading. The idealized minor work, what should never promote autonomy (and Lloyd does not explain how 'autonomous ethical identity' is achieved aesthetically or otherwise for the artwork), must be unshackled from a reading that privileges one political discourse, namely, nationalism, only so that its categorization as properly 'minor'[7] can be justified on the basis of how it embodies another political worldview that is oppositional to imperialist, cultural hegemony. Lloyd's argument also rests on a reading of aesthetic education in Schiller that sees it as a formalizing process that restores 'man's wholeness' as an image or 'artificer of the State'. In other words, the unified identity an aesthetic education produces is modelled on an idealized notion of the political State; personal sovereignty implies political sovereignty. Even though Lloyd is right to suggest that too prescriptive an approach to such a model can lead to a situation where the 'individual experience is evacuated of its specific content' (1987:16), we will see in the chapters that follow that many of the leading advocates of a humanities education credit the humanities with instilling civic virtues that prepare the student for public life. Whether such virtues are to be discredited because they speak for the actions of an 'autonomous ethical identity' is something Lloyd does not make clear. This brief examination of humanities traditions as different 'nationalities' must ultimately return us to the context of either discourse and to the site of teaching. It is the site of teaching that introduces students to literature and that enables them to critically evaluate how literature negotiates such topics as nationalism and imperialism. Whereas each humanities tradition undoubtedly exhibits elements of national character, the liberal education and universality that the humanities privileges must ultimately work to counter readings that promote a particularist approach to knowledge and human potential. In chapters 3 and 4, I return to this argument in discussing the work of Newman and Leavis.

The final account of the humanities that is also important for this study is the somewhat 'suspicious' examination of the traditional humanities subjects in the French university system by Pierre Bourdieu. Bourdieu's work is perhaps of singular importance in documenting issues related to cultural capital and hierarchization in society as perpetuated by the university, and I examine more closely Bourdieu's position in chapter 5. Bourdieu argues that the traditional humanities subjects are often guilty of disseminating a cultural arbitrary that has little value apart from serving to perpetuate the hegemony of a cultural elite in society. This cultural materialist evaluation of the university is important for assessing the value of the humanities at a time of crisis. The humanities model in the Irish university has rarely, if ever, undergone such a self-examination. As J. J. Lee again reminds us, 'there is a certain irony in the reluctance of the knowledge industry to acquire knowledge of itself!' (1989:636). At different times in the chapters that follow, I will return to these perspectives on the humanities in order to examine different aspects of the humanities in the Irish university.

It is also important to look more closely at the definition of the word 'humanities'. A search for 'humanities' in the online *OED* retrieves no results; one must look under 'humanity'. The second definition for 'humanity' has a further two possible meanings. The first tells us that 'the humanities' in the singular and plural form *describes* '[l]iterary learning or scholarship; secular letters as opposed to theology; *esp.* the study of ancient Latin and Greek language, literature, and intellectual culture (as grammar, rhetoric, history, and philosophy); classical scholarship'. Its 'later' *singular* use describes 'the study of Latin language and literature', and one of the 'special uses' is *literae humaniores*, a title used for a course at Oxford University and elsewhere that focuses on Classics. However, the second meaning for humanity in the plural form and usually with the prefix 'the' describes '[t]he branch of learning concerned with human culture; the academic subjects collectively comprising this branch of learning, as history, literature, ancient and modern languages, law, philosophy, art, and music. Hence also in *sing.*: any one of these subjects'. This meaning, therefore, is not defined in terms of an opposition between 'secular' subjects and 'theology'. In the modern university, it is, typically, the second sense that prevails, one that regards the humanities as the branch of subjects collectively comprising the body of learning concerned with human culture. This definition departs from the earlier meaning that regards the humanities as concerned primarily with secular subjects. Therefore, religious studies, theology and comparative religion are included today in the humanities divisions of most of the major humanities universities: the Arts and Humanities division of Harvard University includes a Committee on the Study of Religion and a Center for Jewish Studies; the Arts and Humanities programme for the University of California, Berkeley, has Buddhist Studies and Jewish Studies programmes, and the Humanities web page of the University of Oxford includes the Faculty of Theology.

It cannot be denied, however, that modern humanities is often traced to the *studia humanitatis* of the fifteenth century and to Renaissance humanism. Geoffrey Galt Harpham reminds us that the *studia humanitatis* 'sought to recall humankind to its divine origins through a rereading of the classical and early Christian texts as an extended meditation on ethics whose ultimate goal of personal salvation was manifestly Christian' (2011:83). This account of the humanities arose in reaction to the work of the universities of the day that were seen to privilege 'rationalism, the study of logic, and natural philosophy' (2011:84).[8] However, it was when the influence of religion in the curriculum began to 'wane' (2011:188) in the nineteenth century that philology, a neglected discipline today and one that may never have been practised in the Irish national universities to any great extent, came into its own both as a discipline in its own right and as a discipline that 'served to anchor the curriculum in many colleges and universities in Europe and the United States' (2011:188).

However, the late nineteenth century also witnessed the emergence of the humanities as a practice and discipline closely aligned with the new understanding of 'culture' emerging most persuasively in the writings of Matthew Arnold. This sense of culture was also shaped by the new understanding of the notion of the 'common' that, for Michael Hardt and Antonio Negri, began to be used for all kinds of practices and forms of interaction in the nineteenth century.[9] Matthew Arnold's opposition between culture and anarchy provides the university with what Harpham argues is the 'antecedent, anchor, and direct reference point of what we now call the humanities' (2011:84). However, it must again be noted that Arnold claimed at the time that modern society was in crisis or in jeopardy precisely because of the 'loss of "Christian knowledge" and the tradition of classical *humanitas* that had complemented that knowledge'. John Henry Newman was therefore not alone in regarding religious investigation and theology as essential subjects in a modern education in the humanities in the nineteenth century.

What is perhaps most striking in Harpham's account of the humanities is that he regards the humanities as understood and practised in most of the leading universities today as an American invention; 'the humanities were made in America as an image of American aspirations, and [...] we ignore, marginalize, or denigrate the humanities at the cost of those aspirations' (2011:189). For Harpham, the version of the humanities that has been practised in the majority of leading universities since the mid-twentieth century can be traced back to

John Adams's belief that the 'humanities themselves are the real American dream' (2011:183). The humanities came to speak for 'notions of personal fulfillment, creativity, and freedom'; it had 'emerged as the core of the liberal arts, the center of "general education", the means of establishing a common culture, and the academic expression of the American character: curious, open-minded, unburdened by fear and want, and eager to explore in a disinterested spirit the full range of opportunities inherent in the human condition' (2011:188–9). This overarching and expansive description of the humanities that has travelled 'across the globe' 'on the same winds as the English language, the dollar, [and] rock and roll' is an 'American discourse whose deepest assumptions and implications resist translation into other cultural settings' (2011:188). This description of the humanities as 'American self-understanding' (2011:190) is quite radical, even evangelical, since it presumes a kind of nationalist ethos that accompanies the teaching and practice of the humanities even if the model has been transported outside America. Even though Harpham admits that the 'deepest assumptions and implications resist translation into other cultural settings' when this model of the humanities is being exported, he does not specify what those 'deepest assumptions and implications' are. If these deepest assumptions are those that assume a state of enquiry that is 'curious, open-minded, unburdened by fear and want, and eager to explore in a disinterested spirit the full range of opportunities inherent in the human condition', then we might well question how any exported model of the humanities can still function if these assumptions resist 'translation'. However, if, and this is more likely the case, the 'deepest assumptions and implications' that Harpham refers to are those that inspire notions of 'self-understanding', freedom, confidence and creativity, then Harpham would seem to be describing a general spirit of the humanities[10] that is more universal. Such a spirit is not uniquely affiliated with American values but with an understanding of universal knowledge that Newman privileges also in *The Idea of a University*.

However, if we step back again and look more generally at the change that came to the humanities in mid-twentieth-century America, it is noteworthy that it is with this mid-twentieth-century American model of the humanities that the most dramatic shift occurs; the humanities is no longer interrogated or contemplated in terms of what it *is* but in terms of what it can *do* and what it can allow students to achieve. The Reports of the Commission on the Humanities of 1964 and 1980 stress that the humanities is to be identified with such attributes and practices as 'critical judgment, aesthetic appreciation, and moral decision making' and that the humanities must 'represent "things of the spirit"' (Harpham, 2011:169). However, since all of these faculties are universal human characteristics, it is still not clear how the American model of the humanities would express a distinctly American dynamic in the way it describes such attributes as 'critical judgment' and 'aesthetic appreciation'.

Stefan Collini's recent work on the university also marks an important intervention in works on the humanities. He might be regarded as offering a UK perspective on the humanities. He sets out in *What are universities for?*, as he puts it, to make a series of 'deliberately intransigent' (2012:85) remarks (one can only assume this is in response to the far more intransigent approach to education evident in 'public discourse' today that, Collini argues, is far too 'dispiriting' in demanding justification for how departments 'help to make more money' (x)) on the humanities that include a description of the field that runs as follows:

> 'the humanities' is now taken to embrace that collection of disciplines which attempt to understand, across barriers of time and culture, the actions and creations of other human beings considered as bearers of meaning, where the emphasis tends to fall on matters to do with individual or cultural distinctiveness and not on matters which are primarily susceptible to characterization in purely statistical or biological terms. (2012:64)

While this description is perhaps consoling for those working in the field, Collini would seem to be presuming too much about the shared proclivities of humanities scholars from 'across barriers of time and culture'. He argues that 'what we admire and respond to in the best work [in the humanities]' are 'certain qualities of noticing and characterizing, certain powers of illuminating and persuading', what, he argues, ultimately might only depend on something as seemingly throwaway as 'the choice of adverbs' (2012:73–4). In a book targeted at all those interested in the university, one is constantly left wondering whose Collini's 'we' is speaking for, especially when sentences begin with such phrases as '[a]lert practical critics will notice [...]' (2012:84).

However, it is interesting to read his account of the development of the university in light of Harpham's perspective on modern humanities as an American invention, especially given the fact that the UK and the United States are today's university powerhouses. Collini argues that the first truly modern university was that of the University of Berlin, established by Wilhelm von Humboldt, the Prussian minister for education, in 1810. Universities now came to be seen as 'centres of "the higher learning"', and '[r]esearch was coming to be seen as part of the defining purpose of the university' both in the sciences and also in 'those fields that were later to be designated as the humanities and social sciences, especially in history, philosophy, philology, and the study of classical literature' (2012:23–4). Collini does admit that even though 'different national systems of higher education each have their own distinctive characteristics, scholarship and science are inherently international enterprises and so no one system can be understood wholly in isolation from the others' (2012:24). He would then appear to resist what we might perceive as Harpham's tendency to align one of the chief disciplines of these early universities with a single national ethos. He does however stress how 'hugely influential' were the German universities by the 'later nineteenth century' especially in the United States. It is also noteworthy from an Irish perspective that he describes the influence of these German universities on the British university in terms of an 'ideal of *wissenschaftlich* "research", which came to be grafted onto the native traditions of teaching and scholarship' (2012:24). Collini does then stress the permeability and transferability of national educational idiosyncrasies onto other 'native traditions' in a manner that Harpham's privileging of the rootedness of the humanities in America might not. Collini agrees with Harpham that the winds had changed by the twentieth century and that it was then that the 'major British and American universities [...] increasingly provided not just the dominant models for emulation elsewhere but also the nearest approximation to the Humboldtian ideal of combining a liberal education with advanced scholarly and scientific research' (2012:24). Collini is careful to trace the obvious international influence of the American university to its affiliations with, and emergence from, the 'Anglo-Saxon university' and even to the 'British Empire': 'The British Empire led directly to the establishment of universities around the world modeled on the "home" institutions, in practice more along the lines of London or the Scottish or larger civic universities than of Oxford and Cambridge' (2012:24). He argues that the 'vast expansion and re-shaping of universities across the world in the later decades of the twentieth century' has been spearheaded by the '"Anglo-Saxon" model setting the pace throughout the world, Europe included' (2012:25), and it must be remembered that Ireland was slow to feel the tides of this influence. It is clear then that the battle lines are still drawn in terms of which 'Empire' is most responsible for the university and the humanities as they exist today. Whether we ground our reading of the origins of the university on the 'British Empire', 'American self-understanding' or the 'Anglo-Saxon model' – what incorporates something from the German model while reading any American influence through its emergence from its British forefather – it is the 'native traditions' and those untranslatable national 'assumptions and implications' that Harpham and Collini admit are still evident in the humanities today. Despite the influence of these models on the humanities in the Irish university, one must still look for those 'native traditions' and 'assumptions and implications' that might speak for an Irish humanities ethos.

Harpham also has much to say about the model of the humanities in the British University. He is quick to note that the British University might be regarded as privileging a different understanding of culture to that espoused by the humanities in the American university. While in the American University an 'explicitly Arnoldian concept of culture has informed the discourse of the humanities for the past hundred years', Harpham argues that the 'highly successful movement known as British Cultural Studies', whose founding principles he takes as representative of larger differences between the humanities in the United States and Britain, espoused a 'new concept of culture' that 'was explicitly allied with the discipline of sociology rather than with literary studies or even the humanities'. Harpham goes on to argue that the 'institutional success of the concept of culture, in this context, came at the cost of its identification with literature and any notion of providing direct service to the state' (2011:87). It might be argued that the twentieth-century Irish university would have followed the American model of culture with its heart if it had not been impoverished both financially and philosophically. However, given its roots in the British model and the emergence of 'Europeanization', it would later draw closer to Europe and also to this British model of the university in terms of academic structure and research practice. The re-emergence of the concept of culture in the 1950s in Britain by way of neo-Marxism and the rise of sociology brought a new understanding of culture that was directly tied to political events in Russia and Europe. Culture was understood against the backdrop of 'working-class experience set against both social-democratic and communist regimes' (2011:87). However, Harpham does not hide his allegiance to the American humanist understanding of culture in saying that the British use of the concept of culture in this neo-Marxist way was 'ironic' because this understanding of the concept of culture had 'begun life, as it were, as a dependent clause within statism' (2011:87). One feels he is not doing justice to the efforts of the British Cultural Studies movement. It was a movement that had Raymond Williams as its 'first scholar' and that worked, as Winfried Fluck argues, to 'regain respect and recognition for cultural forms that had been dismissed or ignored by the elites' (2005:11).

However, it is likely that Irish society, albeit somewhat intuitively, shared this regard for culture espoused by the cultural studies movement, a movement Harpham sees as too uninspiring for the American model of the university and the humanities. Harpham is at pains to argue that the British and European model of the university is completely different to that in the United States particularly in relation to the humanities. For Americans, he argues, the British model is 'not properly humanistic at all but rather something that belongs to the "human sciences", or, more exactly, to the assemblage of disciplines Wilhelm Dilthey called *Geisteswissenschaften*, including religion, psychology, law, politics, and economics' (2011:93). It is also noteworthy that he focuses, like Collini, on the 'strategic aims' of the British Arts and Humanities Research Council (AHRC). However, while Collini is less scathing about these 'aims' in suggesting that the sciences and the arts subjects should be judged against the same criteria, Harpham argues that to 'American eyes' the language of the 'aims' is 'strikingly deficient with respect to uplifting rhetoric'. He laments the fact that there is 'no fine discourses about values, sensibility, the imagination, humanity, much less about the need to counter tyranny and terror [...] Breathes there the man with soul so dead!' (2011:94). However, in recognizing that the AHRC aims are less than inspiring, the rhetoric and jargon of the humanities often make it its own worst enemy. As Mel A. Topf notes, humanities conferences often describe a litany of vacuities, and the word humanities itself can often appear as the most 'recent bastard notion of doubtful definition' (in Harpham, 2011:171). Ultimately, it is perhaps the political acumen of those neo-Marxists that is needed today as the western model of the humanities negotiates with the Asian humanities and with a largely Chinese-funded model of the university that has a great deal of 'native' traditions of its own. Uplifting rhetoric is only useful when teacher and students are all singing from the same hymn sheet, and this is definitely not the case in Asia today for western academics, and it may not have been the case in Ireland for much of the twentieth century.

Another important consideration in any discussion of the humanities is the place of religion, and this is perhaps the most pressing concern in the history of the humanities in the Irish university. As I will discuss in the next chapter, the restrictions on religious education in the National University of Ireland (NUI) resulted in a university system that was denied the option of including religion and theology departments in its humanities programmes. Of course, it must be acknowledged that there is a long-running debate on the question of whether religion should be part of the humanities. Writing in 1963, Clyde A. Holbrook argues that despite the fact that 'it is evident that there no longer exists on any major scale that close identification of religion with higher education which we have seen was once taken for granted in Europe and America' (1963:24), it is nevertheless a fact that despite the 'freedom of secular learning from theological pursuits' [...] 'studies in religion [...] for purposes of their intrinsic or humane value have flourished' (1963:24). Holbrook's definition of the humanities describes how spiritual and secular views of self-examination can coincide and overlap. He argues that the 'humanities find their characteristic subject matter in those significant achievements of the human race which illuminate and illustrate the distinctive characteristics of man as a rational and spiritual being' (1963:41). He also notes that Thomas More, a Christian humanist who 'could see no reason to give up either Christian truth or the enrichments of classical learning' (1963:15), explained how the secular can serve to lead a scholar back to the religious or the spiritual: 'There are some who through knowledge of things natural construct a ladder by which to rise to the contemplation of things supernatural; they build a path to theology through Philosophy and the Liberal Arts' (1963:15). Holbrook also describes how the balancing of religious studies and philosophy in the curriculum brought a 'theological renaissance' to the American university in the 1940s and 1950s. The 'fresh excitement in the religious classroom' that passed through American universities at the time did not come 'from an insistence upon traditional "humane" virtues or from an invitation to flee to otherworldliness' but from the 'kind of teaching that challenges the polite gentilities of liberalism by speaking of the spiritual and moral ambiguities of man's historic and contemporary experience' (1963:68). It is clearly evident then that religious investigation and spiritual enquiry have long been integral to the humanities in many leading universities. This kind of breadth of learning was denied the Irish scholar and student of the NUI in the twentieth century. While the humanities should, of course, never be 'governed' by any one discipline, especially the 'religious' – a tendency Seamus Heaney advises against so beautifully for poetry so as to prevent the poem becoming a 'nun of language' with its 'luxuriant locks' barbered 'down to a stubble of moral and ethical goads' (1990:100) – the humanities are most engaging when the spiritual, the ethical, the philosophical and aesthetics are examined alongside one another.

Notes

1 J. J. Lee notes that at least up until the 1960s, '[u]niversity staff in education did little to encourage research on the role of education in society' (1989:586). Dónal Mulcahy argues that '[n]o books which dealt with wider aspects of education' (1981:18) were published in Ireland between 1922 and 1962 and that at no time since independence 'has any sustained assessment and critical analysis been undertaken in regard to the overall purposes and programmes of post-primary education' (1). The humanities has also suffered from this lack of research.

2 It is interesting to note that the Irish philosopher George Berkeley also supported the admission of Catholics to Trinity College without obliging them to 'attend Chapel, catechism or divinity lectures' only so that it would ultimately 'prevent the prejudices of a foreign education' (*The Querist*; Kearney, 1985:154).

3 Seamus Deane argues in his introduction to the *Field Day Anthology of Irish Writing* that 'national, vernacular literatures, institutionalized in university departments and courses, were the articulators of the "national tradition". If Englishness or Irishness were to be sought, literature would provide it' (1991:xxii). He also argues that '"[r]econciliation" is a key term in art criticism, in translation theory and in political crisis. In Ireland, the linkages between these fields are so close that there is scarcely a distinction in the vocabulary employed for each' (1991:xxvi).

4 For Alasdair MacIntyre, the emergence of our modern notion of 'university' is also aligned with a practical concern for teaching: 'The concept of a university finds fully fledged application only later, at the end of the thirteenth century, when there is mutual recognition by universities of their distinctive function and status, a recognition signaled by an acknowledgement, at least in theory, that a master's degree from any university conferred the *ius ubique docendi*, the right of teaching anywhere' (2009:65).

5 Newman argues in Discourse VII that the 'universal knowledge' his university will teach will prepare the student 'to fill any post with credit, and to master any subject with facility' (1976:154).

6 Geoffrey Galt Harpham notes that 'Public Law 89–209, the bill that created the NEH [National Endowment for the Humanities]' in defining the kind of humanities work to be supported, ends with the following: 'the study and application of the humanities to the current conditions of national life' (2011:91).

7 John Guillory argues in *Cultural Capital* that such genres or classifications ultimately become reified in the classroom as the 'noncanonical' (1994:9).

8 Alasdair MacIntyre notes that '[e]arlier education in monastic and cathedral schools had been designed primarily, although not only, for those who would proceed beyond the seven liberal arts to the study of theology. But from the early twelfth century onward both teachers and students in the liberal arts had increasingly secular preoccupations' (2009:62).

9 Michael Hardt and Antonio Negri argue in *Commonwealth* that 'early modern European social theorists' such as John Locke 'conceive of the common as the bounty of nature available to humanity, including the fertile land to work and the fruits of the earth'. However, they argue that a second, later understanding of the common 'that blurs the division between nature and culture' – what they describe as a 'biopolitical' common – is a more 'dynamic' concept where the 'common is not only the earth we share but also the languages we create, the social practices we establish, the modes of sociality that define our relationships, and so forth' (2009:139).

10 This sense might also be related to what Kant has described in relation to the role of the university as a shared sense of humanity: 'For there is something in us that we cannot cease to wonder at when we have once seen it, the same thing that raises *humanity* in its Idea to a dignity we should never have suspected in *man* as an object of experience' (1979:105).

2

The humanities in the Irish context

An 'anomalous state': unique problems for the humanities in Ireland

Ireland was a deeply religious country throughout the twentieth century,[1] but its National University never established, or provided public support for, a theology or religion department. The official first language of Ireland is Irish but virtually all teaching in the universities is done in English.[2] These are two of the paradoxes that lay at the heart of the Irish university experience in the humanities in the twentieth century. The debates over the religion and language questions plagued early political efforts to found representative universities in Ireland. When Ireland became independent, the charters binding the constituent colleges of its National University remained largely unchanged. J. J. Lee argues that the 'new university' was one of many 'major missed opportunities' of the 'official mind' of Irish society and that it made 'little contribution to the modernization of Irish society' in the years leading up to independence and in the early years of the Free State (2008:132–3). The effects of the 1908 Universities Act would be felt for many years to come. Garret Fitzgerald, the former chancellor of the National University of Ireland (NUI), writing in 2008, argues that '[o]ne way or the other the whole shape of Irish education came to be determined, and remains shaped today, by nineteenth- or early twentieth-century reactions to the seventeenth- and eighteenth-century Anglican monopoly of Irish education' (in Dunne, 2008:xvi). This book argues that the implications of such a reactionary and inert approach to the institutionalization of education were felt nowhere more deeply than in the humanities.

The '*de jure* non-denominational status' (Parkes, 2010:567) of education in the universities where 'no money was to be provided for theological teaching' (2010:566) remained a moot point throughout the century. Of course, the roots of this institutional arrangement lay much further back. Susan M. Parkes reminds us that the 'fundamental clash in the middle of the nineteenth century between the secular and religious concept of a university was to have a long-lasting effect on the history of Irish higher education'

(2010:547). It resulted in the rather anomalous situation whereby by 1933, the then Taoiseach Éamon de Valera could claim at the World Education Conference held in Dublin that '[...] the beginning and end of true education, is the development of religious and moral character' (in Farren, 1995:140) while no student or scholar of the National University could officially study in a theology or religion department the nature of Ireland's 'religious character' and how it might relate to such alien concerns as education and morality. Patrick J. Corish points out that it had long been acknowledged that the 'absence of theology from the Irish universities was a "strange anomaly"' (1995:416). Desmond M. Clarke, writing in the 1980s, notes that a further aspect of the 'anomalous state of Irish education' was that even if Irish taxpayers, who were predominantly Catholic and who bore 'the major share of the financial cost of education at every level', did wish for religion to be part of the curriculum that it would have meant very little since they were 'systematically excluded from any significant influence in education' (1985:196). Most commentators would seem to blame the Church for this 'anomalous state' of Irish education. However, J. J. Lee is also quick to note that even though the 'nature of Irish Catholicism cannot be ignored in discussing any major question of social significance in modern Ireland, it is by no means the only factor requiring scrutiny' (1989:621) and that '[i]nsofar as clerical hostility to independent thought was a factor it offers only a very partial explanation of Irish intellectual retardation' (1989:610). Given that the National University was criticized by so many precisely because it didn't have enough religion, it is perhaps disingenuous then to blame the Church for all its institutional shortcomings. It was a vicious circle; the 'official mind' of Irish society saw little need for further 'self-awareness' because there was no tradition of 'social research', but institutions for such research would only be established if that same 'official mind' (a 'mind' reliant on the Church for moral guidance) could be pursuaded otherwise.[3]

Theology was long regarded as the 'strongest faculty' (Corish, 1995:392) of Maynooth's Pontifical University, and it had long held alive – to no avail – the 'hope of integrating the teaching of Theology into the Arts courses of the National University' (Corish, 1995:398). Today's NUI, Maynooth, was founded as Royal College of St. Patrick's, Maynooth, in 1795. Garret Fitzgerald explains in his foreword to *The National University of Ireland 1908–2008* from 2008 that 'it was financed by the British government with a view to enabling Roman Catholic priests to be educated in Ireland rather than in revolutionary France. That college's attempt to extend its role to the education of Catholic laymen as well as future priests met, however, with government disapproval, as threatening the higher education monopoly enjoyed by the Anglican Dublin University with its single Trinity College.

The attendance of lay students was terminated in 1807' (2008:xiii). However, when the university was later confirmed as a Recognised College of the NUI federal structure in 1910, it became subject to the same constitutional requirements as the other constituent colleges. Even though its curriculum included courses in theology and canon law, Séamus Smyth explains that the then president of the college Daniel Mannix submitted a list of professors and lecturers to the Senate of the NUI 'including those in the faculties of theology and canon law, who would of course have no role to play in the arts faculty of the recognised college' (Dunne, 2008:105). Recognition was restricted to the faculties of arts, philosophy and Celtic studies with the Faculty of Science being recognized in 1913. Patrick J. Corish argues that the Faculty of Theology remained in 'splendid isolation' (1995:264). Fitzgerald argues in the same foreword that 'this has resulted in TCD still being the only university to offer degrees in theology on its own campus, though NUI now awards degrees in theology at its Recognised College Milltown Institute [the Milltown Institute became a 'recognized' college of the NUI in 2005] and there are higher diplomas in religious studies in University College Cork' (2008:xiv). UCC also established a Study of Religions department in 2007, and the Irish Society for the Academic Study of Religions was established in 2011. The number of students enrolled on 'Religion' has also jumped in recent years despite there still being no theology department in the National University. The Higher Education Authority (HEA) statistics for full-time and part-time enrolments for 'Religion' at HEA-funded institutions for 2011/12 reveal there were 131 students enrolled on taught Masters courses on 'Religion' and 62 students enrolled for PhDs in 'Religion' (www.hea.ie/en/node/1488).

Donal McCartney argues that because theology or divinity could not be financed by the state, 'philosophy became the discipline in which the teaching of the Catholic Church could be most assiduously promoted' (1999:216). However, McCartney also makes the point that it was only at the meetings of the Presidents' and Bishops' Liaison Committee in 1953 and 1954 that the 'provision of courses in general philosophy for non-clerical undergraduates was approved' (1999:191). Writing in response to Michael Tierney's 'Memorandum on University Question. No. 1. Jan, 1951', Alfred O'Rahilly, the then president of UCC, could also still argue that it was 'unfair' to 'blame the lack of philosophy and theology for lay students in the NUI colleges on their Charters' (McCartney, 1999:186). General philosophy courses for lay students would also then be a long time coming. When philosophy did belatedly appear as an option for all Arts students in the 1950s and 1960s, it was always likely that it would suffer from having to sneak Catholic theology in the back door. The restrictions of the 1908 Act, therefore, not only prevented theology and religion departments from being established but also severely limited the range of another core humanities subject, philosophy. McCartney reminds us that there was 'little tradition of lay Catholic philosophers' in the country. In the Faculty of Philosophy at UCD, the Department of Metaphysics was staffed entirely by clergy until 1962, and McCartney argues: 'there was none who were not Thomists among its philosophers' (1999:226). Instead of removing any academic lacuna resulting from the lack of theology and religion departments in the universities, the 'Catholic ethos' may instead have served to exacerbate it by transforming philosophy – the other core university subject for Newman and Kant – into a kind of watered-down theology. Patrick J. Corish notes how the teaching of such a style of philosophy, the kind a seminarian required, raised similar problems for Maynooth in the 1950s: 'The pass BA course was further bedevilled by the fact that it had to incorporate the philosophy component required of seminarians. This was not good for the humanities, but neither was it good for philosophy' (1995:349). Corish also makes the point that even in Maynooth, where there was a tradition of teaching theology to seminarians in the Pontifical University, there was uncertainty about how to teach philosophy as a National University subject. The reaction of the 1933 Congregation for Seminaries and Universities to proposals for revising the statutes of Pontifical institutions was unhelpful, Corish argues, because the 'Congregation was far from clear on the interlocking of Pontifical and National University courses in Philosophy' (1995:318). The influence of the dictates of the 1908 Act, therefore, affected all the core humanities subjects. Of course, encroaching secularization in the 1970s and 1980s did bring change. This was despite the fact that in 1972, Rev. Fergal O'Connor OP could still 'beg' his new colleague Tom Garvin in UCD's Department of Ethics and Politics not to make a particular speech 'on the grounds that "it would bring the archbishop down on us"' (1999:218) and given the fact that the largest department of philosophy in the country was still headed by a future cardinal well into the 1980s. In the 1990s, when this writer was a philosophy undergraduate student in the National University, there was still no hint of a theology or religion department emerging, and any obvious trace of the pervasive 'Catholic ethos' (1999:159) in the philosophy department had been well and truly extirpated by a heady mix of logic, nomadic subjectivity and deconstruction.

Despite the lack of religion and theology departments in the National University, it is generally accepted that the Church ruled the roost in Irish life. For Lee, religion was the 'main barrier between a reasonably civilized civil society and the untrammelled predatory instincts of individual and pressure-group selfishness' (1989:656). Despite the fact that there was a 'lack of a viable civic culture' (1989:650) in Irish society, Lee does discern some basis for a civic culture in Irish society that was only sustained by 'institutional religion'.[4] Writing in 1989 and before the recent scandals in the Church, Lee is also quick to point out that '[i]f religion were to no longer fulfill its historic civilizing

mission as a substitute for internalized values of civic responsibility, the consequences for the country no less that for the church could be lethal' (1989:657).[5]
However, Lee's prescient, if somewhat exaggerated, claims in regard to religion raise an important question for Irish society. If this rudimentary practice
of civic culture and of the 'public good' was only sustained in Irish society by
an 'institutional religion' whose ethics were almost entirely absent from the
curricula of the state's National University, did this result in something of a
schism in society between those who internalized whatever values could be
garnered from academic study and those who followed the dictates of 'institutional religion'? It would of course be nothing new from a European perspective to have a town/gown dichotomy in operation in society; however, because
there was a lack of a 'viable civic culture' in Irish society and also an unwillingness to speak in terms of class consciousness, any division between an educated elite and the general public was likely to be pronounced precisely because
it was under-examined. New initiatives for social reform spearheaded by academics were likely to be regarded as nothing more than a 'disturbance of the
natural order of things, as willed by God' (Lee, 1989:650). Either side would
also lack the vocabulary to explain its position to the other since 'Irish society'
lacked a 'viable civic culture' (what those in university presumably knew more
about) and those at university lacked a discourse that enabled them to square
their religious beliefs with societal advances in other fields.[6]

The effects of a lack of academic discourse that could put Catholic teaching
and social thought in conversation went far beyond the walls of the universities.
The discussions surrounding the referenda on divorce and abortion demonstrated how far Irish society was behind some of its neighbours in regard to
secularization. Lee argues in relation to Article 44 of the Constitution on the
'special position' of the Catholic Church and Section 17 of the Criminal Law
Amendment Act 1935, which prohibited the importation and sale of contra-
ceptives that 'it was difficult to avoid the impression that the state considered
it a duty to impose specifically Catholic doctrine on all citizens, irrespective
of their personal convictions' (1989:203). However, it should be remembered
that these prohibitions did not exist in a vacuum. Patrick Hannon, professor of
moral theology at Maynooth, argues in an article on the abortion question in
Ireland that the 'poverty' of 'public discussion of religious and moral matters'
in relation to such issues as abortion and contraception can be traced to the
'virtually total absence of theology from the university' (in Mackey, 130).
Ruth Barrington sees a similar lack of public discussion on science and morality. She asks why Ireland, with its 'proud legal and human rights tradition' is
'so backward in relation to handling the great ethical issues of our time'
(2002:147).[7] Once again, Barrington traces this lack of public debate back to
the lack of debate in the universities. She notes, writing in 2002, that 'to this
day there is no chair of bioethics in any Irish university' (2002:147). That the

Irish people might be considered somewhat backward in their response to such social revolutions should not be disconnected from the intellectual life of the Irish universities. The fact that religion and theology were not taught in the majority of the colleges of the National University did not mean that Irish education was progressively secular. On the contrary, the unnatural division that was instigated in the Irish universities between the humanities discourses and the intellectual examination of religious faith and belief meant that even Irish students and scholars were unsure of how to relate many revolutionary philosophical and social issues with the practice of their faith.

Desmond M. Clarke, a leading Irish academic philosopher, has written at length on the influence of the Church on primary and secondary schooling in Ireland, but he is strangely silent on the university and religion. He argues in *Church & State* that the 'outside observer of Irish educational development, especially at primary and secondary level, is tempted to conclude that the churches want to control education because they wish to determine the religious and moral beliefs of citizens'. He goes on to argue that 'on closer examination [...] it becomes apparent that this conclusion is consistent with the explicit educational policy' of the 'majority church' (1985:215). Since Clarke has already clearly demonstrated in his book how far the reach of the Church extends in Irish life, it is surprising that in a lengthy and detailed chapter on 'Education', he makes very little mention of the universities. However, his points clearly show that the Irish student would be most likely to experience something of a paradigm shift in moving from the strictly Catholic ethos of the secondary school to a university where there could be no public support for theology or religion.[8] It led many Irish people to remain disinterested in the moral system and vocabulary underpinning religious beliefs. It is somewhat revealing nevertheless that one of the leading professional philosophers in the National University system writing on Church & State politics in the 1980s says little about this anomalous position in his own institution.

However, Clarke does explain in clear philosophical language how Church control worked in Ireland and how it created a somewhat reactionary political climate in the country. He writes of the Church's espousal of an 'illusion of infallibility' (1985:88) that directed its actions in Ireland. He argues that this 'illusion of infallibility' and the Church's adherence to an outmoded Thomistic version of 'natural law' – what Clarke regards as the 'pseudo-reasonable mask of a religious belief' (1985:68) – deprived Ireland of a modernizing democratic tendency found in 'other Western democracies such as Holland' (1985:88). Clarke explains that a non-denominational, democratic ethos is important for the civic education of a people. He believes tolerance is a central aspect of such modern democracies, and, writing in the 1980s, he believes that the influence of the Church in public and private life in Ireland has resulted in an 'entrenched philosophy of intolerance': 'An insular people, taught by a majority "infallible" church, and cultivated for many decades by an explicit government policy of fostering a nationalist ideal of religious and cultural homogeneity, is hardly likely to provide a paradigm of political and religious tolerance' (1985:89).

Clarke is not alone in relating the Church's influence in Irish life to larger philosophical issues that should have been discussed in the National University. The former chancellor of the NUI and former Taoiseach Garret Fitzgerald has written more recently, in a book published in 2003, that Irish Catholics – and this then referred to the vast majority of Irish people – have been 'left without an adequate sense of civic morality' (2003:246) because the Catholic Church 'made a mistake by not stressing the extent to which its moral teaching is largely grounded on principles of ethics that exist independently of the church' (2003:246). This view is shared by the Australian writer Vincent Buckley who argues in *Memory Ireland* in 1985 that 'when you come right down to it, there is almost no civic sense at all [in Ireland]; that concept is too wide for people's life-experience' and that people have no sense of a '*polis*' (1985:48–50). Now it seems obvious that if the Church itself was reluctant to reveal that its moral teaching was grounded on such principles of ethics that the obvious place to have informed intelligent and interested members of the public about this would have been in the humanities departments of its universities. If, as Newman and others have expressed, a humanities education should have subjects such as theology and religion at its core, then a university should provide a space for investigating how ethics and religious belief are related. Fitzgerald goes on to argue that this lack of an 'adequate sense of civic morality' in the Irish people has 'greatly weakened the fabric of a society that is today much less strongly infused with Christian morality than used to be the case' (2003:246). Fitzgerald would seem to agree with Patrick Hannon who 'regrets the absence of theology from most of our universities', and he argues that this and other institutional factors have meant that Irish people seem to 'lack the capacity to take religious issues seriously':

> The serious debate about religious issues in the lay press on the Continent, even in countries where the churches do not command the allegiance and participation of a majority of the population, has little or no Irish equivalent. It is as if we lack the capacity to take religious issues seriously. This may in part reflect what has always seemed to me to be a pre-occupation of Irish – as well as English – intellectuals with literary matters, to the virtual exclusion of philosophy and political ideas – let alone theology. (Fitzgerald, 2003:272)

It is a somewhat surprising admission by a man who was Chancellor of the National University up until 2009. But what is perhaps more shocking is that very little was done in the National University to deal with these lacunae in its curricula. Fitzgerald also regards Irish society as increasingly 'amoral' because it has 'been left without an adequate sense of civic morality'. He argues that this is so chiefly because of 'the Catholic Church's past insistence on grounding its moral teaching exclusively on authority, without explaining the rational basis for the main principles of this teaching'. Once again, as is the case in most of the leading universities in the UK and the United States, a humanities education that allows for open discussion and investigation between the disciplines of religion, theology, philosophy and politics provides an educational environment that is promoting of the kind of 'civic morality' that Fitzgerald is advocating. Geoffrey Galt Harpham refers to this aspect of the humanities education in the American context in terms of its bestowing of 'moral citizenship' (2011:185), and it is timely that the place the humanities play in imparting 'moral citizenship' in Irish society is closely examined. If the educated young people of a population are not given the opportunity to take their religious questioning seriously, then it is very likely that they will come to regard their religious faith and whatever system of morals it possesses as something that does not necessitate serious investigation or as a set of rules that has no relation to philosophy and politics.

Because traditions of religious belief and traditions of intellectual and scholarly learning had been separated for so long in the institutions of the National University, any attempt to question either one on the grounds of the other only led to recriminations and reactionary rhetoric. Irish students and scholars and Irish people in general lacked an important space for intelligent debate that would have allowed their religious belief to change with the times. However, the impact of this unnatural division should not only be regarded as working in one direction. While it is important to note that it may have resulted in a less than progressive national psyche, it must be acknowledged that the division also meant that a wholesome university education in the humanities in the national universities was hindered because of this division between the public life of believers and the philosophical and ethical aspects of a humanities education. John Dewey, in writing on education more generally, argues that 'the school cannot be a preparation for social life excepting as it reproduces, within itself, typical conditions of social life' (1909:13). The Irish university did not, from a European perspective, reproduce 'typical conditions of social life' in which informed, intelligent debate on spirituality and religious belief accommodated discourse on contemporary social issues. For Dewey, it is the training in regard to this 'social life' that is representative of true morality as 'moral ideas', namely, those 'ideas of any sort whatsoever which take effect in conduct and improve it' (1909:5). However, the National University rarely reproduced the 'typical conditions of social life' in Ireland. Irish people, like their writers, had a perhaps profound, yet unspoken, understanding of how belief and learning were related. However, while Ireland's writers were experimenting by bringing literary motifs, philosophical ideas and theological analogues together in such radical and illuminating ways, Ireland's university students were unable to study the full scope and range of these experiments.

The other key factor for humanities education in the Irish university system was the language question. The language of instruction in the humanities in UK and US universities went hand in hand with notions of national aspiration and sovereignty. The history of the language in these countries in founding a national spirit was deeply embedded in any respective 'spirit of the language' in education, something I examine in relation to F. R. Leavis's work in chapter 4. Educational theories in the United States and in the UK consistently refer back to the founding documents of these nations, be it the Declaration of Independence, the Constitutional Amendments or Parliamentary Acts. There is a clear sense that the aspirations of the people in education are embedded in the language describing the founding political aspirations of the nation. There was no resentment, be it openly expressed or repressed, towards the language of key political documents or the language of instruction in education when it was assumed to be English. There was no tendency to regard too close a textual interest in this language's history and place in national life as reminding the reader or writer, as Thomas Kinsella has argued, of his or her 'divided mind'. Irish would always be the first official language of the Irish people, and documents fundamental to the political identity of the State, such as The Proclamation of the Republic of 1916 and Bunreacht na hÉireann, begin in Irish even though debate on, and scrutiny of, the contemporary ramifications of their different provisions and articles is conducted in English in the principal chamber (Dáil Éireann) of the Irish Parliament (Oireachtas) and in the leading academic journals. Therefore it cannot be assumed that the peculiar sense of detachment from English that Kinsella describes for the Irish writer did not inaugurate a political equivalent that led many Irish people to feel detached from the language of daily political life in Irish society. However, before moving to a closer examination of this issue for the university, I want to briefly examine the relationship between secondary and university education in regard to the religion and language issues.

Secondary education and university education

If university education in the humanities in Irish universities was curtailed by the need to balance the demands of the Irish constitution, the 1908 University Act and Church and nationalist dictates, preuniversity education in Ireland had been dealing with similar issues for a longer period. In many respects, public debate on the place of religion in primary and secondary education was more advanced than it was for the university. Rory O'Connell argues that given the fact that the Irish are a 'religious people' living in a pluralist society who 'wish to respect the rights of religious freedom and equality' (1999–2000:500), an accommodation approach to education would be most effective for Irish society. The accommodation approach, he argues, seeks a return to 'the system of separate secular and religious education' (1999–2000:496) that had been the 'official policy' (1999–2000:497) in Irish education from 1831 to 1965, even though it 'was eroded in practice'. This official policy changed in 1965 when the government recognized the denominational status of schools and later introduced the integrated curriculum in 1971. However, O'Connell notes that the Catholic Church's reaction to attempts in the nineteenth century to 'support religious education', for what it called 'sectarian proselytising institutions', demonstrates that 'religion is simply too delicate an issue for the State to involve itself with' (1999–2000:493). For O'Connell, the Constitution Review Group's Report of 1996 argues that the 'current system of education was incompatible with the constitutional text' (1999–2000:491). This is in regard to 'the constitutionality of the integrated curriculum and the financing of chaplains' (1999–2000:490). He therefore argues that an accommodation approach would be most suitable for Irish schools. For O'Connell, it is the 'State as the Supporter of Denominational Education' approach that has been the 'view traditionally articulated by the people who historically have provided much of the education in Ireland, that is the different Churches' (1999–2000:439). Such an approach to education, what is closely associated with Catholic teaching, exalts 'parental rights over state rights' (1999–2000:440). Religion is regarded as 'the high point and pervasive element of education' (1999–2000:440), and we will see this echoed to a degree in the next section when we look at Newman and MacIntyre on the university and the Catholic philosophical tradition. However, according to this approach to education, the 'State has no competence in respect of religious instruction'. The State 'may not regulate this area, even though it is obliged to fund its provision' (1999–2000:441). There was then a key difference in policy after 1908 between the place of religion in preuniversity education and the place of religion in regard to the university.

The accommodation approach to education, on the other hand, advocates that the State 'provides only for secular education, but seeks to accommodate religious activities in such a way as to secure religious liberty and equality for all' (1999–2000:437). Ultimately, in such an approach, O'Connell argues, the State 'may not decide matters of religious faith, may not engage in religious proselytizing or education, or fund such activities, even on a non-discriminatory basis' (1999–2000:439). The State may 'only pay for the secular elements of the education', thus requiring a clear demarcation between the secular and the religious. The State may also not fund an educational institution where the curriculum is permeated throughout with a religious ethos, nor may it 'pay the salaries of religion teachers or chaplains, or establish syllabi or create tests in matters religious' (1999–2000:439). This is remarkably similar then to the dictates on religious education outlined for the National University in the 1908 Act that I examine in the next chapter. O'Connell argues that it is also constitutional since, as he puts it, Article 42 '*does* recognize the primacy of parental rights and accords the State what appears to be a secondary role' but it does not make religious instruction compulsory, or establish it as the basis for all education, or 'recognize any specific role for religious bodies in education, or explicitly sanction state funding of religious activity' (1999–2000:459). However, whereas the similarities between the proposed accommodation approach to preuniversity education and the constitutional requirements in regard to religion in the colleges of the National University after 1908 would be quite similar, at no point did the debate about the place of religion in education reach this advanced level in discussions of university policy. Even if the university was practising an accommodation approach to education, its students were not informed of how the dictates of the 1908 Act conformed with such an approach. In arguing for the appropriateness of such an approach for primary and secondary education, however, one cannot assume that such arguments would also justify the exclusion of religion and theology from the university curriculum. The argument goes to the heart of what it means to be a university. Whereas for many educationalists, religious instruction and a religious ethos are core aspects of denominational and even non-denominational education, neither religious instruction nor the reliance on a pervasive, if unacknowledged, religious ethos is sufficient for a humanities education that includes religion or theology on its curriculum. The university should promote enquiry and open debate on issues important to the identity and character of a people, and any curricular exclusions or omissions even if regarded as constitutional should be a matter of public debate. It is also important to note that given that Ireland, unlike the United States, has few, if any, religiously run colleges,[9] that there is less case law available in Ireland on the distinction between secondary education and college education in regard to the teaching of religion. O'Connell reminds us that the US Supreme Court has drawn a 'distinction between college education and education of younger people at the different stages of development. The Court's case law permits state funding of religiously run colleges, provided a number of conditions are met' (1999–2000:501). Such a clear and rigorous judicial distinction in regard to the place of religion in preuniversity and university-level education with such a quantity of case law behind it is unlikely to exist in Ireland. Ultimately, it meant that the majority of Irish students would pass from one educational stratosphere that was denominational and had a strong religious ethos to another where religious questions could not be professionally interrogated.

Since native teachers and lecturers at these universities were products of the Irish education system, their understanding of humanities subjects was marked by a secondary school education where, as Séamas Ó Buachalla writes as recently as 1989, the churches represented the 'single most extensive presence in the provision of primary and secondary education. [...] Their presence and power have been increased significantly in the course of this century and have been further consolidated by the expansion of education provision in the last two decades' (248). It was not a philosophy of education that was of interest to the churches and to the successive governments that sought to keep in step with church ecumenicals over the course of the century so much as the putting into practice of a system of schooling that would enact the Catholic and nationalistic principles that had made the dream of an Irish education system a reality. And yet, this would work in complete isolation from the university system that could not involve itself in religious education after 1908. The year after the Irish people, guided by de Valera, passed the national plebiscite on the Constitution of Ireland, in Atlantic City, John Dewey returned to the Kappa Delta Pi Society to give its tenth annual lecture at the Chelsea Hotel. De Valera and Dewey would appear to have had quite different opinions on education. In the Kappa Delta Pi address, Dewey stresses that the school should be a 'kind of institution sharply marked off from any other form of social organization' (1938:3). He also gives a warning to educationalists that would prove to be particularly relevant to the burgeoning Irish education system: 'There is always the danger in a new movement that in rejecting the aims and methods of that which it would supplant, it may develop its principles negatively rather than positively and constructively' (1938:6). It seems that the Irish government did not even go so far as rejection or supplanting in trying to reimagine university education in Ireland. Since it did not have the practical knowledge or experience to implement a more advanced third-level programme for education, it adopted a policy of continuity tinged with quietist forbearance, presumably hoping that any programme devised by the Empire that had given the world Oxford, Cambridge and their 'silent sister' Trinity would be good enough for Ireland despite the rhetoric about national identity and 'religious character'.

While Irish government policy was in these early days representative of a 'new movement', its rush to implement what would be a truly Irish system of education neglected to consider whether it was developing these principles negatively, as Dewey suggests. Dewey notes that 'any theory and set of practices is dogmatic which is not based upon critical examination of its own underlying principles' (1938:10). This was nowhere more evident in Irish education than in regard to the language question. With the constitution of 1922, the government introduced an education system where schooling in all subjects through Irish would be compulsory in primary schools, a completely new approach to education for a less than bilingual people. Beyond a sense of duty to nationalist ideals, the 'underlying principles' for such a measure were never interrogated at its introduction or even when a former president of the Irish National Teachers' Organisation (INTO) questioned whether the policy was ultimately aimed at 'ousting English from the schools' (Farren, 1995:149). Twenty years later, in 1942, the president of the INTO, J. P. Griffith, argued at the organization's congress that by excluding English, the 'home language' from the 'infant departments' we have 'placed each child – each little budding sensitive soul – straight into a linguistic strait-jacket in which he cannot reveal the mysterious workings of his opening mind. We tried this strange experiment but I fear it has not yielded the results claimed for it' (qtd. in Farren, 1995:190). The INTO's report of 1941 which also served to 'dispel many illusions' in regard to the Irish language and education suffered the 'wrath of officialdom' from the then Minister of Education Tom Derrig who 'bitterly and success-fully resisted demands for an inquiry, even from the teachers themselves, into the effectiveness of the official approach' (Lee, 1989:671). However, even with such a reaction from primary teachers, coupled with an earlier report of 1940–41 from the secondary school teachers' organization, the Association of Secondary Teachers of Ireland (ASTI), which claimed that 'after the experi-ence of twenty years the time is ripe for stock taking and we demand an enquiry into the position of Irish in the curriculum' (*ibid.* 190), the govern-ment replied by restating its commitment to the policy of 1922 and by blaming the teachers themselves. It claimed that they had not abided by official regula-tions and recommendations for the teaching of Irish. If children in primary and secondary schools were therefore being schooled in a language they would never use to detail their ambitions or personal philosophies, they would be far less proficient in English and far less expectant in regard to courses and cur-ricula, when they finally arrived in a teaching environment that used English.

The first full-scale review of education policy would not come for another twenty years in 1947, and 'no action was ever taken on the basis of [its] report' (Farren, 1995:201). It is hardly surprising, then, that an education system that could not agree on the language of instruction until well into the 1960s lagged far behind other national education systems in terms of a philosophy or theory of education. J. J. Lee argues that the policy of Irish in national schools may have 'accounted in some measure for the educational retardation of Irish chil-dren compared with English children up to university level' (1989:134). When the Irish government finally decided in the 1960s that English would be a more fitting language of instruction, it still had to contend with the 'church influence and control over the schools' that 'was probably unparalleled else-where in the western world' (Farren, 1995:247). When Irish education had finally limited the effects of these linguistic and moral restraints, it had already begun to feel the influences of another encroaching and somewhat alien force that would further distract educationalists from the pressing concerns at hand, namely, Europeanization. For a less than visionary educational system, the emergence of the liberal yet corporate influence of Europeanization would quickly fill the void left by the unshackling of Irish education policy both from exclusive Church influence and from the narrow philosophical confines of many of the arguments that focused purely on the language question.

On many occasions in the history of state education in Ireland, the universi-ties became embroiled in these contentious issues. At the founding of the NUI in 1908, there was a rare instance of dissent within the church. Dr Walter McDonald, professor of dogmatic theology in Maynooth, made public his differences with church policy in regard to the university question and the management of schools. He suggested 'making terms with Trinity' (Ó Buachalla, 1988:219) by setting up a Catholic college within Dublin. In *The Irish Educational Review* of 1908, he also questioned the validity of the clerical right of direct control of state-endowed schools:

> In schools endowed by the state, churchmen as such have no right to direct control, but only to indirect supervision to see that the laws of religion and morality are observed. Those who provide the funds, the people in all democratic states, have direct control involving the right of appointing teachers, inspectors and other officers as well as of prescribing courses and textbooks. The Church has a right to see that in all this religion and morality do not suffer loss. (qtd. in Ó Buachalla, 1988:219)

McDonald suggests that the church should base its claim for directing state education on the 'presumed delegation of the children's parents who are the taxpayers and electors' (*ibid.* 220). The fact that a similar suggestion would again have to be made by a professor of Catholic philosophy at one of the National University's over sixty years later only demonstrates how slow the government and the Church were to unsettle the status quo and separate state education from the church. Dr. James Good of UCC writes in 1970: 'One must wonder whether control of second-level education should necessarily rest in the hands of the Catholic hierarchy in order that it continues to be suitable for Catholics' (in Ó Buachalla, 1988:220). The universities were not exempt from these institutional questions. Indeed, it might even be suggested that the National University system was set up for the purpose of offering a Catholic university education. Since the Catholic leadership claimed that Trinity College was a Protestant university even though it had opened its doors to Catholics in 1793 with the 'catholic relief act' (Parkes, 2010:541), the numbers of Catholics entering remained low until the 1950s (Ó Buachalla, 1988:207). The three constituent universities of the National University also appeared to have a clear agenda marked out for them in the eyes of the state and the Church. This, as well as the restrictions on religious education and the teaching of theology, would surely affect university autonomy in relation to drawing up courses and curricula for humanities subjects that dealt with ethics and morals[10]. However, the Irish government was at times quite explicit in describing what kind of educational ethos or philosophy it expected in the Irish system. In 1948, the then Minister of Education, Richard Mulcahy, addressed the Conference of Convent Secondary Schools: 'What is wanted is a council which will recognise and proclaim the Catholic philosophy upon which our Irish system is based' (Ó Buachalla, 1988:154). Since the national universities had been founded under this philosophical remit, it is important to investigate not only how subsequent humanities education was affected by this 'Catholic philosophy' but also whether any such philosophy ever existed. For, as Séamas Ó Buachalla writes, throughout 'this century the inherited educational structures of the nineteenth century have been conserved and indeed consolidated' (1988:77).

Identity and education

There is a noted lack of work on the relationship between education and identity in the Irish context. Kevin Williams and Gerry McNamara argue in 2003 that the 'theme of Irish identity [...] features little in the literature' (2003:367) on curriculum inquiry by Irish researchers. J. J. Lee argues, in relation to Irish language policy in education, that identity 'posed so formidable a challenge for the relatively homogenous Republic' (1989:674). For so long, the Irish identity crisis was all about, as Kevin O'Connor suggests in 1985, 'finding a way to cast off the protective skin of nationalism and still say "we are Irish"'.[11] David R. Shumway points out too that the humanities are traditionally, albeit somewhat disavowedly, bound up with nationalism: '[t]he constitutive role of nationalism in the humanities belies their claims to be apolitical and disinterested' (1998:357). However, this does not imply that cultural nationalism can be a substitute for a humanities programme, as many might have sought to imply at different times in Irish university history. If we take curriculum and educational policy to be necessary for a sense of identity in Irish society, it is also important to note that researchers argue that 'we don't have a coherent, integrated curriculum policy' (McCormack qtd. in Williams, 2003:371) in Irish education and they describe existing policy in terms of 'innovation without change' (Gleeson qtd. in Williams, 2003:373). Williams and McNamara argue that the theme of Irish identity 'remains conspicuously undertheorized' (2003:376) in work on curriculum studies and educational policy in Ireland. This seems especially surprising if we read the ideals for education outlined at the founding of the state at the National Programme Conference in 1921. Seán Farren reads the report of the conference as laying out a policy of education that would 'inculcate future generations with a deep sense of their Gaelic heritage' (1995:55). The teaching of history in schools curriculums was to

> [D]evelop the best traits of the national character [...] inculcate national pride and self-respect. This will not be attained by the examining of dates and details but rather by showing that the Irish race has fulfilled a great mission in the advancement of civilisation and that, on the whole, the Irish nation has amply justified its existence. (*ibid.* 55)

The curriculum for English also set out to bring the teaching of literature and culture in Irish schools closer to the culture of Europe, what may appear now as a progressive policy in light of the Bologna Accord, even though at the time, such policy was most likely introduced as a result of an 'Anglophobia' evident in national policy. However, the fact that an international team of educationalists, writing on Irish education policy eighty years later, would find questions of 'Irish identity' lacking in education policy studies can only be partially a result of the nature of the 'Irish identity' espoused in education policy at that time. The national ethos implicit in education policy in those early years was a regard for 'Irish identity' that would be carried into Article 42 of the Irish constitution on education policy in 1937 and through to the 'first full-scale review of educational structures conducted by the Department of Education in the south' (Farren, 1995:201) in 1947, a report on which no action was ever taken. Article 42.1 of the Irish constitution makes a clear connection between education and the 'duty' of parents to bring children up in line with their Catholic faith: '[...] the primary and natural educator of the child is the Family and [the constitution] recognises the inalienable right and duty of parents to provide, according to their means, for the religious and moral, intellectual, physical and social education of their children' (1995:140). As we have seen, this was made apparent when Éamon de Valera, speaking at the World Education Conference held in Dublin in 1933, proposed that the '[...] the beginning and end of true education, is the development of religious and moral character' (Farren, 1995:140). Successive governments would prove slow in advancing the cause of a secular educational philosophy where a broad humanities programme in the National University could freely explore the relationship between identity, knowledge and 'Catholic faith'.

Writing in 1989, Thomas Kellaghan describes the patchy state of educational policy research in Ireland: 'In Ireland, there is relatively little legislation relating to education; hence, one has to rely on other sources. Indeed, such other sources are not very plentiful either and do not always contain explicit and comprehensive statements of the objectives of educational policy' (Mulcahy, 1981:193). Kellaghan also makes direct reference to the lack of any clear philosophy of education in Irish education policy:

> Historical and philosophical research has also been undertaken but, as yet, there has been little evidence of the approaches which are being proposed elsewhere as an alternative to empirical research, such as interpretive studies (analytic, phenomenological, and hermeneutic) and critical theory (neomarxist). The lack of popularity of such approaches may arise at least in part from the fact that their use raises a host of problems for researchers and policy makers who have grown up in more empirical traditions. (1989:194)

Denis O'Sullivan, also writing in 1989, goes so far as to claim that Irish educational thought is 'conceptually and analytically weak, paradigmatically insulated and ideologically sanitised' (1989:220). These observations are also evident in the Government White Papers that in the absence of academic publications on Irish educational policy must go someway towards filling in the detail in relation to education policy and a coherent philosophy of education. J. J. Lee has pointed out that the chapter on third-level education in the government's 1984 White Paper on education, entitled the *Programme for action in education 1984–1987*, 'fails to make a solitary mention of the significance of the quality of social thought, or indeed of any thought, for the well being of society' (qtd. in Mulcahy, 1989:117). As future Government White Papers will continue to do, this document assumes that vocational preparation is, as Patrick Clancy argues, the 'prime purpose of higher education and that the main justification for state expenditure on higher education is its contribution to technological development and economic growth' (qtd. in Mulcahy, 1989:117). Seamus Ó Buachalla admits that the provision for education policy increased in the 1960s when Ireland experienced a relatively stable economic climate. However, once again it was through collaborations with other state educators in Europe and not through any solely Irish initiative that certain reviews were called for in relation to policy on education. Following an OECD conference on education in Washington in 1961, Ireland became one of the participants in the Education Investment Programme for developed countries in Europe. In 1962, a national survey team was established under Professor Patrick Lynch as director. Even though the survey's only recommendation was the establishment of a planning and development branch within the Department of Education, the survey did also comment on the lack of educational resources available. It draws attention 'to the inadequacy of the statistical data available on the system' (Ó Buachalla, 1988:72). The lack of initiative in matters relating to education policy, epitomized by the reaction to this national survey, is linked by Ó Buachalla to what he suggests was the 'caution and pragmatism characteristic of Fianna Fail in government in relation to education' (Ó Buachalla, 1988:73). The sluggishness on the part of Fianna Fail was noted by Fine Gael when, under Liam Cosgrave in 1966, the party prepared a set of policies with the general heading *The just society*. In the document, Cosgrave complained that 'we had been for half a century content to tinker with the system but had never really attempted to reform it' (Ó Buachalla, 1988:71). Unfortunately, little action was taken on the document. The lack of any clear philosophy of education in the system and the failure to redress the make-up of 'Irish identity' as outlined in the educational ideals committed to in the Constitution and implicit ever after in subsequent government documents on education meant that Irish education policy was liable to be bowled over by the waves of Europeanization that were beginning to break across Ireland in the later decades of the century and following Ireland's admission to the European Economic Community (EEC).

Williams and McNamara put forward some reasons for why this might be the case. They suggest that it was not until 1999 that the Department of Education introduced a document that would no longer commit the State to a 'direct endorsement' in schools 'of the Christian view of human destiny'. In other words, until 1999, the State required the 'maintenance of a religious ethos in all primary schools' (2003:377). They also argue that the issue of identity, in the context of the Northern conflict, 'is fraught with potential disagreement and so tends to be avoided' (2003:377) and that it is now time for 'sustained critical inquiry regarding the relationship among religion, politics, culture, and the curriculum' (2003:377). They are correct in noting that the majority of work done in curriculum studies and on anything approaching a philosophy of education in Ireland has been jump-started to a certain extent by the language of policy documents from Europe. The Europeanization of education in Ireland requires at the very least that Irish educationalists understand the philosophical background to continental educational movements that Ireland must now draw level with in many areas. In curriculum research on Irish education, there is an 'almost universally shared view that the European dimension to political and cultural life is to be welcomed and vigorously promoted' (2003:377). Such 'Euroawareness' found its way into Irish schools firstly through a policy drafted at the Council of Ministers for Education on 9 February 1976. It was decided that a 'European dimension' would have to be introduced, in a 'formal' way, to the 'experience of teachers and students in the primary and secondary schools in the European Community' (*Education in a Single Europe*, 2000:220). Following this initial agreement, a further declaration was taken at Fontainebleau in June 1984 that drafted practical means through which this policy of Euroawareness might be introduced. It was agreed that the teaching of foreign languages would be promoted, measures to encourage contacts between students from different European countries would be introduced, the European dimension would be highlighted in teacher training courses and measures were taken to 'underscore the European dimension in the existing curriculum' (*ibid.* 221). It might seem strange then that the curriculum would stress a European dimension while at the same time never making any concerted effort to mediate an interrogation of 'Irish identity'.

Denis O'Sullivan points to important omissions in the educational policies promoted at the time. He suggests that even though Irish educationalists were keen to suggest that they were not promoting any educational ideologies, their institutional dragging of heels in relation to influences from outside was representative of an ideology in itself:

> And when innovations, such as the comprehensive school idea which originated from a social as well as an educational critique, were imported into Irish educational discourse, there was a conscious effort to jettison all elements of social reconstruction. In effect, therefore, by specifically attempting to avoid ideology (considered as social critique or reconstruction), Irish educational planners have acted ideologically, i.e. in the interests of those social groups who benefit from existing social and educational structures. (in Mulcahy, 1989:243)

Another reason for the sluggish approach of the Irish government and of Irish educationalists to detailing a coherent philosophy of education that could complement anything like an 'Irish identity' was that Irish humanities divisions assumed that employing Oxbridge or American academics would somehow graft the foreign humanities ethos onto native academic institutions even if the same range of subjects was not being taught in these institutions. However, it is well known that higher education has existed in the United States 'for longer than the nation itself' (Heller, 2004:50). Harvard College, founded in 1636, was the first higher education institution in the colonies. Donald E. Heller reminds us that even though the 'earliest colleges were private, state support of higher education began with public allocations to these largely church-chartered institutions' (2004:50). The first truly 'public' institutions of higher education were not chartered until late in the eighteenth century. Even though these institutions received direct state subsidies, Heller argues that they were in reality 'quasi-public' because of the 'degree of autonomy granted to their trustees' (2004:50).

The situation in Ireland could not have been more dissimilar. There were no philanthropic trustees or entrepreneurial financial magnates willing to charter higher education institutions in even the early years of twentieth-century Ireland.[12] The Irish National University was, on the contrary, a late legislative response to the dire needs of a monetarily and educationally impoverished people. The fact that the American institutions were founded before the nation itself may also have allowed for a degree of separation between identity and thought about identity, or between nationalism and thought about nationalism, that was not possible in Irish society. In many ways, national identity and sovereignty were forged for the American people in the universities. This is one of the reasons why American national identity, what Harpham equates with the modern humanities themselves, is such a durable and influential ideology. David R. Shumway argues that the 'nationalist foundation of most American social sciences is fairly obvious to anyone willing to look just beneath ground level. American political science, for example, has historically assumed American political institutions to be the center of its object and research' (1998:358). If we see the major national literatures, as David Lloyd argues, as distinctive precisely because they are 'directed toward the production of an autonomous ethical identity of the subject' (1987:20), then we might begin to see why Irish national education policy was slow to tackle the theme of identity. Shumway argues that even though American Studies, like Irish Studies, was 'born out of a postcolonial rhetoric' (1998:369), American writers such as Emerson, Thoreau and Whitman were already describing such an 'ethical identity of the subject' for the American people by the middle of the nineteenth century. Irish writers, as Lloyd argues, would only be recognized, on the other hand, as describing a kind of character who works against such an identity, where the 'subject is denied autonomous status' (1987:21), in the twentieth century. Irish universities therefore were neither founded with, nor helped foster, some autonomous notion of national identity grounded on a reasoned response to the 'ethical identity of the subject'. Even though the Irish National University was inaugurated fourteen years before the founding of the Irish state, it was the national question that influenced all policy for the Irish people, especially policy for education, as Pearse's writings clearly show. Harvard and other early institutions in the United States might have been chiefly 'church-chartered' institutions, but the religious dictates of the founding fathers were not so rigidly aligned with the institution's philosophy of education because the institution was not emerging out of a history of religious oppression. The motivating force of the Irish people in achieving independence was an intoxicating embrace of 'national identity' that was always inextricably tied to their Catholic faith. That their National University would then be exempt from practising or professing this faith would only stunt further their appreciation of identity.

While Irish government policy on education was to struggle to reconcile what it felt were its debts to the Church and its understanding of national identity for most of the twentieth century, American education policy had already in 1819, under the leadership of Thomas Jefferson, inaugurated the first 'real state university' which was 'founded to be free of domination by any and all religious sects' (Heller, 2004:51). If Irish educationalists are then to regard the American liberal arts programmes as substitutes for the Oxbridge model for Irish educational institutions, they must not be blind to these fundamental differences between the genealogies of the two national education systems. However, there are reasons to suggest that Irish universities are now moving closer to the American model. The streamlining of Irish universities in terms of fewer faculties and departments has meant that traditional humanities subjects are moving institutionally closer, at any rate, to disciplines that were previously regarded as being at a remove from the concerns of Arts subjects. Irish humanities undergraduates in history, sociology and even literature follow their American counterparts in regularly gaining credits in courses devoted to techniques of research and to 'methods of inquiry' rather than to 'speculation' and 'substance' (Aronowitz, 2000:136). For Stanley Aronowitz, this approach to academic learning was spearheaded by the philosophy of the core curriculum of Harvard University's Faculty of Arts and Sciences. Its agenda 'spelled out in its 1979–80 catalog' (2000:136) 'does not define intellectual breadth as the mastery of a set of Great Books, or the digestion of a specific quantum of information, or the surveying of current knowledge in [a] certain field but, instead, [seeks] to introduce students to the major approaches to knowledge in areas that the faculty considers indispensable to undergraduate education' (2000:136). Aronowitz views this approach somewhat negatively in arguing that 'we are encouraged to digest, not knowledge, but techniques of research. Hence the invocation to the student to master "skills" such as quantitative reasoning and writing' (2000:136). While a concentration on quantitative reasoning and writing might enable humanities departments to throw off lingering questions about 'identity' and lingering fears about the lack of any coherent 'philosophy of education' in their bids to imitate more successful international departments, the 'substance' of the core subjects cannot be neglected by any methodological approach to learning that values the humanities tradition.

The Irish university and a Catholic philosophical tradition

Alasdair MacIntyre has recently argued that an 'educated Catholic laity needs to understand a good deal more about Catholic philosophical thought than it now does' (2009:1). Writing in 1967, Robert J. McNamara argues, in relation to theology in the American universities, that 'the large scale introduction and continuance of a Ph.D. program in theology on the Catholic university campuses could be the beginning of a major break-through for the intellectual life of the American Catholic Church' (1967:85). It seems that the Irish universities have never given themselves the opportunity to experience such a 'major break-through for the intellectual life' of their campuses. MacIntyre argues that Catholic philosophy should be understood as a 'continuing conversation through centuries, in which we turn and return to dialogue with the most important voices from our past, in order to carry forward that conversation in our own time' (2009:1). MacIntyre's argument would appear to be particularly relevant to the Irish context given the fact that the Irish university and Irish educational philosophy in general has been strongly influenced by Newman's *Idea of a University*,[13] possibly the most respected modern expression of such a Catholic philosophy for university education. MacIntyre also examines what it might mean for a university 'not to be Godless' (2009:17). Since the Queen's Colleges had famously been described by Daniel O'Connell as 'godless colleges' (Parkes, 2010:546), one would imagine that the later university developments in Ireland such as the Catholic University, the Royal University and the National University would have a degree of godliness attached despite the legal requirement against religious education in the non-denominational National University. However, MacIntyre argues that any such not entirely 'Godless' university would need to teach theology and philosophy together in the curriculum: '[t]heology would be taught both for its own sake and as a key to that overall understanding [of such a university]. And it would be a central task of philosophy in such a university to enquire into the nature of the relationship between theology and the secular disciplines' (2009:17). These two aspects of a Catholic philosophical tradition in the university were largely absent from the National University throughout the twentieth century.

MacIntyre goes so far as to argue that 'in all three of the great medieval theistic civilizations, that of Byzantine Christianity, of Islam, and of the Latin West, it is not just that belief in God is so nearly universal that it is, for the most part, taken for granted, but that it is a presupposition of all secular enquiry and activity' (2009:61). He argues that theology is the 'hegemonic academic discipline' for these 'three theistic cultures' to the extent that it often guides the study of the 'secular disciplines' (2009: 61). Newman, rather like Kant in the 1790s, makes a similar point for his Catholic University in 1852. Even though it is generally accepted that the modern understanding of the humanities departs from such a rigid structure, theology and religious enquiry have retained an important position alongside philosophy in many of the leading humanities programmes.

MacIntyre also explains how the Catholic philosophical tradition he traces in the teachings of possibly its most influential theologian, philosopher and educator, Thomas Aquinas, relates to civic morality. For Aquinas, the basis for all reasoned appreciation of law is grounded on the 'eternal law' by which 'God rules the universe' (2009:88). The natural law describes the individual's reasoned apprehension of this eternal law in terms of its applicability to human affairs. MacIntyre argues that Aquinas's teachings essentially describe how '[b]y developing habits of obedience to the natural law, habits that are also expressed in the exercise of the virtues, we direct ourselves toward the achievement not only of the common goods of social life, but also of our individual good, that good by the achievement of which our lives are perfected and completed' (2009:89). Obedience to the natural law is therefore a process essential for the harmonization of one's ambitions with those of a society, and it requires that one balances philosophical speculation with theological sensitivity. For a Catholic society, civic morality would then appear to be grounded on an appreciation of this essential relationship between theology and philosophy. Irish university students were often denied an opportunity for practising such enquiry. The student of the Catholic university education that embodies Aquinas's teachings would begin with logic, grammar and mathematics. When these subjects were mastered, only then would such a student move on to 'moral and political philosophy'. Metaphysics and theology were the final subjects such a student would study (2009:94). MacIntyre argues that the sense of 'unity' which such programmes granted the students is still practised today in 'Paris' and Oxford (2009:93). However, he notes, in moving to a discussion of Newman, that a 'good moral character' cannot be presumed to result from such programmes. MacIntyre reminds us that Newman was keenly aware of how 'knowledge' can 'refine' the mind to such a degree that disgust in the face of 'enormities of evil' (in MacIntyre,

2009:148) does not arise solely from 'genuine moral disgust' but from an aesthetic attribute, namely, that of having a 'fastidious self-regard, a wish to be able to think well of oneself' (2009:148). Universities can therefore foster a 'simulacrum of morality', what MacIntyre describes as an 'aesthetic distaste' (2009:148). His unapologetic Catholic approach to solving this confusing of aesthetic distaste with 'moral revulsion' is only to be found, for a Catholic community, when the 'university community is attentive to that in the moral teaching of the Catholic Church that makes the distinction between the moral and the aesthetic evident' (2009:148). Despite de Valera's and successive education ministers' claims that the foundation of Irish education was the Catholic faith, Ireland's 'university community' was never likely to focus on such an important distinction.

The writer's perspective: Joyce on education

In 1899, in a university matriculation essay written while a student of the University College (formerly the Catholic University), James Joyce displays his acute awareness of the subtle relationship between literature and the sciences. In an age of academic capitalism, when the disciplines are clearly demarcated for funding and capital investment purposes, Joyce's words may seem quaint. However, Joyce describes a consistent feature of progressive and enlightened work in either field:

> For that which ennobles the study of mathematics in the eyes of the wise, is the fact that it proceeds with regular course, that there is a science, a knowledge of the facts, in contradistinction to literature, which is in the more elegant aspect of it, imaginary and notional. This draws a line of demarcation between the two; and yet as Mathematics and the Sciences of Numbers partake of the nature of that beauty which is omnipresent, which is expressed, almost noiselessly, in the order and symmetry of Mathematics, as in the charms of literature; so does literature in turn share in the neatness and regularity of Mathematics. (2000b:13)

Both disciplines share in the 'nature of that beauty which is omnipresent' and 'in the neatness and regularity of Mathematics'. Writing some years later as an expat in Trieste in 1907, on the eve of the creation of the National University, Joyce also discusses education in Ireland. He is disparaging of the existing 'education system' that was only now 'allowing some streams of modern thought to filter slowly into the arid earth' (2000b:121). He recognizes that the 'wave of democracy' that shook England at the founding of the House of the Commons 'washed out on Irish shores' and that the 'dates of the Lutheran Reformation and the French Revolution mean nothing to an Irishman' (2000b:120), a point taken up by Michael J. O'Sullivan in his recent book *Ireland and the Global Question*. O'Sullivan refers to an argument made by

Daniel Cohen in *La mondialisation et ses ennemis*. Cohen, in writing on the relative isolation of the Islamic world and China from the western world from the sixteenth century onwards, argues that 'renaissance, reformation and scientific revolution went unseen', in these lands. Perhaps to still the orientalist tone of such arguments, O'Sullivan suggests that the same kind of argument could be made in relation to Ireland which also 'missed out on these experiences largely because of its occupation, something which in turn has left a heavy Anglo-Saxon [as opposed to European] footprint on cultural and social life' (O'Sullivan, 2006:43). However, Joyce respected his culture too much to leave it there. His formal odyssey in writing strives to bring the three r's (renaissance, reformation and revolution) to the Irish scene of enquiry all at once. But Joyce, like Stephen Dedalus, was no ordinary teacher. We recall Stephen's sense of himself as a betrayer (not of the Word, but the word) in 'Nestor'. He is Peter and Judas rolled into one. Sitting at Deasy's desk, having his crowns and shillings doled out to him like the silver pieces Judas earns, his sense of his location, profession and self in a job he despises hounds him like the three cock crows that provide the soundtrack to Peter's betrayal: 'The same room and hour, the same wisdom: and I the same. Three times now. Three nooses round me here. Well. I can break them in this instant if I will' (1992:36). And Joyce does break them. He gives up teaching the prescribed courses in language in order to invent his own.

Joyce, one of Ireland's most energetic Europeans, gave talks on Ireland and Irish education at Trieste, on the cusp of Europe, in 1907, a pivotal moment in the history of Irish education. After 1908, Irish university education would never be the same. The university education in the humanities that Joyce received bore marked differences, at least officially, to what would be practised in Irish universities after 1908. In his lecture to the assembled guests in Trieste, Joyce was careful to note that the island of Ireland had once been a 'true centre' of 'intellectualism and sanctity', a mix that he would strive to retain in his own later works. However, when Joyce speaks here of a lost paradise of intellectualism and sanctity, he does not refer to the doctrine or dogma of the religious worldview popular in the Ireland that he had, to a certain extent, turned his back on. Joyce had experienced his own particular 'religious defection' (Ellmann, 1972:60) well before writing his matriculation piece, 'The Study of Languages' in 1899, a fact made clear in his lecture at Trieste. In the lecture, he looks forward to a time when '[p]erhaps [...] there will be a gradual reawakening of the Irish consciousness' when 'perhaps, four or five centuries after the Diet of Worms, we shall witness a monk in Ireland throw off his cowl, run off with a nun, and proclaim aloud the end of the coherent absurdity that is Catholicism, and the beginning of the incoherent absurdity that is Protestantism' (2000b:121). If Eamon Casey's very public throwing off of the cowl almost a century later can be regarded as fulfilling

Joyce's prophecy, then the unshackling of the 'Irish consciousness' from its dependence on even the 'coherent absurdity' of Catholicism would be a long time coming. However, Joyce's description of the connections between mathematics and languages would also suggest that he appreciated how the humanities were rooted in such formal disciplines as philology. David R. Shumway argues that the modern humanities have 'all descended from German philology, a critical/scientific project that constituted a radical break from the rhetorically based studies preceding it' (1998:360).[14]

Joyce's university education with the Jesuits also enabled him to investigate how art, philosophy and theology complemented one another. When Joyce was a student at UCD, the Royal University, the examining body for the College, specified that examinations would be in secular subjects. However, Joyce's university education in subjects such as literature would have been influenced by the strong religious views of his professors. It was an education that helped formulate his later artistic trajectory through the philosophy of Aquinas in his quest to discover his own personal philosophy and, ultimately, his own literary voice. Despite the 1879 university act which established the Royal University of Ireland and which specified that there was to be 'no teaching or examining in theology' (Parkes, 2010:560), Joyce's University College maintained much of its Catholic outlook when it was renamed University College Dublin in 1882 and especially when it was placed under the management of the Society of Jesus the following year. The president of the college, Father William Delany, noted that the 'effect of having at least half the faculty in surplices was profounder than it might seem to the outside' (Ellmann, 1972:59). Joyce's university education served up its own mixture of 'intellectualism and sanctity' that sought to impart to students how a grounding in the religious philosophy of thinkers such as Aquinas could enhance the understanding of 'moral history' and ethics.

However, Joyce might also be regarded as sharing some of the educational ideals of the American pragmatists. Louis Menand's *The Metaphysical Club* plots a genealogy of pragmatism in America. In 1896, a few years before Joyce described his own understanding of the principal disciplines of a university education, William James was lecturing for the first time on the new philosophy of pragmatism, at a university named after Joyce's compatriot, Berkeley. In the lecture, entitled 'Philosophical Conceptions and Practical Results', delivered at the University of California, Berkeley, James put forward his first explanation of the method of pragmatism, an idea that he credited to Charles Sanders Peirce but which James appropriated and transformed. The influence of both a Protestant ethic and a pragmatist ethos provided a metaphysical backdrop for many turn-of-the-century American aesthetic theories. Formal and syntactic advances were foregrounded at the expense of the transcendental or epiphanic moment of the aesthetic. Menand writes of a resurgent and vibrant dualism that appeared in the American psyche towards the end of the nineteenth century, and Joyce may have caught the scent of this philosophical and cultural advance and its movement out of religious thought while teaching English in continental Europe. The pragmatism of Louis Agassiz and Benjamin Peirce also sought to redefine the relationship between the individual and the environment, as does Joyce's examination of perception, through Aquinas, in *A Portrait*. Agassiz's theory of recapitulation sees the process by which the universe 'becomes itself as replicated in the life history of the individual' (Menand, 2002:108), and Peirce also saw 'in every form of material manifestation [...] a corresponding form of human thought, so that the human mind is as wide in its range of thought as the physical universe which it thinks' (Menand, 2002:156). This is an empowering re-contextualization of individual agency in terms of the everyday. environment. In some ways, it repeats formally aspects of Stephen Dedalus's appreciation of the artistic moment whereby the 'artist presents his image in immediate relation to himself' (Joyce, 2000a:180). This pragmatist, post-Romantic philosophy was often grounded in a Protestant ethos, just as Joyce's own philosophy of art was also arrived at through his own study of the Catholic philosophical tradition. Both philosophies, in dispensing with dogma, mined the metaphysical foundations of the respective spiritual discourses for theological analogues that could help explain the new worldviews.

Joyce's university education offers a picture of the humanities that may have been closer to the American idea of the humanities than what was experienced by Irish students of the National University at least up until the 1950s. It combined spiritual enquiry with the study of art, and even though Joyce's Jesuit teachers, as Declan Kiberd argues, had 'asked him to believe that there was a radical difference between the methods of religion and science', Joyce 'couldn't agree' (2009:254). Joyce's education played an important role in enabling him to see theological analogues in daily life. In *A Portrait* – what Kiberd describes as a 'sustained meditation on true and false pedagogy' (Kiberd, 2009:54) – Joyce's alter ego, Stephen Dedalus, is an aspiring artist who describes his work as that of a 'priest of the eternal imagination' (2000b:186). Even though, as Ellmann points out, Joyce had already decided to leave the Church by way of 'transmutation', he would still 'retain faith, but with different objects' (Ellmann, 1972:67). He tries to understand the world about him, both as 'moral history' and as inspiration for art through the prism of the education he received in Catholic philosophy. Stephen does not profess any belief in what these religious questions ultimately lead up to, but they provide a linguistic and theoretical background against which the questioning of art and aesthetic theory are enriched and, in a sense, opened out to a wider, non-specialized field of enquiry. In one late section from *A Portrait*, Joyce reveals, through his alter ego,

Stephen Dedalus, how a university education that includes reference to such Catholic thinkers as Aquinas can enable him to attain a more profound understanding of artistic inspiration and perception:

> Aquinas uses a term which seems to be inexact. It baffled me for a long time. It would lead you to believe that he had in mind symbolism or idealism, the supreme quality of beauty being a light from some other world, the idea of which the matter is but the shadow. I thought he might mean that *claritas* is the artistic discovery and representation of the divine purpose in anything or a force of generalization which would make the esthetic image a universal one, make it outshine its proper conditions. But that is literary talk. I understand it so. (2000a:179)

Even though Stephen has moved beyond the Thomistic approach, he reveals here how his understanding of the aesthetic and of perception had been guided by the work of Aquinas. Joyce, together with his alter ego Stephen, will move beyond Aquinas's theory of perception in creating a democratizing understanding of art that sees art as engrained in the transcendental where 'God' is the 'shout in the street' (1992:42). In like manner, John Dewey, whose own work on education grew out of pragmatism, also describes how theology and religious thought influence a moral education that is accepting of everyday 'lapses':

> One of the most instructive things in all human history is the system of concessions, tolerances, mitigations and reprieves which the Catholic Church with its official supernatural morality has devised for the multitude. Elevation of the spirit above everything natural is tempered by organized leniency for the frailties of flesh. To uphold an aloof realm of strictly ideal realities is admitted to be possible only for a few. Protestantism, except in its most zealous forms, has accomplished the same result by a sharp separation between religion and morality in which a higher justification by faith disposes at one stroke of daily lapses into the gregarian morals of average conduct. (1974:64)

However, when Joyce left Irish education behind forever in October 1904, it was only four years before theology and all forms of religious education would be officially excluded from the National University curriculum. The humanities curriculum would not offer the potential for interdisciplinary work in aesthetics, theology and philosophy that Joyce took to heart. For the recognized 'religious people' (O'Connell, 1999–2000:436) that the Irish were, and constitutionally still are, a void emerged in humanities education that could only be filled by the dogmatic tone the government and Church would take in all matters relating to secular education in primary and secondary schools. Irish students would never again find their educational footing in quite the same way or be privy to the same sort of philosophical and theological soul searching that Joyce's *alter ego* is, as he makes his existential discoveries about himself and his homeland through his understanding of art and literature.

Notes

1 Even though it must be acknowledged that Ireland is becoming 'an increasingly secular society', Dympna Glendenning argues, writing in 1998, that 'religion and education are still closely intertwined and this is mirrored in the constitutional provisions underpinning education' (1998:80).

2 Between 1% and 2% of all full-time Arts and Humanities undergraduate enrolments are on courses where the teaching is predominantly through Irish. These courses include Irish and a small number of other courses. For the 2010/11 academic year, there were nineteen students enrolled on Early and Modern Irish at Trinity, thirty-two on Modern Irish (Major) and fifty-two on Modern Irish (Joint) at University College Dublin (UCD), forty-one on Irish and New Media at the University of Limerick, sixty on the BA Joint Hons (languages) at University College Cork (UCC), forty-two on the Bachelor of Arts with Irish Studies at National University of Ireland, Galway (NUIG), and thirteen on Baitsiléir Sna Dána (Gaeilge and Léann an Aistriúcháin) at NUIG. A minority of students also study Irish in First Arts in the different universities. The total number of students being taught predominantly through Irish for 2010/11 was less than 0.5% of the 111,874 total enrolments on full-time and part-time courses in the university and IT sectors (www.hea.ie/en/node/1480).

3 J. J. Lee notes that university education in the humanities and social sciences was not only affected by the language question and by the lack of religion or theology departments. While economics, history and education were established subjects in the university, these were 'exceptionally advanced' compared with related subjects: 'Few lectureships, much less, chairs, were established in sociology, political science, anthropology, international relations, law, geography, social psychology, or economic history, until long after economics had achieved a secure position as a standard university subject' (1989:584). A chair of Catholic sociology was established at Maynooth in 1937 and in sociology in UCC in the same year. A chair in sociology was not created at UCD until 1966 and at Trinity until 1974. University College Galway (UCG) only established a joint chair of politics and sociology in 1969, and UCD separated a chair of politics from that of ethics in 1983. UCC did not create a politics department until much later. Lee also notes that '[l]aw as serious academic subject developed mainly after 1960' (1989:584–5).

4 Lee's sense of the 'civic' here should be distinguished from the sense of civility R. F. Foster highlights in his reading of the plantations in seventeenth century Ireland in terms of a move to 'inculcate English civility' in Ireland (1989:63).

5 However, Lee also notes that any supposed 'decline in religious observance' prior to the 1970s was never of a 'type to prompt the development of empirical religious sociology' (609). It must also be noted that Maynooth established a chair of Catholic sociology in 1937.

6 J. J. Lee suggests in speaking for the state of the universities up to 1965, and possibly beyond, that '[a]ll universities' in the early decades of the State had to 'cope with severely limited resources'. He also suggests that more money would most likely not have improved the situation. He puts this down to the fact that 'so many of the relevant subjects [he is thinking here primarily of sociology and the political

sciences] were not even taught in the institutions'. He continues: 'Only a handful of the former academics among university administrators were familiar with social thought [...] As late as 1965, a Danish consultant expressed his surprise at the scant support for the social sciences' (1989:613).

7 Barrington is referring here to the fact that by 2002, Ireland had neither legislation on nor a 'national body' with responsibility for bioethics that could oversee regulation for human stem cell research. At this time, Ireland had also not signed the Council of Europe Convention on Human Rights and Biomedicine (2002:147).

8 In 1908, the UCD experienced a 'paradigm shift' of its own when it was brought together with the former Queen's Colleges. Donal McCartney points out that '[w]hen the NUI experiment began, the University College and the Catholic Medical School (which became the medical faculty in UCD) had been in their origins and ethos ashamedly Catholic. The former Queen's colleges by contrast were legally undenominational' (*The National University*, 90).

9 Robert J. McNamara notes, writing in 1967, that 'from 1786 to 1957 no less than 268 Catholic colleges for men were founded in the United States, but 185 of them were subsequently closed. Since 1900, 74 such colleges were founded and 47 of them (64 percent) have already been closed' (1967:93).

10 Stanley Aronowitz reminds us in *The Knowledge Factory: Dismantling the Corporate University and Creating True Higher Learning* that the Harvard 'core philosophy' for the undergraduate courses in the Faculty of Arts and Sciences 'purports to balance student interests with the faculty's conviction that such areas as "moral reasoning" correspond to a well-rounded liberal education' (2000:137).

11 K. D. O'Connor 'Ireland – a nation caught in the middle of an identity crisis', *Irish Independent*, 20 July, 1985.

12 An OECD report from 2006 reveals that 'Ireland spends only 0.3% of GDP from private sources on higher education' (2006:175).

13 UCD's website describes Newman's philosophy of education as 'a source of inspiration' for its 'current educational philosophy'. See www.ucd.ie/universityrelations/about-ucd/index.html.

14 As Susan M. Parkes notes, by the 1870s, the university was 'no longer seen as custodian and propagator of received knowledge but rather, in the German tradition, as a centre of informed judgment and open discussion in which scholarship and research were paramount' (2010:557).

3

Newman and the origins of the National University

Early educational ideals in Ireland: Newman and *The Idea of a University*

John Henry Newman is regarded by many as the most eloquent champion of the liberal education the university must impart. For Newman, ethics and civic virtue are bound up with an education in theology.[1] Newman's *The Idea of a University*, a series of discourses delivered to mark the inauguration of the Catholic University in Dublin in 1852, is widely regarded as the most influential work ever to have been written on university education. In his celebrated introduction to the Oxford edition, I. T. Ker writes: 'if it can be said without gross exaggeration that "modern thinking on university education is a series of footnotes to Newman's lectures and essays", then some more formal footnotes in the shape of a critical edition of what is also one of the greatest English prose classics seems long overdue' (1976:v). Walter Pater described the discourses as the 'perfect execution of a theory' (in Newman, 1976:v). Frank M. Turner argues that Newman 'articulated a vision of the university against which alternative visions despite their relevance, usefulness, and practicality make the activity of the university seem intellectually and morally diminished' (1996:282):

> His [Newman's] language has established the style and the essential mode of discourse with which to speak and write of the academic life. Virtually everything else written about universities has lacked his harmony and style and the capacity of his ideas to resonate with the desire that the educational process, whatever it may do, rise above the humdrum of everyday existence, and transform the immature into the nature, the unformed into the formed, the unreflective into the reflective, the youth into the adult. (1996:283)

The largest university in Ireland today, University College Dublin (UCD), also proudly states on its website that its roots lie firmly in Newman's educational philosophy. Newman's *The Idea of the University* is perhaps the earliest mission statement for the university in Ireland. Newman's vision speaks most eloquently for what Alasdair MacIntyre regards as an enduring, yet under-examined, Catholic philosophical tradition in education. In Discourse V, Newman writes that 'the majestic vision of the Middle Ages, which grew steadily to perfection in the course of the centuries, the University of Paris, or Bologna, or Oxford, has almost gone out in the night. A philosophical comprehensiveness, an orderly expansiveness, an elastic constructiveness, men have lost them, and cannot make out why. This is why: because they have lost the idea of unity' (2010:142). He believed, therefore, as do the authors of another, more recent document on education also inspired by the educational history associated with Bologna University, namely, the Bologna Accord, that the disparate elements of European culture had to be united under a common vision. Whereas Newman aligned his educational vision for unity with a strong religious faith – 'the new social order that was arising in Europe demanded a spiritual principle and that it could only find this principle in Catholicism' (Ryan, 1945:214) – contemporary Europeanization does not aspire to such a principle and has instead removed references to religion or spirituality from its principle education policy documents and indeed from its constitution. However, Newman's vision for Europe does share contemporary Europe's principle aim of striving to unite the different cultures of education subservient to the Bologna Agreement. The system of liberal education Newman envisaged for Ireland in these discourses, an educational vision that strongly influenced university strategies internationally, lay down rules and regulations for liberal education that an economically impoverished and burgeoning nation[2] would always find it difficult to meet in practice. While it was always unlikely that Irish educationalists and universities would live up to Newman's expectations, it is timely that his vision be reassessed in light of what followed.

Although Newman's *The Idea of a University* predates the National University by over fifty years, his discourses address the issues raised in chapter 1 in relation to the humanities and the nature of the National University established in 1908. The most celebrated section of *The Idea*, entitled 'Nine Discourses Delivered to the Catholics of Dublin', is chiefly concerned with explaining why religion and theology are essential subjects for a university, since, he argues, a university must teach 'Universal Knowledge' (2010:Discourse IX, 184). Newman repeats the argument a number of times. In Discourse XI, he argues that for a Catholic society, what applies to the Irish societies of the nineteenth and twentieth centuries, '[i]f the Catholic Faith is true, a University cannot exist externally to the Catholic pale, for it cannot teach Universal Knowledge if it does not teach Catholic theology'[3] (1976:184). He goes so far as to argue in Discourse II that a 'University which makes no religious profession' cannot claim to teach universal knowledge and therefore cannot be considered a university:

> If, then, in an Institution which professes all knowledge, nothing is professed, nothing is taught about the Supreme Being, it is fair to infer that every individual in the number of those who advocate that Institution, supposing him consistent, distinctly holds that nothing is known for certain about the Supreme Being {...} If, on the other hand it turns out that something considerable *is* known [and one would have to imagine that this was the case for the vast majority of Irish people in the nineteenth and twentieth centuries], whether from Reason or Revelation, then the Institution in question professes every science, and yet leaves out the foremost of them. In a word, strong as may appear the assertion, I do not see how I can avoid making it, and bear with me, Gentlemen, while I do so, viz., such an Institution cannot be what it professes, if there be a God. (1976:37)

However, Newman is also quick to point out that his examination of the university chiefly in regard to the question of theology and the Catholic Church is to be considered as a 'philosophical and practical, rather than as a theological question' (IX, 1976:182). He stresses in Discourse VIII that the kind of knowledge that is taught in such a university must be a 'Liberal Knowledge', a knowledge that is to be regarded as 'its own reward' (1976:156). However, he stresses again that if such knowledge is to be taught in the university, '[p]hilosophy must be its *form*; or, in other words, that its matter must not be admitted into the mind passively [...] but must be mastered and appropriated as a system consisting of parts related one to the other' (1976:156). Newman is therefore at pains to stress that his mission, albeit strongly religious in tone, should be applicable to all rational justifications for 'Universal Knowledge' and for the 'University'. Indeed it is hardly surprising that Newman's philosophical discourses foreground the religious to such a degree since he reminds us in the Preface that he is coming to a foreign, Catholic society because the 'Holy See' and the 'Irish Hierarchy' have entrusted him with the task of establishing a 'Catholic University' (1976:6). He therefore acknowledges that it is 'to Catholics of course this Volume is primarily addressed' (1976:6).

However, Newman's *Idea* should not only be regarded as an exemplary work of prose that is only relevant to Catholic institutions. Many of his arguments prefigure contemporary issues on the crisis in the humanities. He is mindful of a distinction between teaching and research in society that today's universities also privilege. He argues that the university must not be chiefly concerned with research but with contemplating students and with their 'exercise and growth in certain habits, moral or intellectual' (1976:6). He argues that there are 'other institutions far more suited to act as instruments of stimulating philosophical inquiry, and extending the boundaries of our knowledge, than a University' such as the old, celebrated 'Academies' of Italy and France (1976:7), a term that has returned to the British educational landscape in recent years albeit in a very different guise. He therefore argues that the 'great object' of a 'Catholic University' – and his later discourses demonstrate that he is in truth speaking for the 'University' more generally – is to 'make its students' into 'something or other' rather than 'simply to protect the interests and advance the dominion of Science' (1976:9). In the age of the research university, where hiring and firing is primarily dependent on research, it is refreshing to read teaching being privileged to such an extent. Newman's emphasis on teaching in the humanities can then be regarded as somewhat ironically prefiguring elements of recent educational policy documents such as the 'Browne Report' or the 'Independent Review of Higher Education Funding and Student Finance'[4] in England from October 2010 that are seen by critics as calling for humanities faculties to become little more than 'teaching institutions'. This review advises that the government 'envisages targeted investment in priority subjects' that will bring huge cuts to humanities budgets. Martin McQuillan, the co-founder of the London Graduate School, argues that the proposals of the review mean that 'Humanities departments in "elite universities" will only survive by piling students high and servicing them at low costs. [...] it impoverishes them and turns all of the arts, humanities and social sciences in England into teaching-focused universities'.[5] In other words, it seems that even if today's humanities faculties are being pushed to become primarily teaching institutions removed from the research-heavy science academies or centres, it is a vision, albeit with very different motivations, that is not without historical precedent.

Stefan Collini has questioned the relevance of Newman's model of the university for the contemporary university. In *What Are Universities For?*, he argues that Newman's *The Idea of a University* was 'addressed to a very specific and now largely forgotten question about establishing a Catholic university in Dublin' (2012:40). One might argue, in recalling Pearse's editorials and de Valera's speeches on education, that the notion of a Catholic university education would be an issue for Irish Catholics for at least a century after Newman's series of talks. However, in saying this, Collini is right to argue that 'the diversity of activities carried on in contemporary universities should make us cautious about appearing to follow Newman in finding a single common purpose or identity for these institutions' (2012:41). Collini argues that Newman's vision for the university predated the establishment of the modern university. The publication history of Newman's book is also noteworthy. Collini reminds us that the 'initial lectures which he [Newman] gave in 1852' were published later that year together with some further lectures which he wrote under the title *Discourses on the Scope and Nature of University Education, addressed to the Catholics of Dublin*. In 1858, he then published a 'selection of the addresses he had subsequently given in Dublin in his role as rector, under the title *Lectures and Essays on University Subjects*'. In 1873, he brought the 'bulk of the contents of these two books together, in revised form, as *The Idea of a University Defined and Illustrated.* This was re-published, with further revisions, in several later editions, culminating in the ninth edition published in 1889, the year before his death' (2012:43). Collini goes on to summarize the publication history and ultimate scope of the work: 'the book that has become such a classic began life as a collection of occasional pieces written to justify the creation of a new institution which was somewhat marginal to English social and cultural traditions and which proved to be for the most part a failure' (2012:43). However, despite the fact that the institution itself proved something of a failure, Newman's vision for the university should not be dismissed on these grounds alone. In fact, in an educational environment that is far more utilitarian than Newman could have imagined, when humanities professors themselves are urging us to embrace 'usefulness' and 'practicality', it is worth remembering, as Frank M. Turner argues, that Newman 'articulated a vision of the university against which alternative visions despite their relevance, usefulness, and practicality make the activity of the university seem intellectually and morally diminished' (1996:282).

Michael D. Higgins, speaking in 1989, has also described, albeit in a very different context, the implications for Irish society of this 'new utilitarianism' coming to education. He argues that the consequences for 'uncritically placing education at the behest of the given economic structures and social forms are only too obvious' for then the 'worse features of the society are fed into the educational experience as "natural"' (2006:49). Higgins traces this new order in education to the sociological idea of 'socialization', an idea I will examine in chapter 5 in regard to the French university system through the work of Pierre Bourdieu. Socialization had dramatic effects on education as it was regarded as a 'basic training in the "rules" of society' and education was expected to follow suit by inaugurating a process of 'acculturation into the ideas and symbols of the existing order' (2006:48). However, despite Sean O'Faolain's claims that the 'Celtic tradition' is responsible for an 'Irish mind' that can 'respect no laws at all' (1947:41), this would seem to be one 'rule' or law that, for Higgins at any rate, Irish society is capable of observing.

Newman, utility and professionalism

Newman's approach to the university is often critiqued, and it is a critique he pre-empts, for underemphasizing the importance of professional study and utility. However, in the wake of 'academic professionalism' and 'academic capitalism', many feel that universities have sacrificed too much at the altar of utility. Ironically, many professors in the liberal arts have embraced the jargon of academic professionalism to such an extent that they are leading the charge in describing students as 'outputs', 'products' or 'captive markets'

(Slaughter & Rhoades, 2004:44) and knowledge as 'a critical raw material to be mined and extracted from any unprotected site; patented, copyrighted, trademarked, or held as a trade secret; then sold in the marketplace for a profit' (2004:4). Whether such descriptions are closer to the academic realities of today than the religious overtones of Newman's discourses is difficult to say. However, such an ideology of academic capitalism has led many undergraduates, as Frank M. Turner argues, to regard the 'undergraduate experience as increasingly academically "professional" while the schools, which are supposed to be narrow, have often become self-espoused advocates of liberal learning, in part as a response to the defective undergraduate education their incoming students have received' (1996:298).

Newman's university ideals pay little attention to the physical sciences or to any discussion of the sciences that is not subservient to what he regards as the ultimate science, namely, theology. While he may have been more likely to accept notions such as 'globalization', it is unlikely that any potential global perspective on his part would have squared with what educationalists nowadays describe in terms of the 'alleged emergence of a homogenous world culture and the extinction of cultural difference and specificity'.[6] Turner also argues that Newman 'championed the values and experiences of early-nineteenth-century unreformed Oxford, where there was little research and virtually no instruction in useful or applied knowledge', the kind of research that might have initiated some kind of outward-looking global perspective. Turner also accuses Newman of being 'backward-looking' (1996:284) and ethnocentric. He tells us that 'he [Newman] first published his book only a few years before the Morrill Act (1862)', an act that 'opened the way for landgrant colleges in the United States, and the founders of Johns Hopkins and Cornell established those institutions as non religious research universities' (1996:284). However, it must be remembered that Newman was surprised and somewhat demoralized to learn that the university he was asked to serve as rector for in 1851 was intended only for Irish Catholics. Newman shared possibly a small portion of the expansive educational outlook that has helped to make globalization such an important concept for educationalists today.

It is inconceivable that a competitive university would today grant theology the position it occupies in the university of Newman's discourses, especially in an era which is explicitly market driven, an era Slaughter and Rhoades refer to in terms of 'academic capitalism'. They argue that conceptions of what the university was meant to be underwent a dramatic transition in the nineteenth century:

> In the last quarter of the nineteenth century, universities integrated with the industrial economy, shifting from a focus on theology, moral philosophy, and the education of gentlemen, overseen by the clergy, to science-based disciplines

ranging from chemistry and engineering to the social sciences. Land-grant institutions played an important role by contributing to the industrialization of agriculture [...].

Generally, the superiority of scientific knowledge over theology – the triumph of a more perfect knowledge – was offered as the theoretical explanation for the institutionalization of the new knowledge in universities. (2004:14)

While the economic infrastructure for such a radical transition did not exist in Ireland in the nineteenth century, the Queen's Universities did offer a secular alternative to Newman's Catholic University and to Trinity by dictating that their institutions be universities of 'mixed education' and that 'religious knowledge' be 'excluded' from the curriculum. Martha McMackin Garland argues that these new Queen's Colleges[7] were 'technically open to students of any denomination and the instructional programs were understood to be non-sectarian. This formulation – open admission, no fixed religious instructional agenda – was referred to as "mixed education", that is, Catholic and Protestant students and curricula in one institution' (in Turner, 1996:276). Colin Barr argues that the 'content of the education provided in the Queen's Colleges [...] differed little from either Trinity or the CUI [Catholic University of Ireland]' (2003:217). However, whereas the material taught at the Queen's Colleges could not be the cause of objections, Barr notes that 'concerned Catholics' did object to the 'lack of religious teaching in any part of the curriculum' and to the 'fact that such potentially contentious topics as history and natural philosophy could be taught by Protestants to Catholic youths' (2003:218). However, given the similarities in the curricula, the strength of the opposition to these 'godless' colleges is all the more striking considering that once the Irish people received its own National University in 1908, they would then rest content with no religion or theology department for at least another century. The Catholic University ultimately failed for a number of reasons, not least because of the British government's unwillingness to grant it a charter for awarding degrees.[8] Barr notes that when Newman left and took his reputation with him, 'Catholic Ireland simply did not have the network of schools necessary to provide students for a university with a rigorously classical curriculum' (2003:223).

Another aspect of Newman's vision for the university and for a liberal education that has come in for much comment in relation to the question of utility is his idea that a liberal education transforms the student into a 'gentleman'. For Newman, the kind of 'gentleman' a liberal education can produce will have a 'cultivated intellect, a delicate taste, a candid, equitable, dispassionate mind, [and] a noble and courteous bearing in the conduct of life', but all this is 'no guarantee for sanctity or even for conscientiousness' (2010:V, 110).[9] Newman emphasizes that he is also strongly against the notion of the 'true gentleman' put forward, he argues, by 'religious Philosophy' and Victorian 'intellectualism', a notion of the gentleman that replaces an interest in 'Revelation' with a 'philosophical theory of life' (1976:IX, 185) that 'teaches men to suppress their feelings' (1976:VIII, 178) and that promotes the 'embellishment of the exterior' (1976:VIII, 175). Newman did also not regard a liberal education as aiming at achieving any 'moral transformation' in the student. For Newman, it was left to the Roman Catholic Church to achieve such an end. Newman, therefore, should not be regarded as being completely devoid of a utilitarian strain even though he privileges the classics and theology in his university.[10] As Colin Barr notes, Newman did not want to limit his university to the 'kind of narrow classical curriculum' that 'Oxford was still largely following'; he went so far as to order his faculty of philosophy and letters to 'ascertain what sort of knowledge was needed by a student wishing to become a member of the Royal Artillery, Home Civil Service, or a civil engineer' (2003:216–7).

Newman's vision for his university provides an education that 'gives a man a clear conscious view of his own opinions and judgments, a truth in developing them, an eloquence in expressing them, and a force in urging them. [...] It prepares him to fill any post with credit, and to master any subject with facility. It shows him how to accommodate himself to others, how to throw himself into their state of mind, how to bring before them his own, how to influence them, how to come to an understanding with them, how to bear with them' (1976:Discourse VII, 154). Collini describes this kind of education as a 'statement of *paideia*, an ideal of the shaping of the whole of a person' and a vision of the university where the university functions as a 'metonymy, a location which is somehow exemplary of the ideals of human life as a whole' (2012:47). However, Newman responds to suggestions that he is too idealistic by challenging Locke on education. Locke argues for utility in education and is scornful, for example, of any learning of the '*Roman language*' for a student intent on a trade, for it is, for Locke, a language the student '*is never to use in the course of life that he is designed to*' (in Newman, 1976:140–1). In response, Newman perhaps explains why his own tone is so exuberant and his prose so evangelical: 'Nothing of course can be more absurd than to neglect in education those matters which are necessary for a boy's future calling; but the tone of Locke's remarks evidently implies more than this, and is condemnatory of any teaching which tends to the general cultivation of the mind' (1976:141). He sums up his differences with Locke and Copleston by arguing that '[i]f then a practical end must be assigned to a University course, I say it is that of training good members of society [...] it aims at raising the intellectual tone of society, at cultivating the public mind, at purifying the national taste [...] at facilitating the exercise of political power, and refining the intercourse of private life' (1976:VII, 154). Ultimately, while the National University, in overlooking theology and religion, would fail to meet Newman's guidelines for universal knowledge, it is also questionable whether it would ever accept Newman's claims that a liberal education should work to purify the 'national taste' or facilitate 'the exercise of political power'.

Newman, Kant and the 'English idea of a University'

It must be acknowledged that Newman's model of liberal education is clearly framed to respond to a prevailing English philosophical tradition of education. This is evident in the time he takes to respond to lengthy quotations from Locke and Edward Copleston on education. He also pre-empts this criticism in his Preface, suggesting that 'some persons may be tempted to complain, that I have servilely followed the English idea of a University' (1976:5). The criticism recalls David R. Shumway's argument that the humanities should really be called the 'nationalities' given that each humanities tradition is chiefly concerned with preserving and disseminating a national culture. On this note, it is also useful to recall the distinction Samuel Weber has highlighted in examining the humanities field. In a paper given in 1984, entitled 'The Ends of the Humanities', Weber alludes to the 'crisis of the humanities' (1987:144) that had already become a conference theme in American universities at that time. It is most likely that any crisis in Irish humanities in the 1980s would have had little to do with the rather deep-set theoretical distinctions Weber describes as plaguing American campuses at that time. However, Weber makes the interesting point that there is 'nothing, in French or German academic discourse, that really corresponds to the English idea of the Humanities; nothing in their discourse, and also nothing in their institutions' (1987:133). Weber continues:

> The English idea of the humanities is not centred on the Spirit, not at least in the sense of Hegel or of Dilthey, nor is it focused primarily on the 'life of the mind.' Rather, it is closer to the ideal of Renaissance humanism, which in turn is related to the Roman origins of the word in the emphasis it places on the more practical, social, and civic virtues felt to derive from the cultivation and mastery of certain 'arts'. (1987:133)

However, given that, as J. J. Lee argues, the Irish university was 'steeped' (1989:621) in the English university ethos for most of the century, can we then say that the National University exhibited this 'English idea of the humanities' that places such an emphasis on 'more practical, social, and civic virtues'? Since Newman was often charged with creating an 'Oxford in Ireland', his Catholic University did perhaps manifest something of this 'idea'. But what of the National University, a university system that was also established by the British government? One might argue that here lies the root of the somewhat schizophrenic approach to the humanities in the Irish university. If there is such a thing as an Irish humanities ethos, then it is very likely to privilege the 'Spirit' and possibly even the 'life of the mind' rather than any system of 'civic virtues'. We have already seen how Fitzgerald, Lee and Buckley all see a distinct lack of civic morality in Irish society. The heart of any Irish ethos would then seem to lie with what is, for Weber, a continental tradition rather than with an 'English idea of the humanities' that privileges the 'more practical, social and civic virtues' that Weber argues have their roots in 'Roman origins'. After all, as Sean O'Faolain reminds us in writing of *The Irish*, the Irish temperament is opposed to what he describes as 'Roman law'. He argues that the 'Irish mind' can be described, following its golden period that ended about the eleventh century, as somewhat 'primitive' (1947:39). What lay in the Irish mind, for O'Faolain, and what he conjectures, writing in 1947, 'still may lie' in the Irish mind, is 'atavistically indestructible, an ineradicable love of individual liberty' (1947:40). Such an 'Irish mind' 'clung to the family unit because there was a good deal of individual liberty inside it. Roman law, which was to come in with the Normans, had another idea' (1947:40). J. J. Lee describes such an idea in terms of a 'communal ethic' that was devised in the absence of a 'viable civic culture'. It would seem then that the 'Irish mind', if we follow O'Faolain's logic, would be fundamentally opposed to what Weber traces the 'English idea of the humanities' back to, namely, its 'Roman origins'. However, given that the National University was regarded as being 'steeped' in the English university ethos and that Trinity was described as the 'silent sister' of Oxford and Cambridge, it can only have produced a somewhat schizophrenic[11] educational outlook in the universities. When such an 'Irish mind' encountered the 'official mind' of the University as it existed in Ireland for much of the twentieth century, especially in those subjects, namely, the humanities, that were closest to exploring all that was unique about Irish identity, intellectually, there was an uneasy truce.

However, Weber's argument is also relevant to the kind of moral and intellectual training that Newman envisaged as the crux of his humanities programme. Newman clearly belongs to the educational tradition that understands the humanities in terms of the 'English idea of the humanities', one that places an emphasis on the 'more practical, social, and civic virtues'. Even though his discourses privilege the place of theology in the curriculum, his university is not to be regarded as a spiritual guide or 'Seminary', but rather as an institution in which to acquire 'Liberal Knowledge', what is of 'great secular utility, as constituting the best and highest formation of the intellect for social and political life' (1976:IX, 183). And although Newman is very much against his age's celebration of a 'Religion of Philosophy' that promotes the figure of the 'true gentleman' (1976:179) invested with an 'ethical character, which the cultivated intellect will form, apart from religious principle'

(1976:180–1), a type he often seems to suggest is the result of a Protestant intellectualism, his brand of spiritualism is one that ultimately prepares the student for civic life. He writes that 'when I speak of Catholicism, [...] I am contemplating Catholicism chiefly as a system of pastoral instruction and moral duty' (1976:VIII, 159) and that 'charity is the fulfilling of the Law' (1976:159). However, when he comes to relate the Catholic faith and its core moral guidelines to 'social and political interests', one must ask if he was ultimately presuming too much on the part of the Irish people's sense of civic virtue simply because they were Catholic: 'Where the country is Catholic, the educated mind takes its articles for granted, by a sort of implicit faith; where it is not, it simply ignores them and the whole subject-matter to which they relate, as not affecting social and political interests' (1976:159). However, unlike English Catholics, the Irish Catholics in the 1850s lacked a university tradition and therefore may have been less 'educated' than Newman had imagined. Irish Catholics may have taken the basic truths of their faith for granted, but it is unlikely that they would have intellectually aligned them with 'social and political interests' in the way Newman had presumed.

Weber's description of the humanities also raises the question of whether an Irish humanities ethos would lie closer to a continental understanding of Spirit inherited from the German model of the university. Weber argues that the sciences are 'generally regarded as the model of cognitive rigor whereas the humanities, preoccupied with values and standards, make their own evaluation difficult, if not impossible' (1987:136). However, in referring to R. S. Crane's lectures, *The Idea of the Humanities*, Weber points out that too many workings in the humanities have themselves employed a 'dogmatism' and a 'spirit of reduction', which tends 'to betray what he [Crane] took to be the essence, the "idea" of the humanities: the concern with "the multiplicity and diversity of human achievements"' (1987:136).[12]

Weber then calls on one of the most influential figures in the history of the European University, Immanuel Kant, to seek enlightenment in regard to how the humanities must strive to balance the particular and the universal. Weber notes that Kant only mentions the humanities once and it is towards the end of *The Critique of the Power of Judgment*. Kant's use of the term humanities is related to the sense of universality that he believes is important for understanding the 'beautiful' and 'aesthetical ideas' (in Weber, 1987:151):

> The propaedeutic to all beautiful art, in respect to the highest degree of its perfection, seems to lie not in precepts, but in the cultivation of those spiritual powers (*in der Kultur der Gemütskräfte*) by means of the pre-cognitions (*Vorkenntnisse*) called the humanities (*Humaniora*): presumably because *humanity* signifies on the one hand the universal *feeling of taking-part* (*Teilnehmungsgefühl*), and on the other, the power of being able to *impart oneself* (*mitteilen*) in the most inward

and universal manner; which properties in combination comprise the *sociability* of human beings, by which they distinguish themselves from the limited character of animality. (*Critique*, Section 60, Kant, 2000:229. Translation modified by Weber; Weber, 1987:143)

Kant's use of the term 'humanities' (*Humaniora*) describes human 'spiritual powers', precognitions or 'prior forms of knowledge'[13] that are to be cultivated in order to introduce the individual to beautiful art. His description of the *Humaniora*, these curious 'precognitions' that must be regarded as grounding and being privileged in humanistic study and the humanities, goes on to relate them to a polity and to the law of a particular land and its 'moral ideas' and 'moral feeling' (Kant, 2000:230). The preparation for the study of 'all beautiful art' and for the 'aesthetical ideas' that are so central to humanistic enquiry and the humanities must take into account 'the age as well as the peoples in which the vigorous drive towards the lawful sociability by means of which a people constitutes an enduring commonwealth wrestled with the great difficulties surrounding the difficult task of uniting freedom (and thus also equality) with coercion' (Kant, 2000:229). Such a people, however, must, firstly, 'discover the art of the reciprocal communication of the ideas of the most educated part with the cruder'; they must discover the 'mean between higher culture and contented nature' (229–30) which 'constitutes the correct standard' for 'taste as a universal human sense'. Kant then warns a 'later age' such as our own. He writes that 'with difficulty will a later age dispense with that model' because it would then lack 'enduring examples of it'. And any future age such as our own needs these 'examples' in order to 'form a concept of the happy union of the lawful constraint of the highest culture with the force and correctness of a free nature, feeling its own worth, in one and the same people' (Kant, 2000:230). Tradition is then important here, and Kant's description of a lawful people puts us in mind of the Irish people's national tradition. It is the people who must then decide on this 'mean' between the 'lawful constraint of the highest culture' and the 'force and correctness of a free nature'. One might well ask how a people is to discover this mean. Kant then returns us to the notion of taste to offer some kind of solution. He argues that the 'people' will know through taste which is a 'faculty for the judging of the sensible rendering of moral ideas' that pleasure which is valid for all mankind and through which it 'is evident that the true propaedeutic for the grounding of taste is the development of moral ideas and the cultivation of the moral feeling' (Kant, 2000:230). Once again, all is based on the 'cultivation of moral feeling' for a 'lawful people'. The humanities are surely the disciplines in the modern university that cultivate most deeply this moral feeling. Since the 'conflict of the faculties' between philosophy and theology, what grounds Kant's description of the university, was lacking from the Irish National University, then this must have had a detrimental effect on the cultivation of the people's 'moral feeling' if we follow Kant's logic.

Kant's understanding of 'humanities' is also grounded on an understanding of humanity that privileges its sociability in terms of a capacity for 'taking-part' and 'impart[ing] oneself' universally. It is an understanding of the humanities that foregrounds the 'spiritual powers' in terms of an approach to beauty through the formation of sociability and participation. It reaffirms the traditional sense of the humanities as a 'socializing force' (Weber, 1987:144); however, this 'imparting' must also never 'entirely overcome its particularity', and this is why any institutional demarcation of the humanities is always fraught with 'ambivalence' and a sense of crisis. It would perhaps speak more than any training in the 'more practical, social, and civic virtues' does for the kind of humanities spirit Irish thought embodies. David Lloyd also aligns an influential strand of Irish nationalism with the kind of national identity and sense of 'spirit' that arose within German Romanticism. For Lloyd, it is the writings of Kant's compatriot and contemporary, J. G. Fichte, that relate the spirit or 'innate, spontaneous tendencies' of a people to their language most powerfully. Lloyd argues that the Young Ireland movement with its 'emphasis on the *spiritual* nature' of nationality was heavily influenced by this European tradition (1987:58). Lloyd sees Fichte's insistence on the '*living* nature of an original language' as bound up 'in a reversible analogy between the "immediate" relations of body to spirit' (1987:65). It is the 'spirit of the nation' that is most important to preserve, and it is a people's language that embodies such a spirit. However, given that by 1800 Irish had ceased to be the 'dominant language of culture' in Ireland (Lloyd, 1987:66), the Irish people had to contend with an irremediable break in this spiritual tradition that German nationalism did not experience. For Lloyd, and it is an argument that haunts the humanities in Ireland, it means that the Irish nationalist is in the position of Fichte's 'foreigner' who is 'dependent on the dead letter of history rather than that continuous correspondence with the past which the "living stream" of an original language provides' (1987:67). However, in accepting this, it cannot be denied that this privileging of a national spirit in terms of an essential connection between identity and speech, even when it became accepted that it would have to be speech in English, would play a central role in the Irish psyche.

Another reason this European notion of the humanities is not to be based on 'precepts' or 'rules' is because the ultimate object of the humanities training intended brings one closer to beauty and 'aesthetical ideas', and Kant reminds us that the representation of such ideas necessitates the interrogation of the 'rules' of language: aesthetical ideas are a 'representation of the imagination associated with a given concept (and) bound up with such a multiplicity of partial representations in its free employment that for it no expression marking a definite concept can be found' (Kant, 2001:160). This points to another important omission in Newman's treatment of the humanities and 'Liberal Knowledge' for the Irish context. While Newman's discourses

undoubtedly appealed to the Catholic sensitivities of his audience in focusing on the intellectual and moral significance of 'Liberal Knowledge', they
rarely, if ever, privilege a discussion of beauty or of the aesthetic. He therefore omits a vital element of Kant's description of what the humanities must
strive to pass on. This continental appreciation for the humanities in terms
of partiality, self-imparting and the aesthetic possibly arose for the first
time with the establishment of the University of Berlin by Wilhelm von
Humboldt in 1810. Both Harpham and Collini regard the creation of this
institution, and the contemporary emergence in Germany of the philology
of F. A. Wolf and the work of the 'neohumanists' (Harpham, 2011:48), as
fundamental to our understanding of the 'modern university' (Collini,
2012:23). The Irish university perhaps failed to balance this humanities
spirit with those educational models it borrowed from the English tradition.
However, there was also an institutional unwillingness to confront the issues
raised by such influences. Michael D. Higgins, speaking in 1989, describes
how the Irish government displayed not only 'unwillingness' but 'down-
right hostility' when it came to facilitating 'debate on the purposes and
functions of education' (2006:46).

Newman also has much to say about the universal knowledge that can be
imparted through a liberal education. At the beginning of Discourse II,
'Theology a Branch of Knowledge', Newman lays down the foundations of
what he believes is 'universal knowledge'. He argues that 'the very name of
University is inconsistent with restrictions of any kind' (1976:33) and that a
'University should teach universal knowledge' (1976:34):

> That there is a real necessity for this universal teaching in the highest schools of
> intellect, I will show by-and-by; here it is sufficient to say that such universality
> is considered by writers on the subject to be the very characteristic of a University,
> as contrasted with other seats of learning. (1976:34)

The privileging of such universality means, for Newman, that Catholics
'putting aside faith or religious duty' 'should be dissatisfied with existing
institutions, which profess to be Universities, and refuse to teach Theology;
and that they should in consequence desire to possess seats of learning,
which are not only more Christian, but *more philosophical in their construction*, and larger and deeper in their provisions? [my italics]' (1976:34). Many
commentators have argued that Newman's educational model is irrelevant
for today's university because of its adherence to religious doctrine. However, such claims rarely investigate the nature of the religious ideology that
Newman wants to put forward in his programme for universal knowledge.
As we can see above, Newman urges the Catholic educationalists to be
'more philosophical in their construction' of a programme for university
teaching. Newman's interest in religious education is philosophical as well

as faith based. In this, he shares with Kant, once again, the desire to make the adherence to religion more 'philosophical', an issue I examine in Derrida's work on the university in chapter 5. This re-imagining of religion through philosophy has emerged more recently in the 'turn to theology' experienced within phenomenology (Janicaud, 2000). Newman goes to great lengths to stress that he does not believe that religion should be regarded as only enhancing the sentiments. He does not go along with the claims of the 'religious world' of his day that 'religion consists' in 'feeling or sentiment' (1976:39). For Newman, there is a direct connection between faith and knowledge. However, he cites an important 'turn' away from this idea in the history of religion that he traces back to the teachings of Luther:

> Thus if you look in the Anglican Prayer Book, you will find definite credenda, as well as definite *agenda*; but in proportion as the Lutheran leaven spread, it became fashionable to say that Faith was, not an acceptance of revealed doctrine, not an act of the intellect, but a feeling, an emotion, an affection, an appetency; and, as this view of Faith obtained, so was the connexion of Faith with Truth and Knowledge more and more either forgotten or denied. At length the identity of this (so-called) spirituality of heart and the virtue of Faith was acknowledged on all hands. (1976:Discourse II, 39–40)

He even goes so far as to aim his attacks at what he refers to as 'this day's philosophy' (1976:43) because it sets up a 'system of universal knowledge' and teaches 'about all things imaginable, except one – and that is, about Him that made all things imaginable, about God' (1976:43). In other words, his grievances with the religious thinking of his day are essentially grievances with the popular, contemporary philosophies of religion. Newman presumes a difference between religion as a private concern and religion and theology as university subjects. Much of his criticism of religious teaching is aimed at urging educationalists to be 'more philosophical'. Newman explains that he is also accepting of those who do not regard 'religious facts' to be true: 'if a man thinks in his heart that these religious facts are short of truth in the sense in which the general fact and the law of the fall of a stone to the earth is true, I understand his excluding Religion from his University, though he professes other reasons for his exclusion' (1976:39). What he does not appear willing to accept is the manner in which such a man is dishonest in offering 'other reasons for his exclusion' and not the primary reason. He argues that 'the varieties of religious opinion under which he [such a man] shelters his conduct, are not only his apology for publicly disowning Religion, but a cause of his privately disbelieving it. He does not think that any thing is known or can be known for certain, about the origin of the world or the end of man' (1976:39). Newman is then willing to accommodate a rational and honest explanation for why religion should be excluded from a university curriculum.

The connection between religion and knowledge is of course vitally important to Newman's discourses.[14] I. T. Ker argues that the logic of Newman's educational propositions should not be dismissed simply because theology has such an important place in them. Newman writes that 'Religion and Knowledge, then are not opposed to each other – and not because they are irrelevant to one another but because they are indivisibly connected, or rather because religion forms part of the subject-matter of knowledge' (1976:184). Ker argues that 'we may, of course, deny the premiss, but we should not allow our disbelief to turn into a misgiving over the logic of what naturally follows from it. It may be provocative, but it is not illogical for Newman to declare: "If the Catholic Faith is true, a University cannot exist eternally to the Catholic pale, for it cannot teach Universal Knowledge if it does not teach Catholic theology"' (*Idea* 1976:184). Once again, such comments beg the question in relation to the programme for education of the National University in Catholic Ireland. However, for Frank M. Turner, there is an important distinction that lies at the heart of Newman's thoughts on education. Turner argues that Newman's 'separation of human history and human life into secular-natural and sacred-supernatural spheres meant that Newman, unlike many persons in the late twentieth century university, labored under no illusion that a liberal education can lead to either moral virtue or religious faith' (1996:288). For Newman, liberal education was perfectly capable of producing a 'gentleman' with a 'cultivated intellect' (1976:181), but, as we have seen, it was not aimed primarily at achieving any 'moral transformation' in the student.

The Universities Act of 1908

In 1902, Douglas Hyde outlined for the Robertson Commission the Gaelic League's understanding of the concept of a national university:

> We believe that the only hope of a new university doing good to Ireland will be to have it frankly and robustly national, in a spiritual and intellectual sense, from the very outset ...We want a university whose aim shall be to give an Irish education to suit Irish needs ... We want an intellectual headquarters for Irish Ireland ... that shall be Irish in the same sense that Oxford and Cambridge are English. (Dunne, 2008:38)

It was always unlikely that the Commission or the subsequent movement for educational reform spearheaded by Augustine Birrell would respond favourably to Hyde's words. The Irish Universities Act that was signed into law on 1 August 1908 established two new universities – the National University of Ireland and Queen's University Belfast – and it abolished the Royal University on 31 October 1909 with its income of £20,000 a year divided equally between the two new universities. It marked the end of what Senia Pašeta describes as 'a long and often bitter dispute which had begun in earnest in the 1850s' (2008:19). Susan M. Parkes argues that the Act 'proved a lasting achievement, and subsequent university development was built on its foundations' (2010:567). Under the Act, the National University became a federal university with its seat in Dublin and with three constituent colleges established by charter: UCD, University College Cork (UCC) and University College Galway. The Queen's Colleges in Cork and Galway were also given an entirely new status and title. The National University was designed as a secular university that would be acceptable to Catholics by what Parkes refers to as a 'legal protection against interference in religious beliefs, and by the *de facto* if not the *de jure* presence of a large number of catholics among the staff and students' (2010:567). It had been founded both to 'fulfill the needs of catholics' and to play a 'crucial role in the creation of a separate national identity' (2010:568). However, given what we have read earlier from Lee and Williams in regard to the lack of a sense of identity in Irish society, it is unclear as to whether it was responsible for fostering a 'separate national identity' across the country.

The strength of the Church was evident on the eve of the passing of the Irish Universities Act. In 1907, the Liberal Government had attempted to introduce the Irish Councils Bill to Ireland. However, it proved unacceptable to the Irish Parliamentary Party. It was prepared by Augustine Birrell, the then Chief Secretary for Ireland and former president of the Board of Education in England, and it was an attempt to do for Ireland what had been done in England with the Balfour Education Act of 1902, i.e. 'give rate aid to denominational schools. It did no more than propose the transfer of certain departments – local government, agriculture and technical instruction, national and intermediate education [...] to a representative Irish council' (McElligott, 1981:100–1). However, when John Redmond tried to gather support for the bill, he met with stiff opposition from the Catholic Church who were in control of most school management boards. They had no wish to 'be subject to popularly elected councils and to have to furnish accounts to laymen or even to have money distributed to them by laymen' (1981:101). When the bill was finally defeated at the National Convention of the United Irish League, Redmond tried to claim that the decision had nothing to do with 'clerical considerations', but it was well known that the Church was to blame. The *Church of Ireland Gazette* regarded the defeat as the triumph of 'the Roman Catholic priests' who 'proved once again that religion is more to them than nationality' (McElligott, 1981:103); it was described as 'perhaps the most spectacular political event brought about by the direct political intervention of the clergy' (1981:103). This defeat, in effect, was an acknowledgement on the part of Redmond of 'his impotence as a leader in the face of the combined hostility of the Church and the party machine' (1981:103–4).

The manner of defeat of the education bill was evidence for a power dynamic between the Church and elected officials that would stymie education reform in Ireland for the rest of the century.

Parkes argues that 'Trinity College and the University of Dublin emerged unchanged by the 1908 universities act'; however, the religious effects of the Act would influence events across the Irish universities for the rest of the century. The Act's recommendations in regard to religion would provide a contentious background for future debates on the university in Ireland. In 1955, Michael Tierney, the then president of UCD, remarked in the *Irish Times* that the 'colleges of the National University' were 'institutions which are precluded by law and by charter, from spending one penny on religious education and from discriminating in the slightest degree as between one religion and another' (Tierney, 1955:4). This was a time when Trinity was still regarded as being 'on its own showing' 'Protestant, or at least non-Catholic, to the extent of 75%'. Tierney is also still citing the words of Judge Webb from Trinity College's Historical Society of 1891 who famously claimed that 'our university was founded by Protestants for Protestants and in Protestant interest. A Protestant spirit has from the first animated every member of its body corporate [...] and Protestant may it ever more remain'. Of course, Tierney says all this in order to defend the fact that UCD had assumed a somewhat 'Catholic complexion', which he regards as hardly 'unfair or unnatural' in a country which is 'well over 90% Catholic'. Even though Tierney can claim that 'we have all lived our lives in an Ireland in which this distinction between Trinity College and University College, Dublin has persisted, and if anyone imagines that it is a trifling distinction [...] I would ask him to reflect on the large number of educated Catholics in Ireland today whose education would not have got very far if it had depended on Trinity College', the situation would slowly change for the better over the next twenty or thirty years. Parkes supports Tierney's view to a certain extent. She argues that because each university 'retained its autonomy and was accepted as offering a suitable educational environment for students of a particular religious tradition' (though some prominent Catholics would disagree), it ended up 'reinforcing, the divisions within Irish society' (2010:570). Since a humanities ethos requires time to develop, it also became clear that the different models of university in Ireland would also end up practising distinctly different approaches to the humanities.

With the passing of the Universities Act, it was not so much what Irish universities were permitted to teach as humanities subjects but what they were prohibited from teaching that created a somewhat anomalous situation for the state in regard to its educational ethos. One of the first clauses of the Act states that

No test whatsoever of religious belief shall be imposed on any person as a condition of his becoming or continuing to be a professor, lecturer, fellow, scholar, exhibitioner, graduate, or student of, or of his holding any office or emolument or exercising any privilege in, either of the two universities, or any constituent college; nor in connection with either of those universities or any such constituent college shall any preference be given to or advantage be withheld from any person on the ground of religious belief. (1920:3)

The Act is therefore quite clear in stating that no privilege would be granted on religious grounds. However, a later clause clarifies under what conditions religious education and education in theology would be admitted. The regulations in regard to 'any theological or religious teaching or study' were so clear that the university boards simply saw them as little less than a ban on all forms of religious education in the university.[15] Article 7.4 of the Universities Act, in a section entitled 'Financial Provisions and Purchase of Land', states:

> Any sums paid under this section shall be applied by the governing body of the university or college, as the case may be, in accordance with their charter or statutes, but no such sum shall be applied for the provisions or maintenance of any church, chapel, or other place of religious worship or observation, or for the provision or maintenance of any theological or religious teaching or study:

> Provided that nothing in this provision shall prevent the recognition by the governing body of the university of any professor of or lecturer in theology or divinity as a professor of the university so long as the professorship is founded and maintained entirely by means of private benefaction, or the use of any building belonging to the university or college for any teaching given by such professor, or for any other religious teaching no part of the cost of which is defrayed out of public funds. But no student shall be compelled to attend any such theological teaching, or religious instruction, and no professor of or lecturer in theology or divinity shall be eligible for membership of the General Board of Studies or of any Faculty other than the Faculty of Theology.[16] (1920:7–8)

The article is therefore quite explicit in exempting the constituent colleges from engaging in religious studies or, specifically, in any kind of education in theology unless the lecturers were to be remunerated from outside sources. The Act also specified that no 'grant' provided to an institution will 'be subject to or conditional upon any religious qualification or be devoted to any religious purpose' (1920:10). The constituent colleges themselves most likely took this to mean that the Act of Parliament establishing the university excluded the teaching of, and granting of degrees in, theology or religion. It did, however, give the new university the right of recognizing other institutions for teaching and granting degrees in nontheological subjects. It was under these terms that the Trustees of Maynooth applied for recognition of the college's nontheological courses in 1909. The following year, St. Patrick's College, Maynooth, became a Recognized College of the National University, with Faculties of Arts, Philosophy and Celtic Studies.

The universities would also be powerless to sanction research on how the philosophy of education embodied by their institutions might mediate, or be subservient to, the educational policy outlined by the Catholic hierarchy in their pastoral letter of 1927:

> The education for a Christian people is education permeated by religion. In Ireland, however we have had to make the most of systems that in theory fall short of that ideal. But for years past in practice, the character of our primary, as of our secondary schools from a religious point of view, depends mainly upon ourselves and there is no ground for complaint in the greater part of Ireland. (qtd. in Ó Buachalla, 1988:212)

Any interdisciplinary approach to the humanities that included such subjects as theology, religious studies or comparative religion, something that had existed in universities elsewhere for some time, would not be possible in Irish universities. The Act continues: 'In accordance with sub-section four of section seven of the Irish Universities Act, 1908, no Professor of or Lecturer in Theology or Divinity is eligible for membership of the General Board of Studies or of any Faculty other than the Faculty of Theology' (1920:34). Even though the Universities Act stressed that 'nothing in the provisions [...] shall prevent the recognition by the Governing Body [...] of any Professor of or Lecturer in Theology or Divinity as a Professor of the University, so long as the Professorship is founded and maintained entirely by means of private benefaction' (1920:35), the universities boards chose not to include these subjects on their curricula at a time when the Church was dictating education policy in the schools. However, the Act did lead to quite dramatic changes in curriculum. UCC created new professorships in 'archaeology [...] economics; education [...] German; hygiene; Irish; mathematical physics; medical jurisprudence; music; ophthalmology; pathology as well as in English and history' (Murphy, 1995:180).

The initial charter also established a Faculty of Arts and a separate Faculty of Philosophy and Sociology. To consider devoting a faculty solely to philosophy and sociology in today's universities, especially at a time when many philosophy departments in the country advise students to pursue doctoral degrees in philosophy at foreign institutions, would be regarded as foolhardy. The Arts subjects included Ethics, Metaphysics and Logic, and the Philosophy subjects included Ethics, History of Philosophy and Metaphysics. These course offerings are quite similar to the courses Newman had outlined for the Catholic University. The omission of theology and divinity from the curriculum would now introduce an element of discontinuity into the teaching of humanities subjects in Ireland. The Act does specify that there may be courses of 'prescribed instruction as cannot conveniently be pursued in a College' (1920:95) and such courses may include 'courses of catechetical instruction'

(1920:96). However, since the university board would not pay for instruction in such courses, it was always unlikely that they would prove very popular.

Ultimately, the Universities Act would get a mixed reaction. P. J. Lennox, then a professor at the Catholic University of America, wrote in the *Catholic University Bulletin* in 1910 that he had 'heard many expressions of misgiving as to the future effect, on the faith and morals of the youth of Ireland, of the teaching of an institution into which religion, if it enters at all, can enter only as a side issue, and not, as it rightfully should, as the head and front of the whole curriculum of studies' (1910:96–7). Almost a century later, J. J. Lee looked back on the fact that the Act 'made only miserable financial provision for the new university'; he argues that '[s]tandards were set exceptionally low, and little emphasis put on research in the social sciences so crucial to solving the problems of Irish society' (2008:132). For Lee, the new Dublin university also failed 'to rouse Trinity College from its slumbers as "the silent sister" of Oxford and Cambridge' (2008:132), and it served to reinforce 'existing inequalities of opportunity in Irish society, for the low standards allowed less gifted children of the middle classes acquire a degree, which increased the status differential between them and clever but poor children, unable to secure a university place through lack of scholarships' (2008:133). One might imagine that in Celtic Tiger Ireland, such inequalities became a thing of the past; however, Kathleen Lynch reminds us, writing in 2005, that '[i]n many societies [and she includes Ireland here] the correlation between social-class background and highest level of education attained has become so strong that education credentials are operating in practice, albeit not in principle, as a kind of state-supported system of inherited privilege' (Lynch, 2005:135).[17] However, Lynch notes that to be able to 'challenge social class inequality in education', the arguments for which can be made most effectively by the humanities and social sciences subjects, requires 'a widening and deepening of education on social class issues' (2005:142). Lynch also notes that the 'social class and other biases encoded in the deep structures of curriculum design and assessment are unlikely to be challenged by experts who are not only socialized into the received wisdom of the codes, but who are the net beneficiaries of the system itself' (2005:141). However, one would have to argue that the abolition of university fees altogether in 1995 that saw third-level attendance levels in Ireland become among the highest in Europe was a step in the right direction.[18]

Pádraig Pearse, the national question and education

If there is any historical figure as important as Newman for furthering debate on educational philosophy in the Irish context, it is Pádraig Pearse. The measure of Pearse's influence in educational matters can be gauged by the fact that he secured financial backing for educational projects to the value of almost

£10,000 between 1908 and 1912. However, unfortunately for Pearse, his 'total liabilities' remained at about £6,000 shortly before the Easter Rising in 1916.[19] Elaine Sisson, writing in 2004, also admits that 'Pearse's legacy is troublesome and that it is perhaps telling of contemporary Irish society that his historical place within Irish history is far from secure' (1), and Norman Atkinson has written in 'The School Structure in the Republic of Ireland' that Pearse's educational philosophy 'is largely overlooked' and that it has made 'remarkable little impact on the school structure of the Irish state which he did so much to create' (1967:68). However, Pearse's editorials, lectures and other publications on education have generated more commentary than any other Irish educationalist of the early twentieth century because they offer more progressive ideas on education than all the early government cabinets combined. Despite the fact that his educational thinking is 'derivative' (Walsh, 2007:70), that he does not cite or 'refer to contemporaneous writings on the subject' (Walsh, 2007:70) and that there is a latter-day focus on language with a 'more overtly militaristic character' (Augusteijn, 2010:209) in his educational curriculum, his early educational theories and practices for secondary schooling often appear more progressive than the contemporary university practices in Ireland. Pearse saw St. Enda's and the education system it offered as breaking down 'existing hierarchies in education', and, as Elaine Sisson notes, he felt that a school 'should be a primary, secondary and university education rolled into one' (2004:33). Since his editorials for *An Claidheamh Soluis* also comment on educational philosophy in general and on the 1908 Universities Act, his work can be seen as speaking for an educational philosophy that could also inform the humanities ethos of an Irish university.

Pearse taught at both secondary and university level and this experience, as Séamas Ó Buachalla describes, 'afforded a solid practical base to his writing and provided an opportunity for keeping in touch with the opinions of teachers and school authorities' (Ó Buachalla, 1980:x). In his short career, Pearse lectured at the University College and in the Gaelic League and was a tutor at his old school, C. B. S. Westland Row. He was also a permanent teacher of Irish at Alexandra College, Earlsfort Terrace. He acted as an extern examiner for the Jesuit University College where he also gave Gaelic League-sponsored Irish classes, which James Joyce attended (Joyce was 'so bored by him that he chose to study Norwegian instead').[20] He also lectured in Coláiste Laighean as well as in other Gaelic League Colleges. These varied experiences in teaching meant he was one of the most informed Irish educators writing on education at the time the Universities Act was passed in 1908. Pearse addressed tirelessly the main issues raised by the Birrell Act and other educational acts that were brought before the British parliament in the early years of the century.

Pearse's editorials for *An Claidheamh Soluis* offered, at times, the only Irish perspective available for an Irish readership on these important education acts that would influence education policies in Ireland for the rest of the century.[21]

The editorials return time and again, between March 1903 and June 1909, to the university question. His concern is chiefly for a 'National University – a University that should represent and summarise in itself the whole national life' (Pearse, 1952b:2). Pearse focuses on the place of the Irish language in the curriculum as a means to achieve this objective. He also campaigns from his earliest editorial on the topic in March 1903 for greater representation from the Irish public on the governing bodies of the proposed universities. Pearse's demands in the editorials become more specific as the precise nature of the National University becomes apparent. In January 1904, he is calling for an institution that provides 'organic means for the due representation of Irish national sentiment in its governing body' (Ó Buachalla, 1980:35). In the same editorial, he argues that the Irish National University must learn from the Welsh university that received its charter in 1893 and that originated in a 'thoroughly popular movement' that 'sprang from the very heart of Welsh popular life' (Ó Buachalla, 1980:36). In December 1904, he argues that the new university 'must borrow its traditions and prestige from no pre-existing institution', and in calling on the Irish people to no longer 'beseech a foreign State' to establish their university, he admits that Newman's Catholic University was 'on (more or less) right lines' (Ó Buachalla, 1980: 71–2).[22] However, after years of frustration, Pearse assumes a more sanguine tone in 1908 on the eve of the Birrell University Bill of the same year. He argues that the University Bill, if passed, 'may embody the nucleus of a University settlement which Ireland, by judicious kneading and shaping, may ultimately mould into such a settlement as, if she were mistress of her own house, she might have herself evolved' (Ó Buachalla, 1980:160). In April of 1908 when the proposed University Bill had been made public, Pearse argues that there is little in it to 'enthuse over' and that it makes 'no appeal to the imagination' (Ó Buachalla, 1980:183) but that it could still produce institutions which could 'formulate Irish ideals' and 'develop an Irish "atmosphere"' (Ó Buachalla, 1980:184). However, once the bill had become a reality, Pearse begins to focus on specific aims in relation to the place of Irish in the curriculum. He argues in May 1908 that 'Irish must be made a compulsory subject up to the point at which the student commences to specialise – that is, up to the point at which English is likely to be made a compulsory subject' (Ó Buachalla, 1980:190). While Pearse did not see this ambition realized, he was more fortunate in regard to his demand for it to be 'obligatory on all students for Matriculation to pass an examination in oral and written Irish' (Ó Buachalla, 1980:205). However, by September of 1908, Pearse must admit that 'we quite understand that Irish cannot be placed at present, on exactly the same footing as English at any examination' (Ó Buachalla, 1980:204–5). In his last year as editor of *An Claidheamh Soluis*, Pearse is still describing the university as the 'nerve-centre' of the Irish educational system. Rather like Joyce writing from Trieste a few years earlier, he laments the fact that there is 'no great national concept of education' in Ireland that is 'permeating through and through the entire school system' (Ó Buachalla, 1980:215).

And he acknowledges that such a 'concept' can only 'grow up at' and be 'disseminated throughout the body at large from a National University – the intellectual nerve-centre, as it has been called, of a nation' (Ó Buachalla, 1980:215). Pearse was therefore perhaps the most energetic contributor to public debate on the scope and ambitions of the Irish National University.

Pearse's writings offer the beginnings of an Irish philosophy of education that is willing to deal with the bilingual question in relation to Ireland and with religion and nationalism.[23] Ó Buachalla argues that Pearse did not want to do away with every element of the 'murder machine', or education system, that was in operation in Ireland in the early years of the century. Even though Pearse does stress the need for a new 'creation', rather than a rejuvenation of existing practices, in regard to education policy in Ireland, Ó Buachalla argues that Pearse sought 'a synthesis which identifies both the major weaknesses in the existing educational system and the essential features which should characterise a true education' (Ó Buachalla, 1980:xiii). When Pearse was writing for *An Claidheamh Soluis*, the only education available to Catholics was that 'provided by the remnants of Newman's Catholic University and in some colleges which prepared students for the examinations of the Royal University' (Ó Buachalla, 1980:xxii), and Pearse's editorials enabled people to look beyond this institution.

Pearse sought to introduce the Irish language and a love of Celtic mythology into the curriculum in his own school, St. Enda's, in a manner that would develop and open up the school system, create an 'Irish atmosphere' and kindle in the souls of the students 'the quenchless fire of patriotism, the setting before them of a great and glowing ideal of *Duty*' (Ó Buachalla, 1980:135).[24] Pearse worked out his ideas on education in St. Enda's school paper *An Macaomh* (The Youth), and these ideas later informed *The Murder Machine* his 'devastating onslaught on British educational administration in Ireland' (Atkinson, 1967:71). Pearse's claim that what is needed in Irish education is 'not reform, not even a revolution, but a vastly bigger thing – a creation' (Atkinson, 1967:72) advocates a school system, which also emphasizes the need for unification, as do Newman and the authors of the Bologna Accord, between the heretofore divided practices of the national, secondary and vocational schools; he speaks of an 'organic unity' that will 'replace a composite freak in which the various members are not only not directed by a single intellect, but are often mutually antagonistic and sometimes engaged in open warfare one with another' (Atkinson, 1967:72). Atkinson argues that it is 'not unlikely that Pearse was feeling his way towards an integrated system on the American model' (Atkinson, 1967:72). His desire to 'discover the individual bents of his pupils, the hidden talent that is in every normal soul' (Atkinson, 1967:71), and to form an educational system based on the notion of the 'child republic', where the aim, as E. G. A. Holmes describes, is 'to foster growth' (in Walsh, 2007:69), places Pearse within the child-centred education tradition.

Nationalism was the driving force behind Pearse's writings on education despite the fact that Joost Augusteijn argues that his 'more strident attitudes had mellowed' (2010:165) by the time of the first issue of *An Macaomh*. However, his cultural nationalism is no more strongly expressed than in *The Murder Machine*, published in 1912. Pearse's introduction gives a harsh account of the education system in Ireland:

> I have spent the greater part of my life in immediate contemplation of the most grotesque and horrible of the English inventions for the debasement of Ireland. I mean their education system. The English once proposed in their Dublin Parliament a measure for the castration of all Irish priests who refused to quit Ireland. The proposal was so filthy that, although it duly passed the House and was transmitted to England with the warm recommendation of the Viceroy, it was not eventually adopted. But the English have actually carried out an even filthier thing. They have planned and established an education system which more wickedly does violence to the elementary human rights of Irish children than would an edict for the general castration of Irish males. (1952:6–7)

Despite the rhetoric, Pearse outlines in *The Murder Machine* and in his other writings what Brendan Walsh describes as a radical new education programme that looks beyond the provisions of the Universities Act of 1908. Pearse included a 'heavy classical curriculum' (Augusteijn, 2010:158), weekly lectures on topics in 'literature, phonetics, philosophy, physics, botany, archaeology, Egyptology, topography and medieval history' (2010:166), while also maintaining that 'religious instruction was central to his perception of good education'[25] (2010:162). He sought to establish, in St. Enda's, a private secondary school to rival schools such as Blackrock, Clongowes Wood and Castleknock for those 'aspirational nationalist middle classes' who regarded such existing schools as 'Anglo-Irish institutions' (2010:158). In fact, the schedule was so progressive that one school inspector described it as 'like a university' (Augusteijn, 2010:181).

Pearse argues that the English have created the 'simulacrum of an education system in Ireland' (1952:7) and that it has 'made of some Irishmen not slaves merely, but very eunuchs, with the indifference and cruelty of eunuchs; kinless beings, who serve for pay a master that they neither love nor hate' (Pearse, 1952b:7). Pearse's suggestion that the education system was both subordinating and emasculating was strategic in that it led many nationalists to believe that their dreams for a future race of free Irish would remain unrealized through this fundamental, yet insidious, evisceration of identity and manhood. Elaine Sisson also regards the theme of masculinity as integral to Pearse's vision of education. Declan Kiberd notes, as I will examine in more detail in chapter 4, that there was a deep division in Irish society in the early years of the century in relation to cultural identity that can be encapsulated by the different arguments of Pearse and Yeats.[26] Pearse's understanding of cultural identity echoed some, though not all, of D. P. Moran's ideas from

The Philosophy of Irish Ireland that saw 'Irish Celticism [as promoted by the Revival] as an insidious anglicised invention and argued vociferously that it was responsible for perpetuating a relationship with English culture that was harmful and subjugating' (Sasson, 2004:10). The embrace of Celticism to the detriment of the 'enormous body of literature in the Irish language' copper-fastened 'imperial cultural dominance' and promoted 'self-hatred' through seeking to '"hibernicize" English conventions in literature rather than reviving a genuinely "authentic" Gaelic'. This argument privileges the literary and educational history in Ireland that is traced back to Columcille. Douglas Hyde describes the origins of this tradition as a glorious era in Irish history: 'By the middle of the sixth century Ireland had been honeycombed from shore to shore with schools, monasteries, colleges, (and foundations of all kinds belonging to the Christian community, and books had multiplied to a marvelous extent)' (1901:193–4). Declan Kiberd goes further in relating this notion of 'self-hatred' to the 'postcolonial psyche' and to a dependency syndrome in Irish society. The debate will also surface much later in Daniel Corkery's and Sean Ó Tuama's work on the question of a national literature in English that I examine in the next chapter. However, it must be noted that Pearse was also realistic in terms of the Irish language. Augusteijn argues that '[a]lthough Irish should be used as a medium of instruction', Pearse believed that 'Irish culture and not the language should be central in education' (2010:165). Augusteijn, in fact, compares this to Yeats's vision of creating a 'purely Irish culture in the English language' (2010:165). The language question is therefore an issue that had untold influence on the teaching of the humanities subjects, specifically literature, in the universities.

Pearse argues that education in Ireland did not need a 'reconstruction of its machinery' but a 'regeneration in spirit', and we recall here Weber's tracing of the European model of the humanities back to the 'Spirit' and the 'life of the mind'. He calls the education system 'mere machinery, a lifeless thing without a soul' (Pearse, 1952b:10):

> [I]t is as devoid of understanding, of sympathy, of imagination, as it is of any other piece of machinery that performs an appointed task. Into it is fed all the raw human material in Ireland; it seizes upon it inexorably and rends and compresses and re-moulds; and what it cannot refashion after the regulation pattern it ejects with all likeness of its former self crushed from it, a bruised and shapeless thing, thereafter accounted waste. (1952:12)

The machine analogy would be employed again almost a century later to describe the experience of education, and specifically graduate education, for many educationalists in the humanities. In a recent publication on the experience of doctoral graduates in the humanities and social sciences at leading universities in America, Marc Bosquet employs the machine analogy and the notion of waste that Pearse alludes to above, to describe the present university education system in these universities. He argues that

> [w]hat needs to be quite clear is that this is not a 'system out of control,' a machine with a thrown rod or a blown gasket. Quite the contrary: it's a smoothly functioning new system with its own easily apprehensible logic, premised entirely on the continuous replacement of degree holders with nondegreed labor (or persons with degrees willing to work on unfavorable terms) [...] like a car's engine idling in the takeout food line, the system's greatest urgency is to dispel most of the degree-holding waste product. (2008:24)

Whereas Pearse and Bosquet are writing almost a century apart, their experiences of different aspects of the education system lead them to the same conclusion: their national programmes of education, whether it be the corporate university of today or the implanted educational system of Pearse's day, are forgetful of the basic tenets of a liberal education. Pearse would have supported the ideals of a liberal humanist education that, as Jennifer Washburn reminds us, should 'instill moral principles, build character, and provide a common core of cultural knowledge as well as emphasize linguistic and literary attainment and critical thinking' (*University Inc.* 2006:28).

Pearse argues that education in Ireland is founded on denial or on what he calls a 'Nego': 'Now, to teach a child to deny is the greatest crime a man or a State can commit. Certain schools in Ireland teach children to deny their religion; nearly all the schools in Ireland teach children to deny their nation' (1952:16). He gives a uniquely Irish description of what education meant traditionally to Irish people, a description that bears many similarities to the ideal of a liberal education. Pearse reminds us that the words 'which the old Irish employed when they spoke of education show that they had gripped the very heart of that problem. To the old Irish the teacher was *aite*, "fosterer," the pupil was *dalta*, "foster-child," the system was *aiteachas*, "fosterage"' (Pearse, 1952b:21). Once again, there are similarities here with the vision of education put forward by Newman that Collini compares to a *paideia*, even though it comes from a very different tradition. Pearse then gives a description of what such a system of education sought to achieve, a system that would embody many of the principles of the liberal education being formulated by John Dewey:[27] 'And is it not the precise aim of education to "foster"? Not to inform, to indoctrinate, to conduct through a course of studies (though these be the dictionary meanings of the word), but, first and last, to "foster" the elements of character native to a soul, to help to bring these to their full perfection rather to implant exotic excellences' (1909:21). Pearse's views on education are also profoundly aware of how the education system incorporated into Ireland was likely to embody rather than address socio-economic disparities: 'Our very divisions into primary, secondary, and university crystallize a snobbishness partly intellectual and partly social' (Pearse, 1952b:27).

Pearse also criticized the approach taken by the universities in response to the restrictions on religious education and theology as outlined by the clauses of the Universities Act of 1908. For Pearse, the inspiration required to create the kind of education system he sought in Ireland would come 'most adequately of all from religion'; 'I do not think there can be any education of which spiritual religion does not form an integral part; as it is the most important part of life, so it should be the most important part of education, which some have defined as a preparation for complete life' (Pearse, 1952b:37). Once again, Pearse is echoing the claims of Newman and MacIntyre that regard the humanities themselves as bound up with a Catholic philosophical tradition.

Pearse also researched bilingual education in detail, travelling on numerous occasions to Belgium to examine how its educational system dealt with the Flemish and French languages.[28] Pearse's foresight and equanimity in regard to bilingual education describes a means for teaching through both languages that the Irish government would not implement for decades. Pearse believed that Irish should be made the language of instruction in districts where it is the 'home language, and English the 'second language' taught as a second subject' (47). He accepted that where English was the 'home language', it 'must of necessity be the 'first language' in the schools'. However, he specified that in such areas, there should be a 'compulsory "second language," and he accepted that this "second language" in five-sixths of the schools would be Irish' (47).

Ó Buachalla places Pearse strongly in the tradition of New Education that had blossomed in Europe in the nineteenth century. The New Education movement arose in opposition to the Instrumentary Education approach of the Victorian Age that had a 'narrow literary curriculum and [a] prescribed methodology' (1980:xiv). 'Real education', Pearse writes, 'is not the imparting of knowledge' but a disciplining and a formation of character, what recalls Newman's notion of the 'whole man': 'the real education consists in the forming of the child's character, the drawing out of his faculties, the disciplining of his intellect [...] and the systemic inculcation of patriotism' (1952b:22–3). Joost Augusteijn argues that Pearse was guided by the philosophy of Herbert Spencer in making these claims for education (2010:148). Augusteijn argues that Pearse had a wide network of advisors in the New Education movement. He corresponded with figures like Weygandt in Philadelphia with the language movements of Finland, France, Wales and Scotland. He also corresponded with academics such as Kuno Meyer, professor of Romance Languages in Queens College, Liverpool (2010:152). Pearse's approach to understanding education and the language question therefore often appears more progressive and more broad-minded than many of the more frequently cited academic debates on language and identity that became popular much later in Irish Studies as practised in the universities.

The element of New Education that was of most importance to the study of the humanities was the notion of '*concentration* in the curriculum', an idea derived from the writings of Johann Friedrich Herbart. Herbartianism espoused a wide curriculum making no distinction between the humanities, the sciences and the practical subjects (Ó Buachalla, 1980:xvii). By the 1880s, these ideas were especially popular in the United States because of the special position accorded to 'those subjects believed most likely to promote character formation i.e. religion, history and literature' (Ó Buachalla, 1980:xvii). This belief would be echoed in the later notion of the 'core curriculum' in American universities. Pearse's understanding of education also paralleled the motivations of the movement for moral education. For Michael Sadler, a prominent advocate of comparative education in England, moral education 'was the heart of the modern educational problem; he saw moral education as offering the only adequate protection against the changes and the weakening of established tradition so characteristic of the modern age' (qtd. in Ó Buachalla, 1980:xviii). The spiritual and political debates that grounded the moral education these writers privileged were often not covered in Irish secondary schools and would also be hampered in the universities by the dictates of the 1908 Act. Of course, these grand ideals for educational establishments were also very often derailed by the exigencies of history. In the twentieth century, the world wars shifted the ideological role of the university. This change was most apparent in the United States, where, as Stanley Aronowitz writes, '[a]s the new war loomed in the mid-1930s, the question of where research and development would take place was fairly quickly resolved: in the division of intellectual labor, private and public universities were assigned the tasks of performing fundamental, that is 'useless' knowledge production, but also of figuring out how to transform basic research into applications for the war effort' (2000:20). Because a university education has now become the imperative that a high school education was in Pearse's day, before the great wars of the twentieth century, it is through his writings, practice and editorials for *An Claidheamh Soluis* that we can discover some estimation of what he might have advised for the evolution of the universities in Ireland. Pearse ultimately lived what he taught. As he advised his own students, 'if your way of life or your profession in life does not allow you to live up to that best that is in you, then you must *change* your way of life, or your profession' (in Edwards, 2006:140), and it was advice he would follow. Once the profession of educator had run aground, he moved unstintingly towards the practice of the revolutionary heroism he had taught for so many years at St. Enda's.

Notes

1 James Joyce also regarded Newman as the 'greater prose writer' (Ellmann, 1972:40).

2 I. T. Ker writes in his introduction to *The Idea of a University* that '[t]he day after his arrival in Dublin 1854, Newman was abruptly informed by the Provincial of the Irish Jesuits, "the first ecclesiastic I called upon", that the "class of youths did not exist in Ireland, who could come to the University", the middle class being too poor and upper classes preferring to send their sons to Trinity College, Dublin, or to universities in England or the Continent' (1976:xx).

3 He describes theology variously as 'the Science of Religion' (1976:III, 58) and as a 'real science' (1976:III, 58).

4 See www.bis.gov.uk/.../10–1208-securing-sustainable-higher-education

5 www.thelondongraduateschool.co.uk/thoughtpiece/if-you-tolerate-this% E2%80%A6-lord-browne-and-the-privatisation-of-the-humanities/.

6 See Jaishree Kak Odin and Peter T. Manikas, *Globalization and Higher Education*, University of Hawaii Press, 2004, p. 8.

7 Colin Barr notes that Trinity College and the Catholic University 'insisted on religious knowledge being a component' of their instruction (2003:218). In explaining how the 'content of the education' at Trinity in the 1850s 'differed little' from that in the Queen's Colleges and the Catholic University, he gives the following list of works that a student at Trinity in the mid-1850s would have been expected to study: '[in the first year] Euclid, Demosthenes (Philippics and Olynthiac Orations), Cicero (Against Catiline), algebra, trigonometry {...} Herodotus, and Livy. The course offerings in the final two years included, for physics: Hart's Mechanics and Hydrostatics, Lloyd's Optics; for Greek: Euripides' Medea, Sophocles' Oedipus Tyrannus, Aeschylus's Prometheus Vinctus; for Latin: Terence's Adelphi, Juvenal's Satires [...], Horace's Odes (Books III and IV); for classics: Aristotle's Ethics (Books I and II), Cicero de Officiis (Books III and IV); Thucydides (Book VII), Tacitus Annals (Book I); for ethics: Stewart's Outlines of Moral Philosophy, Butler's Analogy, and Paley's Evidences. Also offered were works in the fields of logic, experimental and mathematical physics, and astronomy. Divinity students – Trinity was the primary Church of Ireland seminary – would naturally follow a different course of study. With the exception of those works in the ethics course (Butler and Paley particularly) which were Anglican in nature, there could be nothing in what Trinity taught its undergraduates that could disturb a Catholic parent or prelate' (2003:217).

8 I. T. Ker notes in his introduction to *The Idea* that '[t]he Catholic University of Ireland survived until 1882 when it was merged in the newly founded Royal University of Ireland. It proved impossible ultimately to attract enough students, partly because of the refusal of the British Government to grant a charter for conferring degrees'. Ker continues: 'Newman had "always advocated" an affiliated connection with the degree-conferring "Queen's University", as opposed to the totally integrated status of one of the constituent "Queen's Colleges"' (Newman, 1976:xxvii).

9 Denis Donoghue also notes in discussing Dickens that one of the values of literature lies in its ability to advance the 'concept of a gentleman as a moral term rather than a term of class' (1970:398).

10 It must also be remembered that Newman stressed that he did not want to turn the university into a seminary. In Discourse IX, he argues: 'If then a University is a direct preparation for this world, let it be what it professes, It is not a Convent, it is not a Seminary; it is a place to fit men of the world for the world' (*Idea* 1976:197). And on the notion of a Christian Literature, he writes: 'if Literature is to be made a study of human nature, you cannot have a Christian Literature. It is a contradiction in terms to attempt a sinless Literature of sinful man' (*Idea* 1976:195).

11 If we see the search for an Irish humanities ethos as confronting the same difficulties as the prospect of a national literature in English in Ireland, then we can also recall Daniel Corkery's assessment of Ireland as a 'two headed calf' in that it has 'literature in English and literature in Irish'. It is a future that Corkery did not seem to want to 'deal head on with' even if such a calf can, for him, 'cry out its hunger through two throats' (in Ó Tuama, 1995a:241).

12 See R. S. Crane, *The Idea of the Humanities*, pp. 13–14.

13 This is Paul Guyer and Eric Matthew's translation of *Vorkenntnisse* (2001).

14 Michael Tierney, president of UCD in the years 1947–1964, proudly asserted that the 'University College derives by an unbroken line' from the Catholic University which Newman founded. He described Newman as 'our first rector and founder' (McCartney, 1999:146).

15 However, it should be noted that once UCC had been founded, the then President Sir Bertram Windle did consider possible routes for introducing Catholic philosophy. He writes in his diary on 1 October 1908: 'To see the Bishop – most cheerful. Tutors – approved Residences. Lectures – Thomistic Philosophy – Yes. Catholic students this time?' (In Murphy, 1995:179).

16 See *The National University of Ireland: Act of Parliament, Charter and Statues (1920)*, pp. 7–8. www.archive.org/details/nationaluniversi00greauoft.

17 Kathleen Lynch and John Baker, 'Equality in education: An equality of condition perspective', *Theory and Research in Education*, Vol. 3(2), 2005, pp. 131–64.

18 Ireland's tertiary education entry rate climbed from 30% to 44% between 2000 and 2007. While this figure is well ahead of the figures for Germany, Mexico and Turkey (34%, 32% and 29%, respectively), it is still far behind Australia, Finland and Poland (86%, 71% and 78%, respectively) (OECD 2010: www.oecd-ilibrary. org/education/tertiary-education-entry-rates_20755120-table2). Ireland's figure for tertiary education graduation rates, however, is far more competitive. At 45%, only Denmark, Finland, Iceland, Poland and New Zealand have higher completion rates among OECD countries in 2007.

19 See Joost Augusteijn, *Patrick Pearse: The Making of a Revolutionary*. London: Palgrave Macmillan, 2010, pp. 154–208.

20 Sisson, p. 34.

21 John A. Murphy also notes in The College that Sir Bertram Windle, the then president of Queen's College Cork, also 'kept the Cork public informed of the course of events [relating to the Bill] through his letters to *The Cork Examiner* and *The Freeman's Journal*' (1995:178).

22 Pearse also outlines his grievances with Trinity College in the editorials. In October 1903, Pearse writes that the 'University of Dublin is obnoxious to the majority of the Irish people' (1952b:7). Pearse discredits the university's standing in terms of

scientific knowledge, and he also laments its contribution to Irish society in terms of nationalism: 'Despite the scientific vanity of the age, these things [the spirit of learning and freedom] are greater than science, and even in science Dublin ranks about tenth rate' (1952b:8). He then asks rhetorically where is 'the evidence of its work for culture and public spirit?' (8). It is also interesting to note that Pearse did not hold the Ireland of the Celtic Revival in very high regard: 'In music, in literature, in the arts, in the professions, compare Dublin of today with Dublin before the Union, when she responded in some degree to the claims of nationality' (1952b:8).

23 Pearse believed 'bilingualism was the appropriate and most effective language policy for Irish schools', and he sought to modernize Fr. O' Growney's Direct Method of education (Augusteijn, 2010:250). The Direct Method was a variation of the Berlitz Method that Joyce would later use in his own classes in Pula.

24 *An Claidheamh Soluis*, 7 Sep. 1907.

25 However, Pearse was also opposed to 'the influence of the Church on anything beyond spiritual matters' (Augusteijn, 2010:168).

26 However, critics who make much of this ideological conflict should not forget that Yeats as director of the Abbey staged performances of Rabindranath Tagore's *Dak Ghar* and Pearse's *An Ri* in 1913 to raise funds for the ailing St. Enda's. He was also a prominent supporter of the school (Augusteijn, 2010:205).

27 Dewey writes in *Moral Principles in Education* that education or 'the school cannot be a preparation for social life excepting as it reproduces, within itself, typical conditions of social life' (1909:13), and Pearse felt too that Irish education was removed from the realities of Irish social life.

28 In his month-long trip to Belgium in 1905, Pearse, accompanied by a 'sixty man strong deputation under the direction of Major John McBride and the old Fenian John O'Leary' (Augusteijn, 2010:149), visited primary schools throughout Flanders; secondary schools in Brussels, Antwerp, Ghent, Malines and Bruges; and 'two universities' and 'the College of Industrial Design' (Augusteijn, 2010:150).

4

The emergence of an Irish humanities ethos

Daniel Corkery, Sean Ó Tuama and a national literature in English

Because the language question was such an important issue for education policy especially in the early years of the State, it is important to look at the work of some of the educationalists and university academics who worked extensively on Irish language literature. One of the first professors of English at University College Cork (UCC), Daniel Corkery, who later spent a great deal of time working on Irish literature, writes in *The Hidden Ireland* that the 'soul of a people is most intimately revealed, perhaps, in their literature' (1984:7). The next sections will therefore examine perspectives on a humanities ethos in Irish universities through the work of academics principally working as literary critics and cultural theorists. In firstly examining the 'literary study' of two literary critics of English and Irish language literature who sought to describe an 'Irish ethos' or 'soul' in such study, it is hoped that we might also come to a better understanding of the perspective of those students and teachers who felt excluded from the 'English idea of the humanities' that was very much part of university practice in the National University and in Trinity. One of Daniel Corkery's English literature students at UCC in 1942 was the renowned Irish literature scholar Seán Ó Tuama. Ó Tuama writes in an essay on Corkery from 1988 that Corkery's 'greatest achievement in *The Hidden Ireland*' is a perception on criticism: it is 'his formulation of the critical viewpoint that the nature of Irish language poetry – its conventions, its diction, its values – is quite different to that of the nature of the central tradition of English poetry'. Corkery argues, for Ó Tuama, that 'Irish/Gaelic poetry of the seventeenth and eighteenth centuries inclined more to the modes of medieval European poetry' and that the 'critical approaches to an evaluation of English post-Renaissance poetry were not always the approaches appropriate to a consideration of Irish poetry' (1995a:246). This is a complex observation that also suggests that Irish literature in English steeped as it often is in the cadences and myths of this Irish language tradition and the Hiberno-English dialect with its inherited leitmotivs, may also not have performed well under those 'critical approaches' appropriate to 'English post-Renaissance poetry'. However, since Ó Tuama explains in his collection *Repossessions*, published in 1995, that '[c]ritical analysis of literature in Irish has as yet scarcely begun' (xiii), it is also possible that the most appropriate 'critical approaches' for the study of Irish literature in English in terms of an Irish literary heritage in English have not yet been found.

One of the most important considerations for Corkery and Ó Tuama is whether Ireland could ever produce a viable national literature in English. In approaching this question, Ó Tuama singles out the work of Synge as that which most successfully embodies the two cultures existing in Ireland during the Celtic Revival, what Ó Tuama describes as the 'rural-based' culture and the 'Dublin-based' culture. Synge was successful at blending these cultures in his work because, Ó Tuama explains, he had his feet in both camps (he had a mother from West Cork and a father and 'numerous childhood nurses' from the 'Wicklow district' (1995c:221)). Ó Tuama's reading is therefore somewhat essentialist in grounding the work in the life and background of the writer; however, he does make a useful observation in pointing to a 'two-way assimilative process' at work in Irish society in the nineteenth century that Synge was carried along with: 'in the nineteenth century just as the mass of Irish people, under increasing pressure from the English political and economic machine, tended to become Anglicized, ironically enough there was a gradual withdrawal of the Anglo-Irish nation from its dependency on the English mother-culture, and an effort to identify with the older Irish culture' (1995c:220). However, for Ó Tuama, it is a process of assimilation between the two groups, the 'mass of Irish people' and the 'Anglo-Irish nation', that only goes so far because the Irish language is lost by the majority and the resulting Anglo-Irish literary tradition will never have an 'individual Irish way of seeing and expressing reality' (1995c:232).[1]

Ó Tuama's reading relies on its positing of a notion of Irishness in Synge's work that is 'characteristically Irish' and that speaks for the 'basic values' of the 'traditional Irish mind'. This kind of Irishness is a 'peasant' Irishness that is also, somewhat paradoxically, a '"high Culture", an aristocratic tradition which lasted strongly in Ireland for practically two thousand years down into the seventeenth century' (1995c:222). Ó Tuama explains that this tradition is responsible for the esteem for music, poetry and 'fine talk' that still exists even today in what he calls the 'characterless modern Ireland' (1995c:222). At this point, one could be forgiven for recalling Bord Fáilte adverts. However, Ó Tuama goes on to argue that Synge went to Aran because 'part, at least, of his psychological make-up responded to that special network of feelings and thinking which is characteristically Irish' (1995c:221); he argues that Synge was 'enhancing his previous intuitive knowledge of the traditional mind' (1995c:221). The singling out of this fading, rarefied notion of Irishness, an essence that if recaptured marks the writer out as truly great, is also then used as a basis for assessing the viability of any future national literature in English. Ó Tuama recalls Corkery's argument that the restoration of the Irish language as 'the main language of communication in Ireland' is essential 'in order to halt the erosion of Irish identity' because 'the Irish mind, the Irish personality – for good or ill – was so bound up with the language' (1995a:238). Despite Ó Tuama's recognition, in this earlier essay from 1972, that Corkery's early work on Synge was possibly not 'racist' (1995a:238), as John A. Murphy describes it, but was really only 'fundamental[ly] dogmatic' (1995:238), he does share Corkery's sense of hopelessness for the future of literature in Ireland. He argues that in 'circumstances' where 'Hiberno-English has clearly lost ground' and where 'standard English is increasingly bringing with it, and imposing on us a "world", a "design for living", a "value-system" at variance with our own, one cannot hope in the long term for a national literature in English, i.e. a literature which shall have an individual Irish way of seeing and expressing reality' (1995c:232). That a leading Irish cultural critic and academic can still be claiming, the year before Ireland joins the EEC, that the alleged use of standard English in Irish society is imposing on the Irish people a 'world', a 'design for living' and a 'value-system' is surely taking to new heights the 'pathology of dependence' that Kiberd observes in Irish society. It suggests that Irish society was not only dependent in the sense of defining its problems in 'conformity with imported assumptions' (Lee, 1989:628) but also in grounding identity on a perpetual sense of disenfranchisement that hides dependency behind a mask of imposition and cultural indoctrination. Joyce was once described as an injustice accumulator, and it seems that the nation itself had taken a page out of his book. That a people would continue to allow themselves to willingly suffer such impositions throughout the century even when they were secure in the knowledge that the 'traditional Irish mind' and the 'aristocratic' 'Irish personality' was still within its grasp surely describes an unparalleled capacity for weathering injustice in that same 'Irish mind'.

Ó Tuama returns to this argument in 1988 under the cover of Corkery's 'fundamental[ly] dogmatic' rhetoric. Ó Tuama goes out of his way to defend Corkery against critics who have a 'misunderstanding of the basic tenets' of Corkery's argument from the 'notorious first chapter' of *Synge and Anglo-Irish Literature* (1995a:239). Seeing as he has made a similar argument of his own in his 1972 essay, he is mostly supportive of Corkery's perspective, as 'cultural philosopher' as opposed to as '*littérateur*', that posits that '[t]here is therefore no means [...] by which Ireland can come on a literature in English [i.e. a national literature in English] [Ó Tuama's insertion] which shall have a way of its own' (and by 'way of its own', Corkery means the capacity of a literature to '*become capable of dealing with universal literary material*' [Ó Tuama's italics]). However, if anyone has taught literature in today's universities in the UK, the United States or Asia, one would be hard-pressed to find a professor of any nationality who did not regard the tradition of Irish literature in English as 'having a way of its own'. It is often regarded as not only a viable literary tradition but as possibly the most important literary tradition of the twentieth century. Ó Tuama's statement, then, coming in 1988, that 'one cannot hope in the long term for a national literature in English, i.e. a literature which shall have an individual Irish way of seeing and expressing reality' (1995c:232) only makes one wonder if his 'Irish way of seeing and expressing reality' is unattainable precisely because illusion has become reality. Ó Tuama is finally gracious enough to suggest that all Irish writing in English since Corkery's time 'from Kavanagh to Heaney, from Joyce to McGahern', has 'dealt quite directly with the values Corkery identifies as basic in Irish culture'. It can then receive Corkery's seal of approval and be described in terms of the 'temporary emergence (at least) of a "genuine Anglo-Irish literature"' (1995a:241). However, to base any account of this body of literature on such rarefied notions of the 'Irish mind', where true Irishness is like amber, a preservative for traditions that Synge had the good fortune to observe among the communities in Aran in 1900 where, as Ó Tuama explains, 'Irish *may* have been its language [my emphasis]' (1995c:221) is surely to misrepresent the protean sensitivity to external influences evident in all these Irish writers who must also embody some kind of 'Irish mind' between them. Whether it is part of a 'cultural philosophy' or a literary evaluation, such characterizing of cultural identity in terms of 'permanency', authenticity and a 'network of feelings and thinking that is characteristically Irish' overlooks basic features of cultural identity such as adaptation and resourcefulness that the anthropologists and linguists Ó Tuama quotes from, writers such as Sapir and Lévi-Strauss, also privilege.[2] Cultures must be understood in terms of how they adapt to changes in their environments as well as in terms of the traditions they embody. To privilege one at the expense of the other is to reduce the unbridled potential of cultural encounter to archival preservation. If the community chooses to adapt to the new environment by adopting a new language and if this remains a working language across the community for a number of centuries, then one is misrepresenting that culture by speaking of this shift in terms of imposition and in terms of a loss of all that is 'characteristically' of that community. Critics and commentators who employ the notion of an 'Irish mind' forever lost with the Irish language seem to invoke a far more troubling sense of 'imposition' in hoisting a notion of cultural identity on the people that prevents the culture from celebrating its resourcefulness and ingenuity in adapting to changes in its history. If the education system in Ireland and specifically in the universities can be accused of being too 'English' in its 'ethos', then those critics who lament a lost sense of pristine Irishness that connects us, despite our current economic impoverishment, to an 'aristocratic' past must also accept some criticism. If we are forever measuring the work of Irish writers in English against a lost 'aristocratic' age that means we can never see a future for Irish literature in English that will 'have an individual Irish way of seeing and expressing reality' (1995c:232), then we are missing the point of much twentieth-century Irish literature in English. However, what these arguments make clear is that the language question that Pearse raised so powerfully in his work had important repercussions for what followed in Irish education and in regard to the development of an Irish cultural self-understanding. Given that the 'soul of a people is most intimately revealed, perhaps, in their literature' (1984:7), to quote Corkery once again, it was to literature that the humanities often looked to explain identity for Irish society beyond academia. However, given that leading academics saw the Anglo-Irish literature that was being taught in the lectures as offering much less than an 'individual Irish way of seeing and expressing reality' (Ó Tuama, 1995:232), it is perhaps no wonder that commentators on university education in Ireland such as Fitzgerald and Lee see this education as partially responsible for the lack of a sense of identity and civic virtue in Irish society.

Denis Donoghue, 'An Irish School of Criticism' and the Leavisite tradition

In moving from the question of a national literature in English to the work of Irish critics who sought to make the tradition of literature in English their own, no critic is more important than Denis Donoghue. However, if the humanities cannot be examined without confronting different forms of cultural nationalism, as Harpham, Lloyd and Weber seem to suggest, English literature, what is for Donoghue and F. R. Leavis at the 'centre' of a liberal education, cannot be separated from notions of tradition. In his 1969 article 'T. S. Eliot and the Life of English Literature', F. R. Leavis argues that the 'university, conceived as a centre of civilization', is the 'only possible organ of the creative effort society has to make' and that 'a vital English School' must be at the 'centre' of such a university (1969:18). As Leavis stresses in an article written over twenty years earlier, the true aims of a 'liberal education' are only to be addressed in the 'field of *literary* study' (1947:593). Such claims made on behalf of the 'English School' and literary study would always sit uncomfortably with the official mind of the Irish university. When Leavis argues that 'literary study, properly pursued', gives an 'incomparable initiation into the idea of tradition (1947:598)', Irish scholars would always be justified in asking 'what tradition?' However, given the fact that the English model of a liberal education, or what Weber describes as the 'English idea of the humanities', was strongly influenced by Leavis's notion of the 'spirit of the language', it is important to examine how critics such as Donoghue have understood this English literary tradition.

Donoghue has been described as a critic of the common reader tradition. This is a tradition that is generally traced back to the emergence in the eighteenth century of a new middle class with increased general literacy. Samuel Johnson describes the common reader as deserving of special praise in the history of reading: 'By the common sense of readers uncorrupted with literary prejudices, after all the refinements of subtlety and the dogmatism of learning, must be finally decided all claim to poetical honours' (in Knight, 2003:153). The common reader was that reader whose 'interests were less identified with any one profession than with the more general ambition to stay informed of events as they transpired on several fronts' (Knight, 2003:7). Of course, the critic who embodies such a tradition today is often regarded as an enlightened public intellectual who appeals to a university-educated readership beyond the ivory tower. Whereas critics from Leavis to Lisa Jardine have argued that 'There isn't a Common Reader any more' (in Knight, 2003:18) and while Geoffrey Hartman has rather scathingly described Donoghue's style in terms of a 'friendship style' (Knight, 2003:53), Donoghue does describe himself as a 'generalist' (in Knight, 2003:56) who has managed to avoid specialization. He is also against seeing criticism as a tool to serve political ends since he regards this as limiting the influence of the artwork: 'I don't want to talk about literature as chiefly exemplifying something that's going on in society. I want to give literature more space to move in, and not to be pressing upon it to disclose its character' (Knight, 2003:68). While this may neglect, to a certain degree, literature's genesis in the political and the societal, it is a style of criticism that, Knight argues, Donoghue practises alongside such distinguished critics as George Steiner and Frank Kermode, a style that may have fallen by the wayside in Irish university departments ever since the heyday of Irish Studies and postcolonialism. The common reader tradition is more psychological and phenomenological in nature. Catherine Gallagher argues that it can even be regarded as describing something unique about the process of reading itself. Gallagher suggests that 'even a theoretically inclined reader might become a Common Reader' if we extend the notion of a common reader to 'the self-reflective entity of the humanist tradition' (Knight, 2003:19). The common reader tradition can then be regarded as spawning a conception of reading that is deeply psychological. Donoghue suggests that this may be a result of a 'new assumption' that also began to 'take root in the mid-eighteenth century' and that 'led to the replacement of politics by psychology as a main source of interest for the writer' (Knight, 2003:74). I therefore wish to examine in this section how Donoghue's style of criticism is representative of a critical perspective and practice that responds well to influential English and American styles of literary criticism that have influenced the respective humanities models. Donoghue is possibly the most respected Irish-educated literary critic of the last fifty years, and his style of reading embodies a critical ethos that is more formalist than much of the criticism discussed so far. Since literature also lies at the heart of the humanities enterprise for such critics as Donoghue, Leavis and Eliot, Donoghue's work can also be read as embodying a distinct understanding of the humanities.

Donoghue was involved in a celebrated humanities debate with Vivian Mercier and Donald Davie in the 1950s on the notion of a correct 'critical method' for the study of literature. As a twenty-seven-year-old, without a PhD to his name, Donoghue published 'Notes Towards a Critical Method' arguing that criticism in Ireland should take up some of the habits of the American New Critics. He argues that the historical approach, much favoured in Irish universities, has 'too often been undertaken in a spirit of almost complete detachment from any consideration of literature as literature' (Donoghue, 1955:187). He describes poems as 'gestures of defiance against the tendency of ordinary living to be wayward' (1955:181). He argues that 'scholars would be profitably occupied in investigating the linguistic, religious and associational development of the more important literary symbols' (1955:189), thereby recognizing the importance of allowing literary analysis to be interdisciplinary in nature and to borrow from religious exegesis. However, in overemphasizing what he calls 'pure scholarship' (1955:187) and an overarching and possibly singular 'critical method' (1955:181), his proposal begins to sound too formulaic. In response, Donald Davie takes him to task in 'Reflections of an English Writer in Ireland' for writing as if he believes that the 'Anglo-Irish tradition is *not* following another course from the English literary situation' (1955:442). Davie wants Irish critics to find their own way and not presume that the English or the American critical traditions are the only shows in town; the 'Irish critic' should not presume that 'he is further back on the one road, behind the clock, twenty or fifty years out of date' (1955:442). However, Davie would appear to regard the Irish critic as something of a critical alchemist who can forge a tradition out of thin air, for he argues that whereas England has had a 'continuous tradition of literary criticism' (1955:440), 'nothing is more striking in the Anglo-Irish literary tradition than the absence of any true critic at all, certainly of any critical tradition' (1955:440). Therefore, whereas the 'Irish tradition of writing in English is now independent', it has no 'critical tradition' to attend to it. However, Davie will then claim that even the Irish tradition of writing in English running through from Yeats to Colum (and Ó Tuama would presumably place these writers in two distinct traditions) is marked by 'discontinuity' precisely because of this 'lack of any continuous and self-respecting tradition of literary criticism' (1955:443). He therefore argues that Irish criticism should avoid trying to catch up, thereby running into the same pitfalls that the New Critics and the Leavisites experienced, and should instead forge its own way by persisting with the 'common reader' approach. As if to fulfil the promise Davie had perceived, Donoghue would go on to become one of the most respected critics of the twentieth century in the common reader mould without relinquishing his New Critical credentials. However, seeing as he spent the greater part of the rest of his academic career practising as a critic on American campuses, it is unlikely that either Donoghue's or Davie's words greatly affected literary criticism in the Irish universities.

However, the debate did have a final instalment. In 1956, Vivian Mercier responded to Davie in the same journal with 'An Irish School of Criticism?'. Mercier admits that the 'gulf between scholarship and criticism seems ever wider and deeper in Ireland than it normally is in other countries' (1956:85). He also commends Donoghue's 'readiness to learn from Americans' something that is 'rare' in Ireland (1956:85). Mercier is reluctant to agree that there is no 'critical tradition' in Ireland. However, when he comes to describe a critical tradition of Anglo-Irish literature in Ireland, he can only mention 'Irish eighteenth-century critics and aestheticians', Myles Dillon's *Early Irish Literature* and Kenneth Jackson's *A Celtic Miscellany* (1956:86). Mercier also argues that 'Yeats's early correspondence alone' amounts to a 'large body of criticism' (1956:85). However, it is presumably professional academic critics that Donoghue and Davie have in mind in bemoaning the lack of a tradition or method. Mercier does make the interesting point nevertheless that 'no native author of a comprehensive work has ever held a university post' (1956:87). It is perhaps ironic that the two university lecturers calling here for an Irish school or tradition would spend their most successful years in foreign universities. Mercier finishes his essay with some advice for the young lecturer who was only ten years his junior: 'If he really believes in his critical method, he should be prepared to use it on work of any period in any language of which he is master. Only by daring to do this can he hope to found an Irish school of criticism' (1956:87). Donoghue would seem to have taken some of Mercier's advice, but the 'Irish school' would remain as imaginary as Leopold Bloom's 'New Bloomusalem in the Nova Hibernia' (Joyce, 1992:606) at least until the emergence of Irish Studies. The professional urgency among leading Irish critics to teach on Irish literature from abroad has also led Irish criticism to regard itself, rather like its literature, as somewhat displaced from itself. However, the questions this literary debate throws up over fifty years later in regard to the practice and institutionalization of key humanities subjects are as relevant as ever.

Donoghue's later criticism would continue to focus on form. He describes his desire to resist the temptation to make the symbolic subservient to a 'content' and his wish to regard criticism in terms of the 'open-ended nature of conversation' (Knight, 2003:52). This creative literary essence that he wishes to preserve from 'ideological' arguments can be compared to Coleridge's 'primary IMAGINATION' (Knight, 2003:75) or to the 'power of exhibition' that Kant assigns to the sublime: '[that] liking [that] is connected with the *mere exhibition or power of the exhibition* (i.e. imagination)' (1976:97). Donoghue also relates his notion of the symbolic imaginary to national identity in his essay 'The American Style of Failure'. He describes the symbolic imagination as 'terrestrial, familial, domestic, and historical' (1974:423), whereas the angelic imagination is more like Kant's sublime, an act of will, 'depending upon its own intensity to keep it going' (1974:423). Donoghue's 'symbolic imaginary' is 'content to live in the daily world', 'making the best of it by using all the resources of analogy and metaphor' (1974:420). However, when exhibited in American literature, Donoghue argues that its powers are grounded in 'conditions representing a radical separation of imagination and reality' that arises 'from the failure of the imagination to find answerable substance in the given world' (1974:409). Donoghue therefore describes a poetic–societal exchange according to which certain communities propagate a rich 'desirability of [poetic] results'. In quoting Whitman, who writes that 'The Americans [...] have probably the fullest poetical nature', Donoghue suggests that such an exchange is not found 'on the demonstrable strength of American poems already written, but on the promising strength of a society in tune with an aesthetic feeling, a certain way of life, a style' (Donoghue, 1988:79). I will examine in chapter 5 how Pierre Bourdieu also regards the French university system as passing on a distinct 'style'. For Donoghue, then, certain societies are in tune with an 'aesthetic feeling' and intimate a 'promising strength' or societal well-being. It seems that the Irish tradition Donoghue and Mercier speak for had not worked out how to embody this 'promising strength of a society in tune with an aesthetic feeling', let alone encapsulate it in a humanities curriculum. However, Donoghue believes that a society can only preserve its 'fundamental values', what must somehow remain aloof from 'needs and drives', through the study of 'artistic form': '[i]ncreasingly fundamental values must be apprehended as living beneath or beyond the structure of needs and drives which, in a consumer society, constitutes normal life. These are values so alien to those of any actual society that they can be sustained only in effigy as the virtualities of artistic form: this is the role of form, to preserve as fundamental truths the values which are otherwise homeless' (Donoghue, 1976:224). While this may beg more questions than it answers, it is representative of a formalist approach to literature in English in the Irish university.

Donoghue and the Leavisite tradition

F. R. Leavis speaks of the English literary tradition in terms of 'cultural continuity' (Leavis, 1969:12). T. S. Eliot describes that same tradition from the perspective of the 'poetic practitioner' as an 'existing order' that 'is complete before the new work arrives' (Eliot, 1975:38). The tradition must be preserved and passed on because it embodies all that is best about a liberal education and the 'spirit of the language'. Donoghue, as we have seen, also assigns a unique 'poetical nature' to the American tradition, and in the next chapter, I will examine how Bourdieu and Derrida also describe a distinctive French approach to the university and a liberal education. However, even though Irish writers and philosophers have been integral to the shaping of the humanities courses in these universities, the nature and ethos of the humanities in Ireland and the tradition it embodies remains something of a mystery. As the chief humanities funding body, the Irish Research Council for the Humanities and Social Sciences (IRCHSS), becomes subsumed under a general Research Council in Ireland that will see 'industry' and 'innovation' once again at the forefront of the 'knowledge industry', it is important that the humanities as taught in the Irish university examines its humanities ethos. This will enable whatever spirit or tradition the humanities embody to be sustained in the Irish university just as Irish writers support the humanities on campuses all over the world.

In an address made to the American Academy of Arts and Sciences in 2004, Denis Donoghue returns to Leavis's 1933 treatment of Joyce. Donoghue would seem to support Leavis's claims that literature speaks of 'feeling', 'need' (in Donoghue, 2004:14) and the force of the 'impulsion from inner life'. In fact, when Leavis comes to sum up the value of a literary tradition, and of what was for him the backbone of university education, he argues that it is valuable because 'language, kept alive and rejuvenated by literature, is certainly an essential means of continuity and transition' (in Donoghue, 2004:15). In an article from 1947, Leavis repeats these claims for the value of an education in the English literary tradition by arguing that only 'the teacher of literature' can demonstrate for a student the 'complete activity' of 'evaluating' the 'change' that has occurred to England as a 'civilized community' between 'seventeenth-century England and the England of today' (1947:605). However, Leavis is already asking in 1933 'how long a cultural tradition can be perpetuated in this way' where language is 'kept alive and rejuvenated by literature' (2004:15). Of course, as a literary critic, he had perhaps too high a regard for literature's role in keeping language 'alive'. Any dominant form of the English language today has splintered into various World Englishes and even though these 'vernaculars' indirectly sustain some notion of a standard English this is most typically not grounded on literature or any 'spirit of the language' but on the belief that English, for however long this may be, possesses cultural capital and economic utility for today's university consumers. However, Leavis's notion of the 'spirit of the language' (in Donoghue, 2004:14) and how it depends on a 'genuinely national culture'[3] (in Donoghue, 2004:14) has been very influential for English departments and, in turn, for the humanities. Once again, the Irish National University may have wished to follow such a vision of the humanities and of a liberal education, but the language question was always the thorn in its side.

When Leavis describes the 'vital English School' as the 'centre' of the university, what is in turn, for him, the 'centre of civilization' (1969:18), he makes repeated references to its imparting of 'order', 'duty' and its creation of a 'civilized community'. Given the arguments already put forward by Fitzgerald, Lee and Buckley in regard to Irish society's lack of a 'viable' civic culture, it would appear that Irish society either did not share Leavis's beliefs or that it was unsuccessful at promoting the civic function of the university. Leavis describes a kind of cultural osmosis that takes place between the people as representative of a 'genuinely national culture' and any 'new influx, ferment and literary efflorescence' (in Donoghue, 2004:14) that comes from abroad. Donoghue replies to Leavis's argument that writers should act in an 'observant relation to' the 'spirit of the language' (2004:18) and to the 'genuinely national culture' bound up with it. For Donoghue, Leavis's understanding of tradition in terms of 'cultural continuity' and the 'spirit of the language' must be rooted in a 'national culture' (2004:15). He argues that Leavis implies that Joyce's later work 'veered from such observance because in Dublin, Paris, Trieste, and Zurich he did not have an adequate national culture or a community to belong to' (2004:18). However, Donoghue is quick to point out that '[s]pirit and genius, as terms of invocation, don't float higher above the rough ground than other words regularly used: *nation, race, culture, Renaissance, Europe*'. Donoghue also takes up Leavis's point that the 'spirit' of the English language has not survived the 'lapse of a national culture' (2004:18). He argues that Leavis was slow to admit that English as a 'national culture', as something embodying the 'spirit of a language' that Shakespeare 'incarnated' (Leavis, 1933:199) through his writing, had become gradually more dissociated from English as the 'dominant international language' (Donoghue, 2004:20). And he suggests that Leavis would have drawn little 'satisfaction' from the rise of English as such a 'dominant' language (2004:20).

In examining what aspects of Leavis's vision for the university would have been applicable to the Irish university, it is important to note that Leavis's vision for liberal education and for university education is bound up with both the 'concrete' and with what he describes as an 'actual living tradition' (1943:18). He is slow to use the word humanities, although he does use the term in quotation marks in the first chapter, 'The Idea of a University', of his 1943 book *Education and the University*, to say that 'humanities' in an 'ancient English university' must be about 'picking up a continuity; carrying on and fostering the essential life of a time-honoured and powerful institution, in this concrete historical England' (1943:19). However, even though Leavis stresses that 'the study of literature' must be at the 'centre' of this liberal education because it is the 'most intimate kind of study, that is, of a concrete

tradition', it must take place in a university where students study 'the literature of their own language and country' (1943:19). Now this argument made
on behalf of English literature in the university curriculum in liberal education in Ireland would always, as we have seen in the last section, be far less
persuasive for students and educators precisely because of the language question. One way early English departments in the universities in Ireland
attempted to alleviate this situation for Irish students' intent on a liberal education that maintained some sense of this 'living tradition' through English
was by naming the literature written in English by writers with a strong association with Ireland, Anglo-Irish Literature. Even in the 1990s when this
writer took these courses, lecturers never attempted to explain what this rather
cumbersome title meant. Were these Irish writers or English writers? Was the
language they wrote in to be academically regarded as Anglo-Irish? We knew
all our great writers were exiles, but the title Anglo-Irish had the effect of
assigning their literature to some liminal, tradition-free enclave where true
creativity was to be found only in the margins of life.

Leavis writes in his 1953 essay 'The "Great Books" and a Liberal Education'
that to say that 'liberal education should be centred in the study of creative literature is a proposition that will perhaps meet with general agreement'
(1953:166). However, while the Irish National University undoubtedly followed Leavis in principle, it must be recognized that the Leavisite vision for the
humanities and for liberal education would never sit comfortably with the
National University because of this sense of disconnect – very often ballooning
to betrayal – that accompanied any model that claimed that the study of English
literature must be at the 'centre' of a liberal education in the Irish university. In
fact, one might go so far as to suggest that because the 'study of literature'
could never claim such an assured position at the centre of liberal education in
the National University, it was the study of history that then assumed a more
prominent position in the academic psyche, hence the presumption in later
years that Irish Studies was synonymous with postcolonial studies.

There is an element of elitism in Leavis's account of a liberal education that
the Irish university would have presumably distanced itself from. Even though
Leavis regards 'academic intellectualism' as detrimental to the spirit of liberal
education and even though he argues that 'it is only when intimately related to
living experience that thought and knowledge in general or historical terms
can have any vitality – can be anything but merely "intellectual" and academic' (1953:168), he also claims in 1947 that 'I am avowedly concerned
with the training of an *élite*' (1947:589). Christopher Hilliard reminds us that
only 335 English undergraduates were admitted to Downing College,
Cambridge, in the years between 1932 and 1960 when Leavis taught there. This
sense of an elite is at odds with the American model of the modern humanities
(2012:260–71). And Leavis seems to have this tradition in his sights when he

argues that 'we' must 'fight against that interpretation of democracy which amounts to the law that no one may have anything everyone can't have' (1947:589). Precisely because Ireland did not possess a visible institutional elitism in the form of an Oxford or a Cambridge – Leavis takes Cambridge as his model – or in the form of the Ivy League or *grandes écoles* models, university culture was in practice potentially more democratic, at least in the American sense that Leavis distrusts.[4] Leavis regards it as a 'clear fact' that 'only a minority is capable of advanced intellectual culture' (1982b:162). In Ireland, there was no discernible difference between the English departments and, in turn, the humanities programmes of each constituent college. However, what the whole Leavisite episode reveals is that the English university model of the humanities subjects, with English literature becoming a progressively more important component throughout most of the century, was a model that the Irish university did attempt to borrow from despite the fact that Leavis's vision was bolstered by his belief that it was English that was representative of national culture and of a 'spirit of the language'. Once again, as with the religion question, this led to a somewhat paradoxical situation in the Irish university in the humanities whereby the overarching model for a liberal education presumed some shared vision with Leavis's account that privileged English while at the same time assuming that if any 'spirit of the language' haunted, or grounded, the university that it was Irish and not English.

Leavis's reading of this 'spirit of the language' is also somewhat problematic. Despite the fact that, for Leavis, this sense of 'spirit' had been created in the English tradition precisely because Shakespeare and the 'national culture' he worked within could infuse and revitalize Renaissance ideas and even the forms and cadences of the artistic creations of other European languages, it was a 'spirit' that was somehow expected to remain pure and pristine despite the numerous revolutions of the Word between Shakespeare's day and that of Leavis. In his 1969 article, he clarifies how the 'spirit of the language' arose within Shakespeare and English literature. He argues that the 'speech' of the 'country-folk of pre-industrial England' (1969:13) created the 'English language that made Shakespeare possible' (1969:14). Their speech developed as 'the articulate utterance of a total organic culture, one that comprehended craft-skills of many kinds, arts of living formed in response to practical exigencies and material necessity through generations of settled habitation, knowledge of life that transcended the experience of any one life-span' (1969:14). Shakespeare was then able to take up this 'marvelously receptive' vernacular in enabling it to accommodate and make its own the influxes of the Renaissance (1969:14). However, Leavis acknowledges that even then this was part of a nationalist enterprise; Shakespeare 'ensured' that 'our language and literature' retained 'an immense advantage over France' (1969:15). It was the industrial revolution, however, what he describes in terms of the 'drive of technologico-Benthamite civilization' (1969:16), that worked an 'inevitable destruction upon the inherited civilization of the people' (1969:15). Later literature, such as the work of Pope, would enforce an 'unprecedented insulation of the sophisticated or "polite" from the popular' (1969:15). However, is it the case that the 'spirit of the language' that had been 'incarnated' by Shakespeare in an existing 'national culture' by infusing and revitalizing foreign influences is then conflated with a sense of tradition that Leavis claims universities must hold up as a benchmark across time, a national template, that educators must 'act in an observant relation to'?

One might also imagine that Irish society, in not experiencing an industrial revolution or a cult of sensibility that separated the polite from the popular, might have preserved for longer this 'living tradition' or 'total organic culture' (1969:14) that was destroyed in England. However, once again, it is the preservation of a national language that grants English culture its 'cultural continuity' despite the industrial revolution. Leavis then argues, in returning to his own time, that it is 'English Literature' (1969:17) and its presence among an 'educated, cultivated and intelligent public' that must sustain this 'cultural continuity' (1969:17). However, there would seem to be a slight contradiction in seeking to preserve a 'spirit of the language' borne out of a 'total organic culture' without a 'polite'/popular distinction through a liberal education that is, for him, 'avowedly concerned with the training of an *élite*' (1947:589). If the Irish universities were then 'steeped' in an English ethos, as Lee claims, did this mean they followed Leavis's model where a liberal education promotes 'cultural continuity' by preserving a 'spirit of the language' rooted in a 'national culture'? If they did, it would obviously have brought deep-seated conflicts to the humanities in the Irish university especially if the force of 'the impulsion from inner life' made one approach the language with what Thomas Kinsella describes, even in 1973, as a 'divided mind'.

Donoghue allows us to imagine what an Irish 'spirit' of the humanities might be. In his essay 'Teaching Literature: The Force of Form', Donoghue argues that the teaching of literature embodies most of what is vital for an education in the humanities. He argues that the language of literature is uniquely rich in value; '[t]he language seems to know not only what it means to say but what it feels about what it says: the movement of the mind through the words is the adjudication of energy and its object'. His essays always privilege the attention to form as the means by which critics such as Kenneth Burke demonstrate how literature reveals 'fundamental human structures and sequences' (1999:12). He argues that 'we should not make any concession in disputes on form' because 'form is the consideration, the value, on which the relative autonomy of the artistic field has depended since about 1835' (1999:20). He reminds us of Bourdieu's words from *Distinction, Language and Symbolic Power* whereby a 'power must be affirmed that belongs to art to constitute everything aesthetically by virtue of form'. Donoghue argues that form is the 'value which permits writers to take part in political conflict, but without weapons' (1999:20). He also privileges the means through which language affects emotions and behaviour; he speaks of the 'movement of mind through the words' as 'the adjudication of energy and its object' (1999:10). Donoghue is a great believer in the power of 'words alone' to both enunciate and incarnate 'feelings' that are essential for the preservation of what is important to humanity. In his early work on Dickens, he commends Dickens for recognizing that one must trust in the 'community of feeling because it is at once particular and general; there can be nothing more intimate than feeling and at the same time nothing more universal' (1970:400). This also recalls Kant's earlier reading of the 'humanities' (*Humaniora*) as 'precognitions' that train one to embody both the taking-part and the act of 'imparting oneself' universally.

Donoghue had little time for the deconstructive and post-structuralist theories of the tradition perhaps most visibly represented in criticism by Paul de Man and Jacques Derrida. He refers to de Man as a 'grim reader' and to Derrida's textual revolution in terms of an 'invidious contrast between the axioms of speech and of writing' (2004:16). However, his work on literature and culture does occasionally move into the same area of investigation that Derrida and de Man highlight. He describes a 'temporal gap between feeling and words' (2004:14) that is always important to seize on in reading literature. He argues that it is generally acknowledged in the treatment of works of literature that 'words as words, in any work of literature, should withdraw themselves – or should at least seem to do so – and disappear among the feelings and perceptions they have produced. That is the proper destiny of words – to die into the further human life they have created. It may be wise not to call this further life "presence," lest that word enforce a stronger ontological claim than we need' (2004:16). Later, in the same essay from 2004, he argues, in regard to Joyce's *Finnegans Wake*, that 'Joyce's words in *Work in Progress* and, later, in *Finnegans Wake* are devised in such forms that they cannot withdraw from the context they enforce. There is nowhere for them to go. They have to remain on the page in the graphic state of what Leavis called "words as words". No wonder so many of them defeat the attention of the elocutionist and can be read only in the sense of being looked at'. This is about as far as Donoghue takes the treatment of signification. His reference to 'presence' and to how words defer meaning for the 'further human life they have created' recalls Derrida's description of logocentrism as a western metaphysical system that privileges speech. However, Donoghue appears unwilling to subject his foundational concepts such as 'form' and the 'symbolic imaginary' to further philosophical investigation because it would relegate the 'literary' or put it out of play.

However, in writing on literary culture as a benchmark from which all good teaching in the humanities must begin, Donoghue can be regarded as speaking for an aspect of the humanities, as embodied by the disciplines of literature and history, that was often pervasive, yet unspoken, in Irish universities over the last fifty years. At its heart, the humanities in Ireland was slow to take to anything postmodern or deconstructive, and this was because of a humanities ethos that worked along the very lines Donoghue describes. The Irish Catholic student and scholar had perhaps an intuitive sense for how literature brought theological analogues into play. The word of literature often functioned as a substitute for the religious Word and a 'spirit of the language' even though this was unspoken because the institutional religious investigation necessary to bring it to fruition was lacking. Donoghue is also a practising Catholic who has spoken of the literary and theological analogues that haunt work on literature. He argues that in the Christian tradition, 'the primal creative principle is identified as the Word of God, God uttering Himself [...] either directly or through the World He created' (in Knight, 2003:110–1). And later, he writes that '[s]ymbol redeems fact, because through symbol the imagination enters experience, as Christ redeemed fact in the Incarnation' (Knight, 2003:117). What Alasdair MacIntyre has recently called the Catholic philosophical tradition was what, for the most part, should possibly have existed in the National University – if we take the university to embody the 'social reality' of its community. However, the dictates of the 1908 Act would mean it could never really, officially, belong to such a tradition.

Donoghue alludes to the influence and reach of the Irish Universities Act of 1908 when he describes the working arrangements of the Department of English of University College Dublin (UCD) in the early 1950s, over ten years after Leavis's book *Education and the University* was written. He writes that Professor Jeremiah J. Hogan was then the professor of English and that he was the 'sole professor: he was in full charge of the Department, in accordance with the ordinance of Departments by the Irish Universities Act of 1908' (2011:1). It would seem most likely then that the National University was still adhering to the dictates of the 1908 Act not only in regard to curriculum but also for organizational matters. Donoghue also explains that 'American literature was not taught' at that time in the National University. It is clear then if we take into account the strict adherence to the 1908 Act and the lack of an American ethos in the curriculum that the National University was more likely to be following the tradition Leavis describes than anything imported from America at that time. Donoghue also reminds us that this situation did not change very much until he returned to UCD from Cambridge in 1967 'partly to propose a reorganization of the English Department' (2011:2). The Irish Universities Act had a strong influence on curriculum and organization right up until the time Ireland began applying for membership to the European Economic Community, and, of course, Ireland would then have to begin aligning itself with the European model of university education to take part fully in such schemes as Erasmus and Socrates.

The advent of Irish Studies and the postcolonial mandate would mean that the National University would move away from Donoghue's formalist style of reading. However, Donoghue has consistently privileged formalist analysis in his discussions of teaching. The humanities as an institutional discourse is, unlike the postcolonial, most often discussed in relation to its human value in terms of its practice and potential for teaching and how it imparts values that extend back to the foundations of Western education. The postcolonial might transgress, reinvent, dispossess and repossess many of the historical and teleological myths of nation, but it is rarely regarded as a discourse that self-reflexively examines the wider educational and humanistic arena that supports it in terms of these foundational texts and practices in the history of education. This book argues that it is important to examine how the humanities can inform educational discussion and teaching in the Irish context. Even though Donoghue's work has often been little more than a refreshing formalist aside for Irish students of the humanities amidst the heyday of the postcolonial paradigm, his works uphold universally acknowledged truths about liberal education that time and again bring us back to the traditions and forms of literary language.

Postcolonialism, Irish Studies and the work of Declan Kiberd

Cultural theory and cultural discourse in the humanities subjects in the National University over the last number of decades has been dominated by postcolonial theory. When this writer made his first excursion into the Irish conference circuit at a postgraduate conference for 'New Voices' at one of the constituent universities of the National University, the invited plenary speaker described Irish Studies as synonymous with postcolonial studies despite the fact that many of the 'New Voices' at the conference were not speaking from a postcolonial perspective. Eóin Flannery argues that 'postcolonial theory has been, and remains, one of the dominant modes of literary and cultural criticism within the broader discourse of Irish studies' (2009:16), and he is referring here principally to 'the discipline of postcolonial studies in Ireland' (2009:16). R. F. Foster has also argued recently that for Irish drama and fiction written after 1970, 'the overarching theme remains history and its negotiations' (2008:171). Nevertheless, Flannery also notes that in both the Irish and the UK university systems, the 'field' has been 'consecrated within the university industry' (2009:111) and that all too often these 'Irish critical debates' descend into 'crass political sloganeering' (37).

However, the benefits of the postcolonial debate for the humanities subjects cannot be overlooked. Luke Gibbons reminds us that the 'postcolonial turn in Irish criticism [...] represents an attempt to extend the horizons of the local to distant and often very different cultures, beyond the comforting cosmopolitanism of the West' (in Flannery, 2009:67). Nevertheless, if the postcolonial discourse that emerged within the disciplines of history and criticism (both might be regarded as part of a larger humanities field that is only an outgrowth of western hegemonic modernization) becomes dislodged from the 'literary and cultural criticism' that originally gave it direction, one wonders what cultural practices will be engaged with in order to sustain the interaction with these 'different cultures'. On this point, it is noteworthy that in Flannery's book of almost 250 pages on the postcolonial and Ireland, a book that stresses the part 'literary and cultural criticism' plays in the discourse, one would be hard-pressed to find a single quotation from a work of literature. Many of the critics whose work is held up as foundational for the postcolonial debate in Ireland, critics such as Bourdieu and Said, borrow heavily from writers such as Flaubert and Austen in drawing down theoretical principles that are then used to define what Bourdieu describes as the 'Rules of Art' and what Said describes as Orientalism. Said's work is deeply rooted in a merging of the aesthetic and the political, and this is why his work is at once appealing to the common reader and politically sensitive. He reminds us in *Orientalism* that it is a tradition of 'thought, imagery, and vocabulary' that has given the 'Orient' its 'reality' in Western writing (Said, 2003:71); he argues that '[u]nderlying all the different units of Orientalist discourse [...] is a set of representative figures, or tropes' (Said, 2000:71). The interrogation of this discourse, by implication, necessitates a proficiency in the analysis of literary 'figures, or tropes'. The danger with the postcolonial debate as it is conducted in Ireland is that it often becomes disconnected from any attention to the primary works that were so important to Said's and Declan Kiberd's influential postcolonial theories. Edward Said has himself warned critics, writing in 1993, that the theory risks becoming 'wrenched' from its proper 'contexts' (in Flannery, 2009:122). To privilege theory at the expense of the imagined communities the artworks speak for removes the discourse from the realm of the aesthetic. However, the postcolonial argument can also help other literary specialisms to keep their feet on the ground and avoid what Claude Levi-Strauss warns is a common 'vice' of structuralist criticism when it becomes 'limited to a play of mirrors, in which it becomes impossible to distinguish the object from its symbolic image in the subject's consciousness' (1976:275). Declan Kiberd, possibly the most persuasive Irish postcolonial critic, follows Said in privileging what Flannery describes as the 'centrality of art' (2009:80) and in advising that we should 'look to artists for inspiration, and not just for ornament' (Kiberd, 1995:652). Even though Graham Huggan rightly points out that postcolonial studies has an 'extraordinary disciplinary range' and that there has been in recent years a pointed interdisciplinary and 'transdisciplinary' approach that marks a 'shift away from a literary focus' (in Flannery, 2009:113) within Irish postcolonial studies, it must be acknowledged that the majority of leading Irish postcolonial critics began their careers in either English or History departments. However, the postcolonial discourse's resourcefulness in attaching itself to new sites of academic enquiry has ensured its durability over the last number of decades. It has also initiated an interdisciplinarity and openness in Irish humanities subjects that has produced important work in Irish Studies, most particularly in gender studies and feminism.

Many critics have also questioned the place of Ireland in postcolonial studies. Anne McClintock criticizes the term 'postcolonialism' for the 'globalising temporality and premature sense of self-congratulation that it sets up' (Carrol, 2003:7). McClintock writes that 'Ireland may, at a pinch, be "postcolonial", but for the inhabitants of British-occupied Northern Ireland [...] there may be nothing "post" about colonialism at all'. McClintock also, as Clare Carrol informs us, 'points out the belatedness that the term "post-colonial" imposes upon colonial cultures. It positions them primarily as an aftereffect of colonial rule and, hence, reads these cultures through the linguistic lens of that rule' (Carrol, 2003:8). While such criticism does suggest that Ireland is indeed still somewhat 'liminal' in relation to the canon of postcolonial discourse as realized in the literatures of Algeria, India and Africa, liminality, as I will examine in the next section, has also a distinct meaning in the field of Irish Studies. Joe Cleary also notes that for all that 'Irish academics avail themselves of the conceptual resources of postcolonial studies as a pedagogical tool', 'there are only two dedicated programmes of study in Ireland that focus on empire and postcolonialism' and these are both Master of Arts programmes.[5]

However, Flannery also points to a darker side of this postcolonial shape-changing that aligns aspects of the discipline with the perpetuation of hegemonic practices and academic careerism. He reminds us of Bourdieu's description of the symbolic power of academic discourse. Bourdieu argues that 'academic language is primarily a mechanism for communication, a mechanism of pedagogical instruction or alternatively a mode of tautological self-preservation, intimately bound to the processes of careerist advancement and the dialectic of consecration' (in Flannery, 2009:143). One way to ensure academic discourse chiefly embodies the first two options, namely, 'communication' and 'pedagogical instruction', is to ground the work in the close analysis of its relevance for pedagogy and teaching. In locating the postcolonial in the history of the humanities, an academic field that is rooted in pedagogical self-examination, we can preserve the more beneficent aspects of academic discourse. Since literature is itself a discipline that is often regarded as the 'centre' of a liberal education where reading is an embodiment in microcosm of the ideal pedagogical performance, it is often in the words of literary texts that we can locate a spirit of enquiry removed from the taint of 'tautological self-preservation' or any 'dialectic of consecration'.

Declan Kiberd and the postcolonial

The work of Declan Kiberd has been at the forefront of the most pressing theoretical debates in literature and history in Irish universities for the last three or four decades. If there is any critic whose work encapsulates what might be regarded as a uniquely Irish postcolonial theoretical perspective in the most privileged humanities subjects, namely, literature and history, then it is Kiberd. His work applies a complex theoretical approach to both the Irish language tradition and the Anglo-Irish tradition. He was one of the first writers to bring the postcolonial debate to Irish Studies, and he has also applied his artistic theories and his perspective on the postcolonial debate by questioning pedagogical practice in the university in Ireland. While it is undeniable that Kiberd's work has brought the Irish tradition closer to the postcolonial experiences of India, Africa and the Middle East, his readings of literature are dominated by how 'Irishness' is defined in relation to the literary tradition and culture of its neighbour, England. His work is very often fighting its own 'war against the past', a title he gives to one of his most pointed essays on Irish nationalism. In fact, Kiberd's work is so painfully aware, linguistically, historically and even psychologically, of how any 'resistance movement' always has 'to adapt itself to the behaviour and character of the colonial power' (2005c:150) that his own work is always haunted by the linguistic and psychological tendencies of the people he speaks for, who 'in submitting [...] to an already loaded language', see the 'revolution' 'taken away' from them 'even as they performed it' (150). His work might be regarded as palimpsestically inscribing itself over a colonial narrative that always shows through no matter how enthralling the 'uncertain future' (2005c:161) he evokes in the attempt to displace the historical perspective from what he calls the 'psychology of literary revivalism' (2005c:162). If we extend Kiberd's revisionist historicist readings to another recently popular figure of the literary critic's trade, namely, prosopopoeia, he might also be regarded as describing the 'madness' of figuration itself, in positing and speaking for the dead through prosopopoeia, even if from a postcolonialist perspective. However, Paul de Man argues that in our 'endless prosopopoeia', in our endless endeavour of 'giving a voice to the absent or dead', we become products of this strategy and not 'its agent'; de Man argues that it would then be 'naïve' to believe that any meaning derived thereof 'can be a source of value' (1979b:68). Even though Kiberd acknowledges, in reference to Conor Cruise O'Brien, that the Irish people are intent on 'commemorating themselves to death' (2005c:163), any account that endlessly corrects the historical misreading may still be giving too much up to the nightmare of history. Kiberd reads Yeats's argument of 1902 about 'pass[ing] into the future the great moral qualities' in order to 'give men the strength to fight' (in Kiberd, 2005c:158) as 'sinister' because the 'fight as a self-sustaining tradition' is privileged at the expense of the 'more humane idea of the culture fought for' (2005c:158). However, Yeats would soften his tone considerably with the passing years until even labour becomes for him 'blossoming or dancing where/ The body is not bruised to pleasure soul'. Yeats therefore moved on from the argument that claimed 'we must live as though it ["the battle"] were to go on endlessly', and it is a lesson that is also important for his critics.

However, if Yeats and the colonizers were hard on the Irish psyche or on the 'Irish personality', it seems Kiberd must go harder and explain how it is inconsolably afflicted by compulsive impersonation, a 'pseudo-self', and a 'pathology of dependence' (2005:185). In drawing on early-twentieth-century literary history to locate the precise contours of these psychological states, he argues that the 'middle-class civil servants and office workers who tittered in 1926 at the urban leprechauns on Sean O'Casey's stage were the same people who, fifteen years earlier, would have accused the same author of mounting Irish shenanigans on stage for the delectation of a Castle audience' (2005d:177). For Kiberd, this is because these civil servants and office workers had fallen for the consoling myth of Yeats's revivalist history, a version of history that had not reckoned with 'the capacity of the occupier to insinuate an entire symbology into his own and his audience's minds' (2005d:177). O'Casey's modern tragedies, while guilty of the 'tragic vision' that Edward Said reminds us is always a 'static one', may also have brought out in their audiences the healthy laughter of catharsis (2000:34). Roy Foster reminds us, in reference to another Irish play, Shaw's *Back to Methuselah*, that Shaw was 'well aware of the mercilessly realistic side of Irish nature, prepared to exploit the past with one hand and jettison it with the other' (2008:184), and it is likely that O'Casey's audiences were also demonstrating this 'mercilessly realistic' side of their nature.

Kiberd deepens his psychological reading to trace this early-twentieth-century false consciousness to a more contemporary Irish malaise. In a revealing reading, he extends his description of the national neurosis to an analysis of the personal relationships between sons and fathers in Irish families. He argues, somewhat quixotically, that '[i]n a colony the revolt by a son against a father is a meaningless gesture because it can have no social effect' (2005:179). However, the logic of this step from the political to the familial is not so clear. Claude Lévi-Strauss reminds us that no matter how consoling myths may appear, '[s]ocieties are not persons' (157). Perhaps Kiberd is suggesting that a revolt that does not achieve its end fails on all counts. However, popular wisdom tells us that a history of heroic failures in Irish history has had quite distinct 'social effect[s]'. Despite the lack or otherwise of social ramifications, psychology also tells us that a child's revolt is always deeply traumatic on a personal level and is far from 'meaningless' for all involved. For literary support, we might also look to Simon Dedalus's somewhat painful ranting about his rebellious son Stephen – 'I won't have her bastard of a nephew [Mulligan] ruin my son' (1992:110) – in the carriage in the 'Hades' chapter of *Ulysses*.

But Kiberd extends this reading of the pseudo-self and of the 'pathology of dependence' to 'weak paternity' and to an uncommon tendency for 'verbal ambiguity' among Irish males in Irish society in general that, in the words of Nancy Scheper-Hughes, 'can provoke schizophrenia in vulnerable individuals' (2005d:185). This capacity to be duped by the colonizer's 'symbology' and to worship the past in some revivalist 'deification of current mediocrity' (2005d:184) is related, in Kiberd's reading of Irish society, to the 'personality structure of the Irish male' (2005d:185) as revealed by census figures in the 1970s. The census figures of 1971 reveal that 'two out of every hundred males in the west of Ireland were in mental hospitals'. The chief psychiatrist of the Eastern Health Board of the day, Ivor Browne, is then quoted in 1976 as arguing that there was a 'growing belief among Irish adults, even in urban areas, that they would never take control of their own lives, government, or economy'. Browne applies the title the 'postcolonial personality' to this male type who displays 'apathy, selflessness and loss of autonomy' as well as 'civic indifference'; it is a state of mind that can only be thrown off by 'his fellow countrymen' casting off 'the security of oppression'. Browne argues that 'we are only concerned with aping our oppressors, with proving to ourselves that we are the same as they were and can use the same methods of oppression on each other' (in Kiberd, 2005d:185). The reference to 'civic indifference' here also recalls Garret Fitzgerald's argument that there is a lack of 'civic morality' in Ireland because of the way the university subjects are taught. However, Kiberd takes the argument much further in tracing a direct line from the Irish people's willingness to be duped by narratives of nationalism and heroism played out on the revivalist stage to the average Irish male's tendency in the 1970s and 1980s to be ensnared by a 'pathology of dependence'.

However, even if we accept the basic structure of Kiberd's argument, we might still find the psychological reading of this national condition both patriarchal and Freudian. Both master narratives have since been blunted by the enlightening post-Freudian and deconstructive theories of writers like Nancy Chodorow, Jacques Derrida and Luce Irigaray. Kiberd's model appears to presume some kind of law of the strong father; anything that departs from this is abnormal and directly linked to an inauthentic relationship with a 'healthy' narrative of national self-determination. Of course, while Freud and Lacan privilege social and sexual maturation from the perspective of the 'little man' in terms of the navigation of the Oedipus and Narcissus complexes, respectively, more recent psychological theories, such as that of Chodorow, have replaced this patriarchal lineage with a concentration on the pre-Oedipal state and on a Law of the mother with a small 'm'. For Chodorow, object cathexis is replaced by object-relations theory and relationships, not drives, are the motivating factors in early development (1999:48); a woman's sense of 'self-in-relation' replaces any patriarchal order where there is a tendency to 'deny relation' (viii). Luce Irigaray has gone further and has asserted that any psychiatric defence mechanism that tries to replace the old Freudian myth of the strong father with the figure of the impotent man – what sounds like Kiberd's 'weak paternity' – is simply another patriarchal ruse to hold on to centre stage even when its foundations are crumbling.[6] In other words, Freudian models, themselves often borrowed from literary narratives and myths, frequently come up short when mapped directly onto contemporary social practices. Irish feminist writers and gender critics of the last number of decades have enabled Irish criticism to advance this mapping of psychological tendencies onto societal practices.

However, even if we do not accept Kiberd's psychological asides, we may also question another aspect of Kiberd's argument. The claim that the social fragmentation evident in Irish society at the end of the twentieth century, and presumably still in evidence today in post-Celtic Tiger Ireland, is a direct result of the capacity to be duped by versions of revivalist history or by a tendency to assume a postcolonialist mentality may assign too much to the redemptive nationalist narrative. R. F. Foster has recently argued that some 'scholars', and he appears to be including Kiberd in this group, have 'interrogated the interventions of "post-nationalists" and "liberal culturalists" in contemporary Ireland and wondered whether this has amounted to a dilution or a transmutation of traditional nationalism' (2008:177).[7] As an example of such an academic venture, he highlights what he calls the 'self-righteous Ireland Institute' that was set up in 1997 by 'among others Declan Kiberd [and] Edna O'Brien'; this institute that Foster argues was 'galvanized by what its founders perceived as the inadequate response to the eightieth anniversary of the 1916 Rising' sets out to 'nurture writing which tackles the revisionist and anti-nationalist stance' (2008:177). However, it may not be that Irish society failed to see through these myths of revivalism or dependency but that it decided that it would be far less painful to risk itself in an exploration of what could be gained from the perpetuation of such myths. The American dream and the dream of a united Europe allowed this calculated culture of dependency to survive and even occasionally flourish over the last number of decades. However, the endless historical debunking of myths of self-determination can become as disempowering as the calculated embrace of these myths. Whether this strengthens O'Brien's claim that there is an inordinate degree of 'civic indifference' in Ireland is unclear. However, one of the places to tackle such indifference is in the universities where a wholesome humanities education can inculcate an interest in civic morality.

However, in an age of globalization and cosmopolitanism, efforts have been made to move this interrogation of the Irish psyche beyond its focus on a cultural dependency inherited from a colonialist 'symbology'. When Ireland was being touted as one of the world's most globalized nations in the early years of the new millennium, Luke Gibbons argued for an embrace of an 'ethics of analogy' and an 'ethics of memory' in Irish Studies. For Gibbons, an ethics of analogy is bound up with the 'historical duty' argument that sees Ireland as having little excuse, given its history, for 'getting it wrong' when it comes to its response to such contemporary issues as immigration. He questions whether in 'the first surge of affluence' of the 1990s, there was, in Ireland, a readiness to 'displace [the] past, not least by placing it in the quarantine of the heritage industry'.[8] By corollary, Gibbons wonders whether this 'readiness' partly arose from 'the protracted crisis in national memory precipitated by three decades of conflict in Northern Ireland'.[9] To counter this, Gibbons postulates an ethics of analogy that would then resituate our encounter with a reconstituted and reconstituting past in terms of responsibility. Mary Robinson has also argued that 'our sense as a people who suffered and survived [...] does not entitle us to a merely private catalogue of memories'.[10] Irish Studies has been thrown into a frantic search for a critical vocabulary that can describe the cultural memory loss or malaise afflicting a people struggling to come to terms with cultural cues that ask them to embrace a dramatic discursive shift from 'Celtic Twilight to Celtic Tiger' and, in turn, from a Tiger economy to a Troika economy. Gibbons reminds us that 'cultural memory is part of a society's continuing dialogue with itself'. However, Ireland's dialogue with itself over the last two decades has struggled to reconcile the multiple accounts of Irishness being disseminated at this time of cultural and economic boom and bust. At such times of uncertainty, the university and its humanities subjects can act as a valuable resource for enabling society to ground itself once again. R. F. Foster has also recently questioned these moves by Irish critics and public intellectuals to apply notions imported from psychology to the understanding of Irish history. He notes that the 'politics of historical commemoration have become a subject for historical commentary in themselves, along with the dangers of projecting imported concepts from psychotherapy and "liberation psychology" such as "collective memory" and "post-stress trauma" on to the historical experience of past centuries. This can lead to crudely airbrushed views that come to resemble exactly the kind of black-and-white, green-and-orange versions from which the Irish supposedly have been trying to liberate themselves' (2008:176). However, in staying with the psychological reading for a little longer, it might be argued that it is not a 'pathology of dependence' or even a belated style of bearing witness that most evocatively describes the Irish mode of self-representation but a form of Nietzschean *ressentiment*. Gilles Deleuze reminds us that, for Nietzsche, '[t]he man of ressentiment experiences every being and object as an offence in exact proportion to its effect on him'. As Nietzsche himself writes: 'One cannot get rid of anything, one cannot get over anything, one cannot repel anything – everything hurts. Men and things obtrude too closely; experiences strike one too deeply; memory becomes a festering wound' (Ecco Homo, I 6, p. 320; Deleuze, 2006:116).

However, it is Kiberd's essays on the teaching of literature in the curriculum in both schools and universities that describe most fully his understanding of the shortcomings of an Irish approach to education in the humanities subjects. In an essay entitled 'Writers in quarantine? The case for Irish Studies' originally published in Mark Hederman and Richard Kearney's *Crane Bag* in 1979, he begins with a combative epigraph from Pádraig Pearse where Pearse is denouncing what he calls the 'Irish-literature-is-English idea' and calling for Yeats to be 'crushed'. Pearse's statement might sound like revolutionary propaganda; however, Kiberd argues that 'Pearse's doctrinaire statement became a major policy of the Gaelic League and this led to an artificial division between writing in Irish and English on the island. Such a division persists in Irish schoolrooms to this very day, where Anglo-Irish literature is studied in one class and literature in the Irish language is considered in another' (2005c:52). Kiberd's main problem with the education in the humanities subjects in Irish universities is therefore in regard to the language question. That he could still be arguing for this as the main oversight in the university curriculum in the late 1970s is surely evidence that the language question remained an issue for most of the century. Kiberd does not question the lack of theology, religious studies or comparative literature in the Irish humanities or the status of philosophy in the universities of the National University. He also does not dwell on what Foster has noted is a recurring argument shared by 'both the Catholic *ancien régime* and the post-revisionist Begrudgers' that supports a 'recurrent hostility to "liberalism"' in Ireland and that sees 'liberalism or pluralism' as 'somehow un-Irish' (2008:188). I have argued in this book that one of the reasons large sections of the Irish people might be regarded as expressing such a view is that some of the core values of a liberal education that deal with how the individual incorporates such notions as spiritual values into a modern-day secular philosophy of identity that does not necessarily see itself as post-nationalist were often absent from the Irish universities.

Kiberd prefers to return his argument to the different traditions that Pearse and Yeats speak for. He argues, writing in 1979, that the most urgent development for the humanities in the Irish university is the bringing together of these two traditions; the work of Pearse and Yeats clearly demonstrated that there were 'now two traditions to be confronted and the more exciting challenge was to forge a literature which would bring into alignment the world of Berkeley, Swift and Burke with that of O'Hussey, Keating and Raftery' (2005c:53). Once again, then, a 'two culture' approach to the Irish question is taken as a given, an approach we have seen in Ó Tuama's essays where one group is described as the 'majority of the Irish people' and the other group as the 'Anglo-Irish nation'; if only the realities of cultural integration organized around demographic groups could be arranged so neatly. Kiberd, like Ó Tuama, credits Synge with having 'succeeded in his search for a bilingual style' (2005c:53), but he says less about how this bilingual style might be taught in the universities and how it might be aligned with an Irish language philosophy of education. In the end, in the face of the resurgence in Ireland of 'writers of English', the leaders of the Gaelic movement 'prayed for the emergence of a writer [in Irish] of European stature who might deliver the language from its bondage' (2005c:53).

Raphaël Ingelbien points to another aspect of Irish Studies and its some-times questionable postcolonial status that has meant that the approach to such subjects as literature and history in the Irish university has departed radically from the European model. He argues that 'in the last three decades, literary criticism in the Anglo-Saxon world' has been 'reshaped by the transformation of English and the gradual eclipse of Comparative Literature' (2009:23). Ingelbien argues that the postcolonial notion of 'writing-back', most famously posited by Ashcroft et al.'s The Empire Writes Back, 'made possible an expan-sion of the corpus of English literature at a time when the discipline was look-ing for new material as well as new approaches, and when multicultural realities made the idea of a Eurocentric canon untenable' (2009:24). Ingelbien reminds us that Edward Said's real intention in supporting the postcolonial cause was to attack the institution of comparative literature, and it would seem that Kiberd is promoting here some notion of comparative literature, even if on a much smaller scale, when he speaks of reading Irish language works and English language works in the same lecture or class. However, it is likely that this Irish–English comparativist approach would have slighted connections with the European model of comparative literature and with those vital Euro-pean influences that so many of the Irish modernists drew from in favour of more home-grown connections. Ingelbien also reminds us that Said moved from comparative literature to the postcolonial precisely because Said's target was the 'discipline's very focus on an idea of Weltliteratur that, while claim-ing to transcend boundaries and ideologies, actually asserted the supremacy of a Western tradition that was, in Said's claim, profoundly implicated in Impe-rial domination' (in Ingelbien, 2009:26). However, when Ingelbien argues that 'multilingualism and a European frame of reference are the two babies that were thrown out with the bathwater of old-style Comparative Literature' in the postcolonial turn, it becomes apparent that the situation was not entirely the same for the Irish university.

By the 1960s or 1970s, the Irish National University had never had a prop-erly European-style comparative literature element, and therefore in embrac-ing the postcolonial turn, it was moving further away from key aspects of the

European model of the humanities such as multilingualism – Ingelbien describes the Irish approach to the postcolonial as largely 'monolingual' – and the 'European frame of reference' precisely at a time when it would have benefitted from integrating these aspects into its humanities programmes. Fortunately, the 1990s would also see the advent of the Bologna documents on education in Europe, and these would push the Irish university back to the European model despite the postcolonial drift. It is perhaps surprising then that one of Ireland's leading postcolonial critics, writing in 1979, neglects to mention this 'death of a discipline' in regard to comparative literature in Europe and beyond in advocating this Irish–English comparativist approach in the Irish classroom and lecture hall. Kiberd argues that '[s]eventy years after the death of Synge, a literary partition between writing in Irish and English divides the classroom of Ireland as surely as a political partition divides the land' (2005c:54). Kiberd reminds us of Thomas MacDonagh's 1916 study *Literature in Ireland*, with the subtitle 'Studies Irish and Anglo-Irish', published some months after his execution in which he speaks of the 'essential continuity of the two traditions' (2005c:63). However, as late as 1941, the professor of English at UCC, Daniel Corkery, had retreated once again to Pearse's position in claiming in *What's That About the Gaelic League* that 'The English language, great as it is, can no more throw up an Irish literature than it can throw up an Indian literature. Neither can Irish nationality have its say in both English and Irish' (Kiberd, 2005c:64).

Kiberd is right to take de Valera's pronouncements on education and Irish in the early decades of the State to task for offering little more than 'rigid prescriptions for Irish writers' (2005c:66) and as inciting a state-sanctioned publishing drive through movements such as An Gúm where 'masterpieces' were rejected and 'sentimental bilge by tenth-rate writers' was celebrated (2005c:66). Kiberd also reminds us that in the early decades of the century, there was 'no critical tradition in Irish over and above the internecine pedantries of rival grammarians' (2005c:66). Once again, Kiberd is quick to extend this situation to the 'partitionist mentality' (2005c:68) of the Irish psyche or 'mind'; he claims that '[e]very Irish person who has passed through the classrooms of the country has emerged from this educational mauling with a chronically divided mind' (2005c:68) and that 'at the root of many a man's inability to live in peace with his neighbours is the inability to live in peace with himself' (2005c:68).

One can argue, however, that such a debate on the state of Irish, at a time when the 'crisis' in the humanities was raging elsewhere in all its post-structuralist and deconstructive splendour, pushed the Irish university further towards academic peripherality or isolation. However, Kiberd only strengthens the argument; he writes that 'it is imperative that wide-ranging courses in Irish Studies be instituted in all schools and universities now'; he describes the situation in terms of a 'battle' that 'will finally be won or lost in thousands of parish schools across the land', and he claims that it is the 'universities [that] have the chance to play a leading role'. This writer began his studies in literature in one of these universities only fifteen years after Kiberd's essay was published. However, it is safe to say that the kind of 'battle' Kiberd describes had been well and truly lost by the mid-1990s. Most of the lecturers who filled the lecture theatres this writer attended in the mid-1990s and who gave inspiring courses on English literature were English men and women who could not speak Irish. Despite the fact that the professor of English, Seán Lucy, at this same department had 'remarked with some gusto' in 1970 that he 'would take no student of Anglo-Irish literature seriously unless that student were bilingual' (in Kiberd, 2005c:68), out of the two or three hundred of us who squeezed into these lectures on Anglo-Irish literature twenty years later, very few would have regarded ourselves as bilingual, at least in Irish and English. In the end, it seems that the reality that Kiberd describes was true for most universities in Ireland at that time: 'those students who tried in their graduate work to vindicate the logic of Sean Lucy's argument have found the doors of Irish academe slammed in their faces' (2005c:68). However, another reason for this failure on the part of Irish universities to hire their own may run much deeper. Irish universities, in feeling somewhat insecure about the doctoral education in the humanities that they have imparted to students in their departments, tend to overlook the graduate student who has done all of his or her work in Ireland in favour of the student who has gone oversees, particularly to Oxford or Cambridge, for graduate study.[11] However, what this debate on the role of the universities in regard to these humanities subjects reveals is that it may have hindered a broader perspective on the plight of the humanities. Edward Said has claimed, in this regard, that the Irish experience of colonialism and subsequently, one would imagine, the Irish version of the postcolonial experience, in both its academic and nonacademic realities, has been somewhat removed from the European experience. He describes how 'the Irish experience and other colonial histories [...] testify to [...] a spiral away and extrapolation from Europe and the West', and Said, in saying this, has sought to wrest Yeats's work away from 'European high modernism' (in Ingelbien, 2009:30). In fact, Said justifies his dismissal of the revisionist claim that Ireland is not a postcolonial nation by arguing that it is ludicrous to assert that 'Ireland is a European nation like France or Germany' (Said, 2003:177; Ingelbien, 2009:30). Raphael Ingelbien also describes Kiberd's attitude to continental Europe in *Inventing Ireland* as one of 'schizophrenic ambivalence'. He argues that, at times, 'Kiberd's "Europe" is synonymous with Western Imperialism, and [that] its literary tradition is – in Saidian fashion – deeply complicit with colonialism' (Ingelbien, 2009:31). It is therefore clear that even though Kiberd has sought to address the situation in the humanities in the Irish university from a comparativist perspective, that, his focus has most often been on the state of Irish in the curriculum.

In a later essay, 'Joyce's Ellmann, Ellmann's Joyce', Kiberd does explain why there was a lack of 'Irish scholar-critics' (2005a:242) in the Irish universities and why there was no discernible 'criticism of the national life' (2005a:243), a phrase he borrows from W. E. B. Du Bois's description of the black American literary tradition in the United States. Kiberd argues that there were many reasons for this, among them 'a belief that oral tradition was paramount and that it was sufficient for any professor to instruct his or her own students in the received wisdom' (2005a:243). He also argues that lecturers and professors were simply overloaded with work, a claim that many foreign scholars might also have claimed for their own careers: 'the sheer weight of the teaching-load, the small numbers in most departments meaning that each person had to teach across a huge range, and the lack of sabbatical facilities' all 'retarded the development of scholarly research' (2005a:243). His claim that 'Irish writing, like that of the American Renaissance, seemed to contain within itself its own auto-criticism, its own essential self-commentary' is another familiar argument made about Irish writing. However, no one has yet explained precisely why *Ulysses* or *Endgame* possesses more self-criticism than *The Wasteland* or the writings of Henry James. It is also now evident after the publication of the collected critical writings of Joyce and Beckett that these writers were capable of good criticism on both Irish writers and foreign writers. If these graduates of the University College and of Trinity could produce good criticism, why did so few follow them? It was clearly because the universities could not, or chose not to, support such work. For the general public, the real writers were always those who emigrated and wrote novels or plays; they did not share Kiberd's views that those who stayed behind and wrote criticism were overworked. What Foster describes as a 'recurrent hostility to "liberalism"' (2008:188) in Irish society may also have extended to the liberal education that was found in the university. Kiberd also suggests that when American critics started arriving in Ireland in the 1940s and 1950s, there was a belief that the 'Americans wrote criticism; the Irish were creative' (2005a:243). However, the belief in the innate creativity of the Irish people also made them believe they had an intuitive gift for understanding literature that made criticism redundant. Kiberd notes how literature was seen to explain everything in Irish society: '[s]omething was clearly askew when the sociology written by outsiders was turning so fast into literature, and the literature produced by insiders was taking on the value of sociology' (2005a:244).

Kiberd explains that 'Irish students' of his day – and the situation may not have been too different in the 1990s – 'suppressed' any central questions they might have had that ran counter to how foreign critics were interpreting the Irish psyche or personality in Joyce, Wilde or Yeats. As Austin Clarke lamented in the *Irish Times* in a series of letters in 1941, there was a distinct 'absence of a developed national criticism' in the Irish university, something that had not really altered when Kiberd was a student in the 1960s and 1970s. Kiberd argues that Irish students suppressed their own questions because they 'had been taught to read literature in our departments as if we were young Londoners or Mancunians. When we wrote of D. H. Lawrence, we did so in the approved manner of a Leavis or a Kermode; when we constructed essays on Joyce, we practiced the style of Ellmann, Hugh Kenner or Walton Linz. Only outside the classroom or the library did we permit ourselves to think that there was something very strange in Ellmann's attitude to Ireland' (2005a:240). And in the 1990s and noughties, this tradition continued as we all tried to write like Derrida or Bloom. This awareness that there was a lack of a certain kind of reader or a certain kind of critical tradition in Irish universities and in Irish society has been echoed more recently by Colm Tóibín who argues that novelists like Higgins, Banville and McGahern had to work in 'a manner that was experimental, personal and innovative' because there was 'no audience here for such books. It was not just that Ireland did not offer a shelter between history and destiny for the novelists to pitch their tents, thus causing them to write at one remove from what was happening. But there was no-one to read the books, no set of educated, curious, open-minded literate people' (in Kiberd, 2005c:163). One could argue that the censorship that was at the heart of the lack of a readership also worked in other forms in the universities where there were obvious gaps too in the humanities curriculum. Kiberd's recognition of the lack of an Irish critical tradition and Tóibín's recognition of the lack of a readership for these 'experimental' and sometimes controversial works of fiction went hand in hand.

Kiberd's most lengthy essay on learning is entitled 'Museums and learning'. However, in examining 'learning' in relation to museums, he has little to say about the universities. In investigating the nature of the learning peculiar to museum culture, he raises important questions about learning in general in Ireland. One is tempted to read the museum as metaphor for the university in his essay. Was the Irish humanities agenda more about preserving old ideas than inspiring new ones? He reminds us that 'the task of curators, of course, is to resist this notion of a knowledge, which has been stabilized once and for all, and to mount displays which recognize that history is an open process, never concluded'; he reminds us that curators struggle 'to give as full as possible an account without lapsing into nationalist apologetics' (2005b:225). One wonders at times whether Kiberd is reminding himself of the tasks of the postcolonialist, nationalist critic who must also read received literary pronouncements against the grain while avoiding such 'nationalist apologetics'. In this regard, he does bring the debate back to the critics when he notes the irony involved in the whole *Field Day* project, a five-volume anthology grounded on what he describes as a 'colonial ideology', namely, the idea that you can 'study a whole civilization from its rise to its demise' (2005b:225).[12] He argues that because museums 'deal in objects' that they 'seem to give material form almost immediately to official versions of the past, reinforcing a type of "public memory" which privileges the social over the personal and so narrows the definition of what the "political" might in fact be' (2005b:226). Kiberd is clearly contrasting the museum display here with other forms of presentation that also claim to give 'official versions of the past' albeit in a less immediate manner. The form of presentation that lies closest to his own heart and that he is presumably connoting here is the historically sensitive reading of cultural artworks and artefacts. It begs the question then as to whether the public institution that supports and puts on display these literary 'versions of the past', namely the university, is to be regarded as exempt from these tendencies to privilege the 'social over the personal' thereby narrowing the definition of the 'political'. After all, Kiberd does argue that '[t]he task of the teacher or curator, like that of the historian, is literally to re-member the past, to put the different parts of its body back together again, and to restore to it the fuller context which once it had' (2005b:230). In response, one might argue that criticism and historical commentary in Ireland, especially in recent years with the rise of the postcolonial reading, has always privileged the social as historical over the personal. The artists have reimagined the personal, and the critics have exploited it for the historical nugget that can service the national. It is only very recently with the rise of feminism and gender studies in Irish criticism that the personal has come more to the fore. A pared-down humanities programme with little concentration on the connections between spirituality, ethics and literature is always likely to produce a pared-down version of the personal.

Irish Studies and the humanities: liminality and hybridity

Irish Studies is the most recent academic movement in the Irish universities to exhibit an important sense of interdisciplinarity and European influence. Irish Studies experienced a theoretical 'turn' in the 1990s in the wake of the postcolonial and post-structuralist revolution on the continent and in America. Despite the moniker Irish, Irish Studies does, as Clare Connolly argues, keep in mind that a 'great many things that have happened and are happening on the island [...] are not primarily concerned with nationality and its discontents'.[13] Irish Studies is then a general studies area that covers recent work on Irish topics in critical theory, gender studies, feminism, postcolonial theory and new media. Without question, it is gender studies and feminism that have been at the forefront of this movement. Connolly argues that theory, as it appears in Irish Studies, has 'helped mark out a space between scepticism and reverence' (2003:10) in Irish cultural criticism. While critics such as Richard Kearney tackled the philosophy head on and brought a strong new voice to the continental school of philosophy, many critics in the humanities working in such fields as English literature, French literature and sociology sought to use somewhat watered-down versions of the very often French theories and tropes for their respective disciplines. Because there was no indigenous philosophy of language or any readily apparent archive of Irish philosophy from which Irish critics working in the humanities could borrow in an age when boundaries between philosophy and criticism were becoming blurred, it became necessary to display some grasp of the rudiments of these new theories and philosophies from the continent. Thomas Duddy writes in the preface to his *A History of Irish Thought* that '[a]part from Richard Kearney's ground-breaking anthology, *The Irish Mind* (1985) no attempt has hitherto been made to write a comprehensive and up-to-date account of Irish thought' (Duddy, 2002:xv) and such a volume has not yet appeared on university reading lists. He continues by suggesting that the 'Irish contribution to the history of thought has been marginalized, partly because thought has been too narrowly understood' (Duddy, 2002:xiv). This section extends Duddy's comments to Irish Studies' relatively recent embrace of the language of post-structuralism for critical theory. For a number of years, Irish Studies has approached the language of critical theory from an overarching postcolonialist persuasion. However, postcolonial and post-structural discourses have distinct habitus since they privilege historical and linguistic roots, respectively. The distinction was not always acknowledged in Irish Studies. Conference titles[14] elicit the discourse's willingness to accept the rhetoric of the 'linguistic turn' inaugurated by post-structuralism and deconstruction without explicitly interrogating the theories of signification and language that have enabled predominantly French and American theorists to develop the guiding philosophies of language. David Lloyd has alluded to the dangers of the reductive historicist gaze in a recent essay 'After History: Historicism and Irish Postcolonial Studies'. He argues that '[h]istoricism reduces the cultural forms and practices of past and subordinated people to mere reaction, folklore, or mythology, and yet depends on them for its own articulation and for its own myth of a finally triumphant progress' (in Carrol, 2003:46). It is with these considerations in mind that I examine here, through one of Irish Studies' most favoured tropes – the trope of liminality – different aspects of postcolonial and critical theory as practised in Ireland.

Irish postcolonial theory frequently employs tropes from post-structuralist and deconstructive analyses of signification to describe an Irish take on cultural identity that privileges history's means for mediating a cultural consciousness that exploits the form of the text, be it literary or otherwise, for its own ends. However, if the figures and tropes of post-structuralism and deconstruction have been accused of working to any critical paradigm, it is most consistently one that is synchronic and not diachronic. Theorists such as Jacques Derrida and Paul de Man, who have most effectively described the means through which signification mediates such notions as hybridity, difference and liminality, terms now pervasive in Irish postcolonial theory, primarily employ these terms in readings of literature and philosophy that view culture in terms of a grammatology or a rhetoric of blindness and insight. The tropes of post-structuralism and deconstruction, while never ascribing wholly to such a clear dichotomy, are grounded in a textual paradigm that approaches culture by way of signification and representation. They privilege formal elements of the text and question the very possibility of our being able to represent directly an easy passage between the text and notions of cultural identity; they revise our notions of how an ontological reality can be mediated by a privileged historical paradigm. If the neologisms and tropes of these disciplines are then stitched back into readings that privilege historicism or cultural nationalism without any interrogation of the role signification plays in such master narratives, then the tropes cannot be presumed to do the same deconstructive or post-structuralist work.

Irish Studies is aware of this dilemma it confronts in trying to bring language and history together. Seamus Deane writes in 'Heroic Styles: The Tradition of an Idea' that 'both literature and history are discourses which are widely recognized to be closely related to one another because they are both subject to various linguistic protocols which, in gross or subtle ways determine the structure and meaning of what is written' (in Connolly, 2003:14). He claims that '[i]n Ireland, however, the two discourses [literature and history] have been kept apart, even though they have between them, created the interpretations of past and present by which we live'. It also must be noted that Homi Bhabha's description of the liminal, on the other hand, what he refers to as a 'borderline' or 'a contingent in-between space', a reading important to Irish postcolonial theory, does not only privilege the 'past and present' implicit in the discourses of literature and history. He writes that the 'borderline work of culture demands an encounter with "newness" that is not part of the continuum of past and present. Such art does not merely recall the past as social cause or aesthetic precedent; it renews the past, refiguring it as a contingent "in-between" space, that innovates and interrupts the performance of the present' (1994:7). He also stresses the formal work of art and culture in terms of how it 'refigur[es]' anything approaching a standard historical narrative. Deane's argument that the Irish have been unable to reconcile the two discourses may then be because there has been a lack of attention paid to how the aesthetic and the philosophy of language are always 'refiguring' how we conceive of history. Irish Studies has always regarded history as more capable of mediating the 'interpretations of past and present by which we live'. There is always the danger that if Irish Studies was to apply post-structuralism's and deconstruction's philosophies of language to its privileged historical frameworks, they would upset the narratives of redemption Irish Studies typically extracts from its handling of literature. However, it might be a risk worth taking. Paul de Man reminds us that the

'best interpretations' of great literature 'question the convergence of the meaning with the linguistic devices used to convey it' (1979a:25) and this is revealing of the textual horizons that inform the sense of liminality implicit in his
interpretations of figures such as chiasmus and metaphor. Derridean deconstruction also invents neologisms such as *différance* and hymen precisely so as
to refigure our understanding of liminality and peripherality (another popular
notion in studies of Irish identity) but only because these notions are bound up
with the articulation of meaning in general. The hymen is representative of
'non-presence'; 'there is no longer any textual difference between the image
and the thing, the empty signifier and the full signified, the imitator and the
imitated' (1983b:209–10). Irish Studies may only overcome the divergence
Deane perceives in its ranks between the discourses of literature and history if
its employment of figures such as liminality for the Irish condition is more
explicit in detailing its understanding of representation.

Border politics and transnational agreements have influenced the course of
Irish history, and it now seems that these notions must also be made to act as
figures for a pervasive sense of Irish cultural identity, a historical complicity
many of Ireland's leading writers sought to contest. Deconstruction's definition of liminality by way of a phenomenology of alterity and difference also
has very different roots to Irish Studies' definition of liminality according to a
particular national or post-national identity. This highlights important differences between the critical theory of the continent and that practised in Irish
Studies. Luke Gibbons points to one possible historical reason for this difference in referring to Edmund Husserl's Vienna lecture of 1935:

> The reason for this [the lack of theory] according to Edmund Husserl in his
> famous Vienna lecture of 1935, is that while all cultures were free to express
> themselves mythically, religiously, or creatively, only the advanced metropolitan
> countries of Europe had the capacity to produce theory, or modes of thought
> consistent with the ordinances of universal reason. (Carrol, 2003:81)

Gibbons' reading of Ireland's distance from the dialectic of enlightenment that
influenced European metropolitan culture of the twentieth century explains the
lack of 'theory' in the early part of the century, but whether Ireland as an
'advanced metropolitan' country has been able to 'produce theory, or modes of
thought consistent with the ordinances of universal reason', is unclear. Jacques
Derrida, whose grammatology and system of tropes is grounded both on a
rigorous critique of Edmund Husserl's 'theory of signs' and on an unsettling of
phallogocentrism, regards the hinge (*brisure*) – a concept important for liminality – as marking 'the impossibility that a sign, the unity of a signifier and a
signified, be produced within the plenitude of a present and an absolute presence' (1998:69). Derrida's account of the hinge is taken from Roger Laporte,
and it has, as with all Derridisms, the double meaning of 'joint' and 'break'.

It speaks of a hinged articulation, of an articulation that is both grounded (embodied) and spanning a break (disembodied). The worth of Derrida's neologisms lies in the fact that they reference ideological states and are also rigorously derived from, and implicated in, the analysis of signification. Irish Studies, however, employs post-structuralist tropes for readings that are essentially historiographic in nature, thereby reincorporating them into a logocentrism that does not explicitly question language's means for narrating or imparting a history or *une histoire*. If there is any kind of oppression that is privileged in Derrida, it is the primordial oppression writing has suffered under speech, what he describes in terms of presence and phallogocentrism. The employment of a rhetoric of deconstruction and post-structuralism in Irish criticism often buries the detail of the 'linguistic turn' beneath an elaboration of how Irishness inherently mediates history, thereby foregoing any interrogation of how to integrate a phenomenology of language into the reception of the discourse of history.

Colin Graham's work has been central to the theoretical 'turn' in Irish Studies. In his 1994 essay, 'Liminal Spaces: Post-Colonial Theory and Irish Culture', Graham introduces the notion of the liminal to the contemporary critical discourse of Irish Studies. Graham explains his understanding of the liminal in a later essay entitled '... Maybe That's Just Blarney: Irish Culture and the Persistence of Authenticity':

> Because of proximity, geography, race and religion the position of the Irish in colonial discourse was and is, as I have suggested elsewhere 'liminal'. Irish culture, at once Western and colonized, white and racially other, imperial and subjugated, became marginal in the sense of existing at the edge of two experiences, with a culture that epitomizes the hybridity, imitation and irony latent in colonial interchanges. (1999:15)

Graham appears to run two distinct problems together here. The claim that Irish Studies has only reluctantly been acknowledged as belonging to the 'canon' of postcolonial discourse and the fact that at the time of colonization (a process that may never really be complete), 'Irish culture' was both 'Western and colonized' are really two quite distinct cases of marginalization or liminality. For many years, postcolonial theory has acknowledged the duplicitous nature of the colonized. Homi Bhabha writes in 1988 that 'despite the "play" in the colonial system which is crucial to its exercise of power, colonial discourse produces the colonized as a social reality which is at once an "other" and yet entirely knowable and visible' (1988:70–1). It should be noted that Bhabha also directly relates this duplicitous colonial nature, what possibly involves some kind of liminality, to narrative: '[I]t resembles a form of narrative whereby the productivity and circulation of subjects and signs are bound in a reformed and recognizable totality' (1988:71). It is unclear, then, what Graham's understanding of the 'liminal' implies for 'Irish culture' and why it might be such a unique arrangement for understanding colonization.

'Liminal' is a rather evocative and versatile word for Graham. It refers to 'marginal in the sense of existing at the edge of two experiences', and yet, how does one exist at the edge of two experiences? The implication is that Irish culture became marginal because it represents this state of being 'at the edge of two experiences'. This representation, or this expression of Irish culture, must then evoke the experience of being Western, colonized, white, racially other, imperial and subjugated, but in this 'marginal' way, so that the representation also 'epitomizes the hybridity, imitation and irony latent in colonial interchanges' (1994:15). This smorgasbord of states that 'Irish culture' must embody resembles then, according to the logic, a 'marginal', 'liminal' hybrid or a complex configuration of a cultural identity whose conditions of manifestation or representation Graham never details. One might also suggest that the particularity of any event or any experience is surely that while being *lived through* it is impossible to perceive its 'edge[s]'. Despite the array of states and marginal identities, Graham's reading of identity would still appear to be of a kind that Thomas Docherty describes as 'criticism [that] is tied firmly to the place-logic of the nation-state' (Smyth, 1998:45). Postcolonialism, decolonialism and the rehistoricizing of Irish cultural identity are the staples of critical theory as it is practised in Irish institutions under the mantle of Irish Studies. Post-structuralism and deconstruction had rather short formal linguistic careers in these institutions; they were quickly deployed to fight the postcolonialist and decolonialist cause. However, in transplanting the remnants and revenants of this old 'place-logic' onto a supposedly more radical textual approach to identity that never offers any theory of signification, we may become blind to the more subtle, yet more exhaustive, strain of economic and consumerist colonialism that inhabits the curricula and the institutional processes that assign us such texts. Gerry Smyth informs us in *Decolonisation and Criticism* that the

> [C]riticism/decolonisation connection constitutes a fundamental aspect of the modern Irish 'cultural' imagination, and that, at least since the late eighteenth century, the debate surrounding the 'function of criticism' has always been a debate about the function of the nation and the relations between colonising and decolonising subjects. (1998:52)

If criticism is so inextricably tied to the notion of nation, no matter how deconstructed or postmodern such a nation might be, then the language of Irish criticism is always taking its cue from a spatial and historical dimension. It is, if you like, never allowed to question whether the analysis of signification and language might rather be initiated from a site, which does not presume a necessary, somewhat essentialist mediation or transfer between language analysis and national history. Jacques Derrida provides Irish Studies with many of its neologisms and tropes. These tropes are developed in his philosophy through a style of analysis that is not practised under an explicit subordination of sig-nification to the discourse of national history. Irish Studies' complicity with a historical subtext very often denies itself the opportunity to investigate the specific nature of the language that mediates such a subtext.

If being at the 'edge of two experiences' is taken to motivate the liminal state of cultural identity in Ireland, there is an implication that a subject's experiences are to be mapped directly onto the language employed to describe the experience; such liminality, then, presumes a degree of authenticity between the experience and its representation. In the essay, 'Ireland and the Persistence of Authenticity', Graham draws a parallel between such authen-ticity and nationalism: both are, he writes, 'reliant upon their antiquity *as* authenticity, yet disparaging of teleologies which destroy the mystique of authenticity' (1999:11). Graham adds that Ireland's 'liminal status', however, 'allows authenticity a less stable role' (1994:15). I wish to suggest otherwise. The unquestioning acceptance of a phrasing of cultural identity as 'colonially marginal', 'liminal' and 'hybrid'[15] may instead hide a thriving and *sub*liminal institutionally accredited authenticity that operates all the better behind this veneer of indeterminability. Derrida informs us of another problem in relation to the cultural dynamic expressed here; he suggests that 'writing can never be thought under the category of the subject' (*Of Grammatology*, 1998:68). Despite the by now jaded textual rhetoric of such comments, Derrida does question this easy complicity between representation and subjective experi-ence. He argues that 'spacing as writing is the becoming-absent and the becoming-unconscious of the subject'. Derrida relates signification to space and, therefore, language to place in a manner very different to that employed by Irish Studies for its postcolonial and decolonial discourses. He writes:

> The relationship between passivity and difference cannot be distinguished from the relationship between the fundamental *unconsciousness* of language (as root-edness within the language) and the *spacing* (pause, blank, punctuation, interval in general, etc.) which constitutes the origin of signification. It is because 'lan-guage is a form and not a substance' [Derrida here quotes from Saussure's *Course in General Linguistics*, 1931:169] that, paradoxically, the activity of speech can and must always draw from it. But if it is a form, it is because 'in language there are only differences' [Saussure once again, 1931:166]. *Spacing* (notice that this word speaks the articulation of space and time, the becoming-space of time and the becoming-time of space) is always the unperceived, the nonpresent, and the nonconscious. (1998:68)

If language is to have any relation with space or place, then this occurs, for Derrida, at the formal and psychological levels. It is the formal markers of the text, namely, pause, blank and punctuation, that grant the *unconsciousness* of language a connection with spacing. For Derrida, the most evocative word for describing the liminal or the merging of separate 'edges' of experience would be the 'trace'. For him, the trace is 'the opening of the first exteriority in general, the enigmatic relationship of the living to its other and of an inside to an outside: [or] spacing' (1998:70). It seems, therefore, that the trace is assigned to a similar kind of moment to the liminal moment Graham seeks to express in relation to Irish Studies, namely, the enigmatic moment between two distinct *spacings* of experience. The fundamental difference, however, is that for Derrida, the trace is associated with language and with ethical encounter and with all that can be derived from the interrogation of the philosophy of language in this regard; language invokes ethical enquiry, but where is the ethical enquiry in Irish Studies? Even though Derrida's grammatology also speaks for the deconstruction of such dichotomies, he grants the representation of such experiences greater potential by interrogating how language itself can embody subjugation (when speech is privileged) and open us up to the genesis of ethical enquiry. Graham's liminality may also only be a revitalized form of the 'peripherality' that J. J. Lee argues became something of a mid-century excuse for Ireland's weak economic performance. Ultimately, the inner conflicts Graham highlights in describing liminality may be as old as Achilles's balancing of immortality and mortality or Jesus's balancing of his identity as God and man despite the deconstructive neologisms. It would all seem to support Gerry Smyth's argument that the function of criticism in Irish Studies 'has always been a debate about the function of the nation and the relations between colonising and decolonising subjects' (Smyth, 1998:52). The reason deconstruction has been so successful in other critical discourses is that it aimed its analysis at the deep structures of language and at ethical encounter, what, once again, recalls civic morality.

Derrida also regards the relationship between language and place as one 'between the fundamental *unconsciousness* of language (as rootedness within the language) and the *spacing* (pause, blank, punctuation, interval in general, etc.) which constitutes the origin of signification'. It is the *unconsciousness* of language that bears a relation with *spacing*. Does Irish Studies neglect the *sub*liminality of language in favour of its liminality? Is there a tendency in Irish Studies to reduce the libidinal to the liminal? Richard Kearney is one of the few Irish critics, along with Joyce, who has reminded us that the 'Irish mind' possesses a 'logic' of its own, most likely due to its overactive libidinal and subliminal economy:

> Could it be that the Irish mind, in its various expressions, often flew in the face of such logocentrism by showing that meaning is not only determined by a logic that centralises and censors but also by a logic which disseminates: a structured dispersal exploring what is *other*, what is irreducibly diverse [...]? (1985:9)

Lacan also informs us that the 'signifying structure interposes itself between perception and consciousness' and it is here that 'the unconscious' or the *sub*liminal 'intervenes' (2006:51). In transplanting the tropes of deconstruction and post-structuralism onto the field of Irish cultural discourse with its hegemonic historical voice, Irish Studies is slow to recognize that cultural memory draws from a conglomeration of recollected experiences that are open to the vicissitudes of a collective *sub*limation. The acceptance of a postmodern rhetoric of a divided or schizophrenic subject, one that is marginalized and liminal, may only work to dress old themes in new clothes.

Another possible oversight in Irish Studies' privileging of postcolonial discourse may be found in its understanding of sovereignty. As I have noted earlier, postcolonial critics such as David Lloyd have highlighted the risks for interpretations that privilege historicism and its 'myth of a finally triumphant progress' (Carrol, 2003:46). This 'triumphant progress' is most often regarded as part of some account of sovereignty. Giorgio Agamben examines something akin to liminality through his interrogation of sovereignty as a 'state of emergency' or a 'state of exception' in *Homo Sacer*. He interrogates sovereignty to a degree that is rarely evident in the political language of the postcolonial and decolonial discourses of Irish criticism. His thesis in *Homo Sacer* is that when sovereignty is the issue, 'the state of exception comes more and more to the foreground as the fundamental political structure and ultimately becomes the rule' (1998:20), an experience Irish society may know only too well. Agamben builds a series of richly rhetorical essays around the paradox of sovereignty whereby the 'sovereign is, at the same time, outside and inside the juridical order' (1998:15). For Agamben, language may also be viewed as the sovereign, 'who in a permanent state of exception, declares that there is nothing outside language and that language is always beyond itself' (1998:21). Language and law are inextricably linked for Agamben; language 'expresses the bond of inclusive exclusion to which a thing is subject because of the fact of being in language, of being named' (1998:21). Agamben then asks whether communities that place their ideals of sovereignty beyond the reach of their political realities, as one might suggest of Irish Studies if it retains the authenticity described above, live within a state of '*being in force without significance*'. For Agamben, this phrase applies to any sovereign force that invests in the 'maintenance of the pure form of the law beyond its own content' (1998:53). The point appears to be that once a culture puts a name to its democratic ideal, once it puts a name to the state it is striving for, it has then consigned 'the pure form of the law' to language. Thus, its identity, its idealizing and its politics are inextricably tied to the workings of language.

Such a link between identity and language is relevant to contemporary historical discourses, such as Irish Studies, which seek to incorporate the postmodern notion of the 'end of history'. The politics of Irish postcolonial discourse necessitates the examination of what remains when a state *survives history*, when 'a State sovereignty [...] maintains itself beyond the accomplishment of its *telos*'; does it become 'a law that is in force without signifying?' In other words, if the sense of belief in an authentic understanding of sovereignty has disappeared, and we are left merely with the tired discourses that replay *sub*liminally the call for such sovereignty, are we writing without significance? In a postmodern age that discredits all metanarratives and 'myth[s] of a finally triumphant progress', where sovereignty is submerged under the economics of globalization, how durable will the postcolonial discourse be for mediating the transformations within language? Agamben tells us that to persevere in the language of such a sovereignty while recognizing that it is without content and significance is akin to believing in a 'transcendental object' which is not a real object but is 'merely the idea of relation' (1998:52), or the liminal, as understood by Graham and other critics of Irish authenticity. In perpetuating a postcolonial language in contemporary critical discourse, does Irish Studies beg the question of what sense of sovereignty its historical narratives engender? Does the borrowing of a post-structuralist surface text voiced through such tropes as liminality, hybridity and marginality still allow the old authenticity of an outmoded sovereignty to pass underneath, in what deconstruction perceives as the fundamentally important *unconsciousness* of language or language's *sub*liminality? One might suggest that in the *realpolitik* of contemporary European political dialogue, sovereignty is no sooner granted than it is willingly imparted to a federalist council of Europe that has yet to finalize its constitution.

And perhaps one must turn, once again, to our writers for assistance when our use of metaphors and tropes is proving limiting. Many European critics[16] return to Kafka's story 'Before the Law' in seeking to elaborate a metaphor for the state of 'liminality' or the 'threshold experience' that literary analysis affords the reader. Samuel Beckett also describes a similar experience:

> my way is in the sand flowing
> between the shingle and the dune
> the summer rain rains on my life
> on me my life harrying fleeing
> to its beginning to its end
>
> my peace is there in the receding mist
> when I may cease from treading these long shifting thresholds
>
> and live the space of a door
> that opens and shuts (1999:59)

The voice in this poem is rather like that of the man from the country in Kafka's parable 'Before the Law'.[17] Kafka's man is not prevented from passing the threshold or entering the Law; the door lies open, but yet he continues to sit outside; his unwillingness to perceive the Law as similar to life is all that provides him with reasons for persisting in seeing them as different: the 'law is all the more pervasive for its total lack of content', writes Agamben in his discussion of this parable (1998:52). Beckett's speaker also desires to 'live the space of a door/that opens and shuts,' or to wait at the threshold, unwilling to disentangle consciousness from its linguistic manifestation, what the shingle and the dune of the space removed from the liminality of the threshold appear to offer. The first verse describes the terror of a stretched consciousness, of the self-awareness that coexists in the 'me' and in the 'my life'. Peace will only reign at the threshold, in the comfortable realization that one is securely liminal. And yet the final word of the poem, 'shuts', suggests how difficult it is to live eternally in liminality. How does one remain at the threshold of a door that persistently opens and shuts? Irish Studies must then continue to tread the 'long shifting thresholds' of ethical, linguistic and psychoanalytic discourses, so as to explore the lessons of linguistic sensitivity that an embrace of our schizophrenic existence reveals.

Richard Kearney and post-nationalist Ireland

If there is any Irish academic who has consistently championed a Francophone philosophy of identity and who is most at home with the French academic tradition of the last fifty years, it is Richard Kearney. Kearney spent the majority of his university education on French-speaking campuses (his BA was at UCD but his MA was at McGill under Charles Taylor and his PhD was at *Université Paris X (Nanterre)* under Paul Ricoeur), and he writes in French and English. His work has consistently promoted what he describes as a 'post-national' Ireland, where, as he wrote as a young academic in a series of articles for the *Irish Times* in 1987, Ireland amidst its recurring crises of identity must move to throw off the 'twin modern ideologies of the centralized nation-state and the autonomous consumer individual' (*Irish Times*, Dec. 31, 1987d:14). In the late 1980s, Kearney argued that Irish society was 'devoid of a guiding ideology' (*Irish Times*, Dec. 25, 1987:8), and he employs the then popular jargon of postmodernity to astutely argue that Ireland can make a virtue of this necessity; Ireland can use its unique ability in being consistently in crisis, unlike 'France, Britain, America', who are able to 'assume a stable and unquestioned identity' (*ibid.*, 1987a:8), to seize hold of the 'collage' effect, the 'regional pluralism' (*ibid.*, 1987a:14) and the 'communitarian' public sphere that the postmodern condition affords. Since the postmodern is concerned with the breaking up of all master narratives and with the dissolution of consoling epistemes and myths of identity, it can channel the Irish unease with any stable qualifiers of identity or nation. Kearney argues that the EU's promise of 'regional pluralism' (1987a:14) and of 'decentralization without provincialism', at a time when 30,000 Irish people were emigrating each year, should not be regarded as coming from a 'geo-political empire made up of servilely dependent provinces but as a multiform community of communities' (1987a:14). It is somewhat ironic that in today's political reality with similar emigration and unemployment figures in Ireland, EU membership should be seen to have produced servile states for reasons Kearney could not have imagined. However, what is perhaps noteworthy from an Irish university perspective is that in early works such as *Transitions* and in this series of articles in the *Irish Times*, Kearney rarely looks to the university to explain this lack of a 'guiding ideology' in Irish society. Ironically, his longest study on education, *The Black Book: An Analysis of Third-Level Education*, was published when he had just begun his BA course at UCD. It perhaps says something about the Irish experience of education that a leading European philosopher of the last fifty years would never return to the subject at such length having completed his studies at the Irish university. When Kearney searches for alternatives to Ireland's 'rhetorical nationalism' and to what he still describes, even in 1987, as the 'Catholic Church's' leading role in 'community, particularly in the areas of education, social welfare, parish activities and public morality', the university and its humanities agenda, the institution whose unique privilege his works embody, is barely mentioned.

Kearney's recent work returns to religious questions and yet he does not examine the cultural and academic impact of the NUI's lack of comparative religion or theology departments. In *Anatheism*, he puts much of his religious reawakening down to his years spent as a secondary school student with the 'Benedictine monks of Glenstal' (2009:xii). He relates how the 'monks had us read cogent arguments against the existence of God – by Feuerbach, Nietzsche, Sartre, and Russell' (2009:xii). Kearney's late return to religion and to his 'philosophical' examination of faith is therefore all the richer and is tied to a personal religious trajectory because of this secondary school education that allowed for a careful interrogation of how philosophy and spiritual enquiry are related. The vast majority of Irish university students, not to mention secondary students, did not have the opportunity to receive such an education where philosophical and religious enquiry are combined at such a young age. When Kearney also comes to describe his general method and style of philosophy, his language is replete with religious terminology. He writes that it is a 'grace of philosophy' that it 'opens a space for the questioning of God where theists and atheists may converse' (2009:xvii). This happens, for Kearney, through his notion of anatheism, what he describes as the experience of 'coming back' or 'returning' to God after a long absence. He also describes his own understanding of philosophy in terms of a vocabulary of faith and belief; he writes that 'the kind of philosophy I speak from' is 'one nourished by the modern theories of phenomenology and existentialism, on the one hand, and by postmodern ideas of poststructuralism and deconstruction on the other'. He has 'learned from the former' a 'belief in the possibility of thinking from concrete embodied experience' (2009:xv) and a 'faith in the power of human imagination and action to transform our world' (2009:xvi). These admissions recall the descriptions of the Catholic philosophical tradition that MacIntyre and Newman have described. However, what Kearney's late turn reveals for the Irish university context is how the most influential Irish philosopher of the last fifty years traces his philosophical perspective back to a grounding in a style of education that merges religious enquiry and philosophy, a kind of education that was not an option for the majority of Irish humanities students in the twentieth century.

It is also worth noting that in the US campuses at which Kearney has taught for the last number of decades, the teaching of religion is most often discussed in terms of its conflict with science education. Despite the fact that it is the humanities that are often regarded as suffering most profoundly when religious study is removed from the curriculum, Kearney has argued for a closer relationship between science and religion in the university. Kearney has claimed that Irish academia has 'often failed us' in not marrying science and religion successfully in the curriculum (1997:170) and that this failure led to an enforced 'dissociation of inquiry' that 'has taken its toll on the Irish intellectual scene' (1997:169). This 'dissociation of inquiry' becomes more noteworthy in the Irish university as humanities divisions internationally move ever closer to a scientific model of enquiry and practice.

As a BA student in 1975, Kearney questions, in a manner somewhat reminiscent of Newman, whether the university should be a 'training centre for the acquisition of skills and specified quantities of knowledge' or an institution that is 'critical of the utilitarian nature' of society. This would be a question of fundamental importance for the Irish university over the next decades. Given that the Irish government would promote education in the 1990s and early noughties in terms of enhancing a 'knowledge industry', it would seem that it was less critical than Kearney of a reductive approach to learning. Kearney argues that the original idea of the university was concerned with exposing the 'state's blind belief in the inevitability of progress' so that it could allow people to 'reassert their humanity in a radically dehumanized world', a point taken up by Kearney's department lecturer at the time at UCD, Seamus Deane. Deane has an essay in Kearney's collection that perhaps says more about literature and the humanities in the Irish context than any other essay written at the time. Deane admits that the 'Humanities' is typically associated with the 'Greek and Roman classics', with 'a certain basic philosophical training' and with the defence of those 'disciplines which we still refer to as the Humanities'. He notes, however, that the 'variations upon this model' are so great that it is difficult to discern 'its presence' in many of the different shapes the university has taken throughout Europe. Deane's argument claims that the heyday of the Humanities, where they played the 'dominant and liberalising role' assigned to them in the universities of classical Germany, did not come to an

end because of the 'growth of the technological sciences' but because the
Greek and Roman classics were replaced by the 'national, vernacular literatures of the great nation states'. These nation-states then did not renew classical learning but instead subjected it to a 'process of *embourgeoisement*'. This
resulted in the situation where in Victorian Britain, the 'body of English literature' was transformed into 'a value system which had more to do with a particular form of class consciousness than it had to do with the literature itself'
or with culture. Pierrre Bourdieu makes a similar argument in relation to the
French university, and I examine this in the next chapter. However, Deane then
admits that even though literature ultimately reveals how the different critical
approaches such as formalism and structuralism are inadequate when it comes
to defining the 'transcendent quality' of literature, we should not get carried
away in assigning this ineffable quality of literature to the 'freedom' that the
humanities is often credited with nurturing. He advises against this because of
the nature of the 'educational framework' in Ireland which, he argues, writing
in 1975, 'has not notably altered in its class stratification and exclusions in fifty
years', and Kathleen Lynch's more recent work has documented how inequality in education is still very much part of the education system.[18] Deane argues
that the 'freedom' the humanities are often seen to nurture is bound up with the
notion that a 'high degree of individuation' is precious for the student. However, Deane advises that because our 'educational systems are not really
humanistic in any serious sense any longer', they are more likely to produce
'uniformity rather than individuation'. For Deane, then, the 'role of the
Humanities' can only be preserved and enhanced by attending to the teacher–
pupil relationship, or to what he describes as the 'teaching-and-taught relationship'. It is an argument that is more urgent than ever today, and it is an approach
to the university, the humanities and professionalism in terms of exclusion and
class consciousness that needs further examination in the Irish context.

Kearney, who has worked with the leading philosophers of his day in leading philosophy departments in Paris and French-speaking Montreal, makes
rather little of the 'ideological crisis' in the humanities and the university system in Ireland in his later work. Once again, there is a rather familiar silence
regarding the state of the humanities in Irish university departments at a time
when Kearney's colleagues in France, professional philosophers such as
Derrida and Ricoeur, were describing a 'theological turn' in philosophy and
creating institutions of philosophy to deal with the institutional crisis in the
humanities. There is often the sense that the Irish philosopher will look to the
national literature in making a claim against the contemporary 'ideological'
state of the nation and its institutions instead of looking at the reality of those
institutions themselves even if these are the institutions that have granted
these philosophers the 'cultural capital' that justifies their claims to be heard
when they speak about events outside the university.

However, Kearney makes some other optimistic claims in relation to Irish society in general. He argues, writing in 1987, that 'Ireland's post-modern project might well serve as a vanguard movement for the wider world' and as a 'pilot-model for its European neighbours' (1987a:8) in balancing the official nation-state discourse and the 'radical pluralism' that the European community fostered. Ireland, mid-austerity, would once again be lauded as the model for another European balancing act for reasons Kearney could never have imagined and this was despite the fact that Irish public opinion was split on the means for moving from a Tiger economy to a Troika economy. Katy Hayward's recent study *Irish nationalism and European integration* also echoes Kearney's claims over twenty years later by arguing that 'Irish official discourse has been able to pose European integration and nation-statehood as mutually complementary' (2009:13) and that 'Ireland is a valuable case study for examining the relationship between European integration and nation-statehood in official nationalist discourse' (2009:6). However, Hayward's study recognizes how Irish 'government elites' have sanctioned an 'official national discourse' that promotes greater European integration while at the same time appealing to 'national interest' by way of a discourse of collective and cultural memory. Hayward argues that the 'premise' on which her 'research relies' is 'that the official discourse of the government elite' is an integral element of political relations, facilitating the 'constant renewal of hegemonic domination' that also takes into account Habermas's definition of the state as the 'representation of the monopolistic discourse' (Hayward, 2009:47). Therefore, whereas Kearney was advocating the 'radical pluralism' of Europe as an alternative to the old order where 'European nation-states have generally camouflaged their inner fragmentation and diversification by opting for strong national leaders (e.g. Thatcher, Mitterrand)', it would appear that any political promotion of such 'radical pluralism' was simply the 'old order' in new clothes. As the EU expanded, the 'government elites' of these nation-states recognized the value of official discourse on Europe for similar acts of political camouflage, and the universities cannot be regarded as other than complicit in this process. Kearney recognizes that even if the 'nationalist ideology' is superseded in his 'postmodern' world, it would still need to play a 'valid role in our cultural and historical memory' (1987:8), and we have seen how Luke Gibbons and others appealed to such cultural memory for an 'ethics of analogy' when Ireland was something of an economic powerhouse. In recognition of this fact, it is important to note that the 1992 Maastricht Treaty (Treaty on European Union, or TEU) uses similar language in transferring the discourse of 'cultural memory' to the European context. The EU must work to:

> contribute to the flowering of the cultures of the member states, while respecting their national and regional diversity and at the same time bringing the common cultural heritage to the fore.

However, Kearney and other academics had little to say on the somewhat anomalous state of the Irish humanities in relation to the humanities programmes of many of the leading European universities at the time. He does argue that as many 'young people as possible' should be provided with 'an advanced education', but he does not go into any detail on what this should consist of in the humanities.

Kearney also begins his 1985 introduction to the edited collection *The Irish Mind* by arguing that 'there has never been a study specifically devoted to Ireland's contribution to the world of thought' because '[t]he existence of an Irish mind has frequently been contested' (1985:7). In recognizing the central place this collection occupies in recent works in Irish Studies, one might respond today by saying that there has never been a study specifically devoted to how those subjects championed in his collection through the writers discussed are taught in Irish universities. The 'Irish mind' exhibited collectively by the writers, philosophers and politicians – all of them men – that Kearney and his fellow contributors privilege, men such as Joyce, Synge, Shaw, Yeats, Berkeley, Swift, Eriugena, Burke and Connolly, is a 'mind' that, if it was educated at university, was either educated at Trinity College Dublin (Synge, Berkeley, Burke and Swift) or at the University College (Joyce). We cannot forget too that Yeats, Shaw and Connolly did not attend university. Is it not important therefore, in light of this celebration of the notion of an 'Irish mind' and over a century after the Irish Universities Act, that we examine how 'Irish mind[s]' have been informed and enlightened in our institutions of learning in relation to those subjects and ideas which these writers and philosophers championed? Kearney cites Matthew Arnold in peddling the familiar claim that the Irish were often portrayed in the nineteenth century as 'incompetent when it came to translating dream into decision, when it came to responsibly ordering and organizing their boundless fancies' (1985:8). However, the irony is that if we posit some detached notion of the 'Irish mind' or of Irishness largely formed before the founding of the State that somehow manifests itself apart from institution and organization, then we may very well be perpetuating another 'boundless' fancy. To posit an identity that even in 'not reveal[ing] itself as a single, fixed, homogenous identity' (1985:9) somehow spans the millennia from Newgrange to News Corp and that is radical because it embodies 'a more dialectical logic of *both/and*' instead of 'a dualist logic of *either/or*' (1985:9) is surely to draw as close as one can to an academic version of this 'boundless fanc[y]'. J. J. Lee has also posited a far more useful definition of an Irish mind that dominated Irish society, what he calls an 'official mind'. Lee argues that Irish society throughout the twentieth century was dominated by an 'official mind' that promoted what he calls a 'possessor ethos' instead of a 'performance ethos'. He argues that in Ireland, 'possession was a pre-requisite for performance' and that 'the primacy of the possessor principle' would survive at least until the second half of the twentieth century; 'The prestige and social rank of the family as a whole depends on the ownership and *not* on the use of the property. Size of farm, not productivity, determines one's place on the class ladder' (1989:392). Lee argues that the same philosophy dominated all areas of Irish society to the extent that it held back the modernization of society.

Kearney notes in his introduction to *The Irish Mind* that the 'cultural myths of the Irish Revival' (1985:31) have long been questioned by critics and historians such as Seamus Deane, Declan Kiberd and others. Deane reminds us that Yeats's 'mythologizing' borne out of his 'intellectual and aesthetic need for coherent "arrangements of history"' was responsible for what Deane identifies as an 'Hegelian rage for retrospective order' (in Kearney, 1985:32). However, is the Yeatsian rage for order only a respectable straw man that we drag on stage when we want to justify our own version of 'retrospective order' that is buoyed up by more sophisticated, psychological notions of 'cultural memory'? The stereotypical Irish disdain for order and for institution should not lead us to imagine that today's 'Irish mind' will be fashioned by a national psyche that is free of the traces of its institutionalized schooling as so much of our heritage appears to be. The 'Irish mind' that rose to the institutional challenges of EU membership, that weathered the judicial introspection of post-Tiger tribunals and that signed up to the organizational commitments of the Troika economy and Bologna with its description of education as a 'knowledge industry' can no longer shirk the institutional responsibilities of this new age. If we want to function successfully in an education environment that has signed up for the reductive self-regulating criteria of middle management while preserving what so many commentators have described as our 'cultural memory', then we will have to momentarily put off the romantic notion of soul-searching that very often accompanies the 'cultural memory' cue so that we can engage in such projects as educational self-assessment. If we do not do so, there will most likely be far fewer Irish professors around to evoke such constructs as cultural memory.

Kearney is perhaps right to suggest that some notion of the 'Irish mind' must be asserted, if only to begin the discussion. He is also right to argue that we have a 'critical duty to demythologize cultural myths and metaphors whenever they assume a reactionary or perverse guise' (1985:33). However, in an era when the 'national' has been liquidated of all authenticity by those servants of the State who invoked the 'national interest' while bleeding it dry, any investigation of Irishness must begin by examining how such an exploitable notion of nation-state identity evolved in, and was mediated by, those institutions of learning that the majority of these government ministers and former *Taoisigh* attended. This book argues that this process should begin by examining the humanities in the Irish context.

Notes

1 Thomas Kinsella also writes as late as 1973 that the Irish writer could not feel 'at home' in 'his use of the English language' (in Lucy, 1973:209). This may also have resulted in an academic reluctance to embrace philosophical dilemmas and enquiries derived from an intertextual and structuralist reading of the text that worked through English. The 'language question' together with a residual reverence for Irish may have created a critical resistance in Irish universities to language-based philosophical and hermeneutic investigations working through English (even if translated from French and German) that were central to the practice of the humanities subjects in Europe and the United States.

2 Claude Lévi-Strauss reminds us that '[a]ll the traits successively cited to define racial differences have turned out to be linked to adaptation phenomena, even if the reasons for their selective value occasionally elude us' (1992:5).

3 Donoghue admits in *Irish Essays* that even though his style of humanities teaching never intentionally had 'any ideological emphasis' (2) except for a 'vague but persistent nationalism', this in itself can be regarded as an 'ideological emphasis' (2).

4 However, as we have seen, Kathleen Lynch, writing in 2005, questions whether the Irish universities are tackling inequality in education today.

5 In Flannery, pp. 116–17.

6 Irigaray believes sexuality has always been examined in relation to a privileging of procreation, with fatherhood being regarded as a 'proof of his potency' (1985:54). However, she argues that any realization of a general impotence has not led men to be more accepting of 'feminine pleasure': 'The problem is that they [men, epitomized in this instance as psychoanalysts] claim to make a law of this impotence itself, and continue to subject women to it' (1985:105).

7 Seamus Deane also argues in relation to such cultural nationalism that '[i]n a country like Ireland, where nationalism had to be politically opposed to the prevailing power-systems, [that] there was a serious attempt to create a counter-culture and to define it as authentic to the nation. In doing so, it used historical and archaeological scholarship in a tendentious and polemical fashion' (Introduction to *Field Day Anthology of Irish* Writing, 1991:xxii).

8 These comments were made as part of a plenary presentation entitled 'From Celtic Twilight to Celtic Tiger' at the annual JASIL conference at Shinwa Women's University, Kobe, Japan, on 26 October 2007.

9 *Ibid.*

10 See the full text of Mary Robinson's speech at Grosse Ile at www.ballinagree. freeservers.com/grosse.html.

11 Many of the core humanities departments in the National University have very few, if any, full-time academic staff among their faculty who have done their doctoral work in the National University. At the time of writing, of the ten full-time academic staff in the Philosophy department of UCC, none did their doctoral work in the National University, and of the fifteen full-time staff in the Philosophy department of UCD, Ireland's largest university, only one did doctoral work in the National University (7%). The situation is reversed for leading humanities departments abroad such as the Yale English department where out of the current

academic staff list of forty-four full-time professors, only one has done doctoral work outside America, this being at Oxford. This situation surely has to change if Ireland's humanities graduate students are to have any belief in the value of a National University of Ireland research degree in these subjects and if Irish graduate programmes in the humanities are to attract the best Irish humanities students. This seems all the more urgent when we consider the numbers enrolled full-time for PhD and MA degrees in Irish universities. There were 1,293 students enrolled full-time for PhD degrees in Arts and Humanities for 2011/12 (an increase of 78% from 2005) and 1,677 students enrolled full-time for taught Master's degrees. The PhD enrolments include 69 in Philosophy and Ethics across the Higher Education Authority (HEA) university sector, 137 for 'Combined Arts and Humanities', 165 for 'Mother Tongue' and 94 for 'Combined Humanities' (www.hea.ie/en/statistics). A large proportion of these would be in English. The annual fee for a graduate research degree in an Arts subject at UCD is €5300.

12 However, we should note that Seamus Deane's introduction to the *Field Day* anthology does not make any such claims for the collection. He is more concerned with cultural authority than with canons. He admits that 'in its necessarily unsuccessful, but nevertheless strenuous, attempt to be comprehensive, this anthology includes a great deal of material that has for long been unknown or unacknowledged' (1991:xxvi). He also writes that there 'is no attempt here to establish a canon. Instead, what we show is an example of the way in which canons are established and the degree to which they operate as systems of ratification and authority' (1991:xix).

13 Introduction to *Theorizing Ireland*, 2.

14 In recent years, conference titles on Irish Studies include 'Liminal Borderlands' (the title of the Nordic Institute of Irish Studies' Biannual Conference held at Dalarna University, June 2004) and 'Double Vision: Liminal Irish Identities', UCD, 18–20 March 2005.

15 In 'Questioning the Frame: Hybridity, Ireland and the Institution', Richard Kirkland regards 'hybridity' as a style of interpretation: 'The relative absence (until recently) of hybridity as a means of analysing Irish identity indicated a wariness about the dangers of a possible cultural relativism unable to do anything more than compare and contrast' (*Ireland and Cultural Theory*, 1998:212). However, how can culture, and whatever identities it may produce, be anything other than hybrid? To transform 'hybridity' into a 'means of analysing' something, even if it is 'Irish identity', also raises the questions of how a cultural characteristic can become a method of analysis. It also appears to presume some steady-state, a priori 'Irish identity' that is to be analysed with the fruits of post-structuralism's own interrogation of language and signification. Once again, it is worthwhile recalling Derrida here. He informs us that the trace (what, for him, institutes difference and dissimulation) 'must be thought before the entity' (*Of Grammatology* 1998:47). Irish Studies appears more inclined to reverse this strategy; it strives to safeguard the entity, which is often Irish identity, against the risks that a prioritization of signification and language might reveal.

16 Jacques Derrida gives a lengthy reading of this parable in 'Before the Law', an essay collected in *Acts of Literature*, ed. Derek Attridge (New York: Routledge, 1992). Giorgio Agamben also discusses the parable in *Homo Sacer* in order to

    elaborate his understanding of the 'state of emergency', what I have compared to the notion of 'liminality' in Irish Studies.

17 The parable of the old man and the doorkeeper, a parable that is named 'Before the Law' by Derrida, runs to just over a page of Kafka's novel *The Trial*. The parable is related to K by a priest and is followed by a few pages of analysis by both the priest and K (Franz Kafka, 1988:120–1).

18 The Clancy Report of 2001 finds that 'nearly 100% of the children of higher professionals and over 80% of the children of employers and managers enter higher education as compared with only around 20% of the children of unskilled and semi-skilled manual workers' (in OECD, 2007:52).

5

International comparisons

Jacques Derrida, Pierre Bourdieu and the French University

The work of leading French academics such as Pierre Bourdieu and Jacques Derrida on education points to key differences in emphasis in the Irish and French university systems. However, the French university system did share, only much earlier, many of the key changes that have come to Irish universities since the 1980s. It experienced a surge in university numbers slightly earlier than its Irish counterpart. Alain Bienayme notes that the French experienced its 'unprecedented growth in its student population' (1984:152) in the 1960s. In 1963, 5% of the French eighteen- to twenty-six-year-old age group was in university. This had risen to 15% by 1988. The numbers taking humanities[1] subjects increased fourfold between the 1960s and the 1980s. In one generation, the number of students in France rose from 50,000 to 600,000 (McCartney, 1999:345). Student numbers in Arts and Social sciences in France also increased by 18.3% between 1981 and 1987 (Lamoure Rontopoulou and Lamoure, 1988:37). The numbers for Irish university graduates, on the other hand, rose most dramatically after the 1980s. Whereas Ireland experienced a 47% increase in the numbers of university graduates between 1998 and 2009, the figure for France was only 13%.[2] However, the French university system, rather like its Irish counterpart, was, for Bienayme, a 'fossilized system' that remained 'fundamentally binary and monolithic' at least up until the 1968 Faure education law that split the old 230,000 student, University of Paris into thirteen 'more manageable autonomous universities' (Bienayme, 1984:154). However, there was one important difference between these national monoliths. The French university had maintained a 'Napoleonic conception' of education that kept the elite *grandes écoles* separate from the universities. The university in the French system was often a 'second choice after failure to enter the selective streams of education' which included 'preparations for entrance examinations for the *grandes écoles*' (Lamoure Rontopoulou, Jeanne and Jean Lamoure). Mary Gallagher argues that the French republican model of education with the *grandes écoles* as 'famous republican incubators of the French elites' is also 'now wobbling under the combined pressure of a growing corporate orientation' in education (2012:74). There is no comparable post-secondary elite body of institutions separate from the universities in Ireland. However, both university systems have experienced more recently the effects of Europeanization in education that has brought greater 'heterogeneity' across universities, more egalitarian academic structures and a 'massive recruitment of teaching staff' (Bienayme, 1984:158).

Pierre Bourdieu's sociological account of the university and of the humanities has been influential in education studies internationally. In *Reproduction: In Education, Society and Culture*, he casts his critical gaze back to Emile Durkheim's *L'évolution pédagogique en France* and to Maurice Halbwachs's preface to this work. The work was published in 1938 (it was taken from a lecture series Durkheim gave between 1904 and 1905 entitled 'The history of education in France'), the year after the Irish Constitution came into force and the issues Halbwachs's preface raises, even though they have not been closely examined in the context of the Irish humanities, could also describe the somewhat conservative university tradition in Ireland for much of the century:

> The organs of education are, in every age, connected with the other institutions of the social body, with customs and beliefs, with the great currents of thoughts. But they also have a life of their own, an evolution which is relatively autonomous in the course of which they conserve many features of their former structure. Sometimes they defend themselves against the past for support. It is impossible to understand, for example, the division of the universities into faculties, the systems of examinations and degrees, boarding-school life, school discipline, without going back a long way into the past, to the period of the construction of the institution whose forms, once created, tend to persist through time, either by a sort of inertia or because they manage to adapt to new conditions. Considered from this standpoint, the pedagogical organization appears to us as more hostile to change, more conservative and traditional perhaps than the Church itself, because it has the function of transmitting to new generations a culture whose roots lie in a remote past. (in Bourdieu, 1977:196)

Whereas the foundations of the Irish university might not lie in such 'a remote past', it has long been acknowledged that the Church has also been a conservative and traditional force in Irish society. However, because it was so influential and because its role in society as a support and as a resource for moral and civic guidance was institutionally at a remove from the role of the university as dictated by the 1908 University Act, it always bore the full force of public criticism when it came to civic matters. Now that the Church has lost its influence in Irish society, it is timely that the universities be assessed in terms of whether they are 'hostile to change' in supporting a 'pedagogical organization'

that is conservative and traditional. Since it is historically the humanities disciplines that serve to articulate a university's mission and purpose, it is to these
disciplines that we must turn in assessing whether a university is unwilling to
change with the times. Bourdieu's argument might be regarded as overly
mechanistic in today's university that is evermore regarded as a consumer's
university where the professors are rated online, evaluated in the classroom
and paid by course. However, despite the shifting nature of today's academic
habitus, Bourdieu's model of assessment still offers much for a national university tradition that lags behind the French, UK and US traditions in terms of
philosophical and institutional self-assessment. Bourdieu's cultural materialist
perspective argues that education considered as 'the process through which a
cultural arbitrary is historically reproduced through the medium of the production of the habitus[3] productive of practices conforming with that cultural arbitrary [...], is the equivalent, in the cultural order, of the transmission of genetic
capital in the biological order' (1977:32). He claims that pedagogic work (PW)
is capable of 'perpetuating the arbitrary it inculcates more lastingly than political coercion', and he also argues that in a Christian society '[r]eligious power'
also 'lastingly informs practices' related to the PW of education (1977:33).
This is a less than flattering description of institutionalized education, and
Bourdieu claims that it is the humanities that are frequently most culpable
when it comes to manufacturing consent for this cultural arbitrary. He speaks
of practices that persist in 'fossilizing' or 'embalming' 'the classics' (1977:58).
Bourdieu takes aim at academic jargon and at the 'allusive, elliptical discourse'
of the academic dissertation that signifies the student's 'complicity' in the
'pedagogic relationship in its traditional form' (1977:111). Of course, if any
discipline is most responsible for the academic jargon and for the allegiance to
'theory' that infiltrated even Irish humanities departments in the 1990s, it is
most likely what has come to be known today as 'French theory', a subgenre
Bourdieu is often, perhaps wrongly, associated with. It might be argued that
the traditionalism of the Irish humanities departments made them react strongly
against such theory; it did not fit with the consolatory historicist readings that
were most prevalent in history and literature departments during the theoretical 'turn'. However, this reluctance to investigate what the theorists were pro-
posing does not imply that these institutions were then less guilty of Bourdieu's
pedagogic reproduction.

Despite the cultural materialist leaning of Bourdieu's argument, it is echoed
by recent commentators on the university; Rolf van der Velden and Emer Smyth
note in regard to the Europeanization of Irish universities in a 'knowledge society' that 'there are strong indications that various "elites" continue to play an
important role *within* mass higher education in many countries, based on strati-
fied higher education, protected labour market positions, or both' (2011:135).

They suggest that Bourdieu's reading of the university in terms of the perpetuation of a cultural arbitrary that acts as a safeguard for forms of hierarchization may have a new element to contend with in today's university where 'tertiary education is increasingly becoming a necessary, but no longer sufficient, condition' (der Velden, 2011:136). In other words, in an age of mass education, there must be new criteria for evaluation; whether this is 'because of the need to guarantee excellence or of the need to protect privileges of the in-group against outsiders, or a combination of both, entry to many professions is subject to an increasingly complex and demanding set of criteria' (der Velden, 2011:136).

Bourdieu's reading of the teaching event questions old-style humanities teaching. He refers to the work of Max Weber who compares the mystified and mystifying lecturer to the priest whose 'status legitimacy' means that the 'responsibility for failure' falls 'neither on the god nor on the priest but solely on the conduct of the faithful' (1977:111). The teacher or lecturer with such 'status legitimacy' who 'suspects he is less than perfectly understood' by his students can simply, 'so long as his status authority is not contested, blame his students when he does not understand their utterances' (1977:111). However, the notion of 'status legitimacy' may point to an important contrast between the French and Irish academic traditions in the humanities. Since, as Durkheim has already outlined in his lectures of 1904–1905, the roots of the French education system 'lie in a remote past', it is a tradition that is more likely to be steeped in, and therefore stunted by, tradition. Bourdieu argues that this is most evident in the humanities subjects where there is what he calls a 'type of relation to language and culture'. The French education system, he argues, has been described 'from Renan to Durkheim' as an education system that is 'so concerned to transmit a *style* [my emphasis]'. This concern to transmit 'a style' as well as content is a practice it owes 'to the humanist tradition inherited from the Jesuit colleges – an academic Christian reinterpretation of the social demands of an aristocracy, which leads distinguished detachment from the professional rank to be seen as the accomplished form of the accomplishment of every distinguished profession' (1977:114–5). Irish society may never have possessed an aristocratic class like that of France, even if we do see the Anglo-Irish ascendancy as inspiring the revivalism that Kiberd bemoans in Yeats and others and even if we do accept with Ó Tuama that 'Irishness' is rooted in 'an aristocratic tradition which lasted strongly in Ireland for practically two thousand years down into the seventeenth century' (1995b:222). Kathleen Lynch's recent work on inequalities in education does note, however, in reference to Bourdieu, that inequalities that exist in Irish and European society have a direct impact on 'lower rates of attainment among students from low-income backgrounds'; '[t]heir educational marginalization' is, she argues, 'economically generated even though it may subsequently take cultural and political manifestations' (Lynch and Baker, 2005:135).

However, despite the egregious nature of contemporary inequalities in education, it is unlikely that the Irish university system ever perpetuated academically, particularly in the humanities, an academic 'style' inherited from an age
of aristocracy or ever had to exorcize such tendencies to the same extent.

Bourdieu is also vitriolic in his treatment of the aged humanities professors
who are experts of 'classic authors' and 'ancient texts', what recalls John
Guillory's reading of the university English curriculum in terms of canonicity,
a disciplinary procedure that embodies many of the practices Bourdieu
describes. Bourdieu asks: '[w]hat indeed is left from long frequentation of
ancient texts or protracted dealings with classic authors, apart from the right
to hear phrases from the pink pages of the dictionary without a blush and, at a
higher degree of academic consecration, the ease and familiarity characteristic of the "relations as between a famous father and his sons or nephews" with
which Girandoux complacently credits *normaliens*, those "intimates of the
great ethics, the great aesthetics and the great authors"?' (1977:124). Once
again, the Irish humanities departments were less likely to possess such an
academic aristocracy capable of producing *normaliens* or dons even if it did
accord possessors of such cultural capital with similar privileges when they
visited or even took up positions. In most international English departments,
the Irish tradition only stretches back to Swift, and it is frequently the 'foreign
expert' who has not necessarily been schooled in Ireland who is the resident
expert. Irish writers, and those who teach them, may still be considered relatively radical despite the writers' long-standing place in the canon. The postcolonial turn in Irish humanities departments has also reinvented these
canonical Irish writers and in aligning them with African and Indian 'subaltern' voices has extended their revolutionary shelf life.

In the end, however, Bourdieu reminds us that it is the humanities that are at
the heart of these cycles of eternal recurrence and 'pedagogic conservatism' in
education and society. Because he regards the traditional 'pillars' of 'humanist
teaching of the 'humanities' such as 'Latin' and 'the agrégation of the literary
thesis' as outmoded and unnecessary, their privileging to this day in certain
models of the humanities in France is evidence for the education system's
'obsession with its self-perpetuation and social conservatism' (1977:198–9).
These practices are, for Bourdieu, representative of the 'traditional pillars of
the literate relation to culture and of the pedagogy by default inherent in humanist teaching of the "humanities", [and they] have always received and still
receive' in France 'constant support' from the 'most conservative fractions of
the dominant classes' (1977:199). Bourdieu argues that these 'aristocratic values' that are 'imposed on the French educational system' are the result of 'its own
tradition' and 'its relations with the privileged classes' (1977:201). Bourdieu
also explains, again from a cultural materialist perspective, how the theory/
practice dichotomy emerged in the university, and he points to a possible

explanation for why the 'theory' pole of this opposition has often been greeted
with suspicion or resilient hostility in Irish humanities departments:

> No doubt this system of specifically academic oppositions would not have the same
> degree of classificatory output and symbolic efficacy if it did not indirectly evoke
> the opposition between theory and practice in which the fundamental division
> between manual and non-manual labour finds expression. In systematically privi-
> leging one of the poles of a series of systematic oppositions (with the pre-eminence
> accorded to the theoretic disciplines, the literary cult of form and the taste for math-
> ematical formalism or the absolute depreciation of technical education), the educa-
> tional system privileges those on whom a family relatively freed from the
> pragmatism imposed by the urgencies of economic necessity has bestowed the
> privilege of the aptitude for symbolic, i.e. initially verbal, mastery of practical
> operations and the detached, distant and 'disinterested' relation to the world and to
> others. (1977, note, 216)

Given that Irish society in the first half of the twentieth century was rarely
'freed from the pragmatism imposed by the urgencies of economic necessity'
and given that Ireland remained a 'primarily agricultural' society for so long,[4] it
was always likely that the same theory/practice dichotomy that Bourdieu traces
to aristocratic roots in France would be slow to take hold in Irish universities.

Bourdieu's *Homo Academicus* extends this critique of education to a more
in-depth analysis of the university, and his analysis of those subjects traditionally aligned with the humanities once again foregrounds his notion of reproduction. He reminds us that French universities are 'strongly hierarchical and
centralized' (1988:75):

> [T]he field of arts and social sciences is organised around a principal opposition
> between two species of power. Specifically university power is founded princi-
> pally on the control of the instruments of reproduction of the professorial body –
> board of examiners the *agrégation*, the Universities Consultative Committee
> (which appoints tenured professors) – that is, this power rests on the possession
> of capital which is acquired in the university, in particular at the Ecole Normale.
> It is a power which is principally held by the professors at the university, the
> *Sorbonne*, and especially by professors of the canonical disciplines who are most
> often themselves children of teachers in secondary or higher education and espe-
> cially of primary school teachers. This kind of power prevails almost exclusively
> throughout the (French) university system. (1984:106; 78 in English translation)

One might argue, again for the reasons mentioned above, that such hierarchization if it exists in the Irish universities is never so centralized; the universities of the National University have, since 1997, a great degree of autonomy,
and Trinity College's governing council operates largely independently of the
dictates of the National University. Bourdieu also goes on to argue that in
France the 'faculty of arts and social sciences' is an institution 'charged with
transmitting legitimate culture and invested therefore with a social function of

consecration and conservation, they are places of specifically social powers, which have as much right as the professors of law and medicine to contribute to the most fundamental structures of the social order' (1988:99–100). The notion of consecration and conservation is undoubtedly important to the humanities in Ireland especially if we think back to Kiberd's essay on museums and learning in Ireland. However, the suggestion that Irish university professors of sociology, literature or history occupy the 'most fundamental structures of the social order' would be met with disbelief by a majority of people in Ireland, something that speaks for the different status of the academy in France.

Bourdieu also explains how the sciences and the humanities are positioned differently in the social fabric in regard to the perpetuation of the cultural arbitrary. He argues that the difference between the sciences and the humanities can be understood in terms of the differences between those agents and institutions 'orientated mostly towards research and scholarly goals or the intellectual field and specifically cultural goals [most likely the sciences]' and those 'which are orientated more towards the reproduction of the cultural order and the body of reproducers and towards the interests associated with the exercise of a temporal power within the cultural order [most likely the humanities]' (1988:74). Therefore, those disciplines that are traditionally more culpable in regard to the cultural arbitrary are the humanities subjects. However, questions about what kind of 'cultural arbitrary' the Irish university perpetuated and whether it was the humanities professors who were most responsible for its 'reproduction' in the 'cultural order' have never received such rigorous analysis in the Irish context. As John Guillory notes for American society, the university there is '*undetermining* with respect to American national culture'. If there is a 'national culture' in Ireland, it is also unlikely to be formed in the university but in what Guillory describes as the 'complex interaction between mass media and regional or ethnic cultures' (2006:35).

Jacques Derrida and the university

As an academic philosopher, Jacques Derrida consistently advocated for the teaching of philosophy both in the early years of secondary school and in disciplines such as Law and Medicine in the French University. In order to achieve these ends, he set up the Group for the Research of the Teaching of Philosophy (Groupe de Recherche sur l'Enseignement Philosophique – GREPH) which 'tried to convince our colleagues and our presidents that philosophy should be taught earlier than in this last grade of the high school'.[5] He has also argued that philosophy must be integral to the founding of any university. In 1982, he presented, with others, a report to the French government 'to justify the founding of an International College as the Collège International de Philosophie' (Ciph) (Derrida, 'Privilege', 2002a:17).

The founding of Ciph in 1983 enabled him to institutionalize a struggle he had taken up 'vigorously and unequivocally' to 'ensure and develop what is often called the threatened "specificity" of the discipline of philosophy' against its 'fragmentation, and even its dissolution into the teaching of the social or human sciences' (*ibid.*, 8). As I have suggested earlier, if there is any core disciplinary ethos in the Irish model of the humanities, then it is likely to lie somewhere between history and literature; philosophy has always been on the sidelines, and the philosophy undergraduate students of at least one of the National universities have consistently been advised to pursue graduate work abroad. However, because philosophy necessitates and privileges self-reflection and self-examination, it is likely that any educational system that gives philosophy pride of place in its humanities programme will foster greater discussion of the objectives and potential of university education in general.

Philosophy embodies a unique privilege for Derrida; he writes that 'the question "what is..." always belongs to philosophy' to such an extent that it is philosophy's privilege. Philosophy, for Derrida, '*would be this privilege*'; it would be 'the power of granting it [this privilege] to itself' (*ibid.*, 7), a description that leaves us with the question of how such '*self-foundation* [emphasis in original]' (2002a:21) straddles the divide between what is philosophical and what is not. The French minister of culture who came to the inauguration of Ciph appeared to acknowledge, however disingenuously, this privilege, saying that the official inauguration of Ciph was really a matter of 'self-foundation'. This incident reveals how the language philosophy often prides itself on practising can occasionally be taken up by government officials, a process that 'professional philosophers' such as Derrida may be uncomfortable with even though it may be an inevitable result of the struggle to prevent the 'fragmentation' of philosophy by appealing to government sanction and funding. This next section sets out to contrast Derrida's deconstructive speculations on the humanities and on the university with those we have examined from Irish educators. Derrida believes that philosophy's place in the university has historically been associated with a notion of privilege (and privilege here may overlook inequality in education), a privilege that recent educational policy on globalization, internationalization and the 'knowledge industry' appears unwilling to recognize.

Derrida was a leading French advocate of the humanities and philosophy; however, his work on the university as an institution is perhaps less well known. University privilege is an important concept in some of Derrida's later writings. His essay 'Privilege' examines the origins of such privilege in regard to philosophy in the university. Derrida received a letter from François Mitterrand in 1981 in which the 'president of the republic' (2004a:213) supported the idea that the 'teaching of philosophy should be preserved and developed' as a 'critical discipline that should better allow everyone to understand the world and their place in it in order to live and act in that world' (2004a:194); Mitterand argues that '[a]t least, the teaching of philosophy should obligatorily figure in all sections of the long second cycle' in the secondary schools. It is hard to imagine Bertie Ahern or Charles Haughey ever writing such a letter to the founders of a new college of philosophy in Ireland.

Derrida's essay 'Privilege: Justificatory Title and Introductory Remarks' gives a new reading of 'conflict' that Kant privileged, as I have discussed, in his treatment of the university. For Kant, according to Derrida's commentary, the university as 'rational institution' finds its 'reflection' in the 'faculty of philosophy'; it has an 'absolute autonomy', and its 'formal' power rests with 'the speculative self-representation of a few professors', with 'books with a limited printing' and with a library 'whose light reaches the public space only extenuated through a series of filters and translations' ('Privilege', 2002a:59). Derrida develops his reading of Kant's *The Conflict of the Faculties* in his essay 'Vacant Chair: Censorship, Mastery, Magisteriality'. Derrida argues that Kant's main objective in *Conflict* is, since censorship is inevitable in the university, to 'give the reason for censorship in a discourse on the university' or 'to speak the truth about censorship from the stance of reason' (2004c:52). Kant's *Conflict* was written after he had received his 'famous reprimand' from Friedrich Wilhelm II in 1793 following the publication of book two of *Religion within the Limits of Reason Alone*. Wilhelm II's Edict of Religion of July 1788 'prohibited everything that appeared to oppose the official religion', and in December of that year, the 'law against the freedom of the press was declared' (Derrida, 2004c:44). For Derrida, censorship is important in any discussion of the different faculties in the university because even in 'industrial societies with supposedly liberal and democratic regimes, even if State censorship is very reduced [...] for the system in general, there are, on the other hand, mechanisms of prohibition, suppression, repression, *without censorship* (*stricto sensu*)' (Derrida, 2004c:51). It is only the university that can properly analyse with authority the ground of this censorship, and it is philosophy, despite its status as a 'lower' faculty and despite its lack of 'power', that must be at the forefront of any analysis of the justification of such 'suppression'.

Since philosophy has never had the same 'privilege' in the Irish university that it has enjoyed in the French and German universities and since the Irish National University had neither a privileged philosophy department nor any kind of Faculty of Theology, it is perhaps not surprising that Irish society experienced a very different kind of censorship. J. J. Lee argues that discussions of censorship in Irish society always return to Cosgrave's Censorship of Publications Act of 1929, an Act that empowered a censorship board to prohibit any work it considered 'indecent or obscene' (1989:158) as well as all literature 'advocating birth control'. This had obvious ramifications for university curricula. However, Lee also argues, as Derrida does for the French context, that censorship in Ireland spoke for privilege in society; it 'served the materialistic values of the propertied classes by fostering the illusion that Ireland was a haven of virtue surrounded by a sea of vice [...] [i]t helped to rivet the remunerative impression that immorality stopped with sex' (1989:158). In recalling Bourdieu's notion of the cultural arbitrary, Lee also points out that such censorship was not 'uniquely Irish'; it served to 'shrivel the domain of "real" morality to those teachings which happen to conveniently coincide with the objective material requirements of the dominant groups in society' (1989:158). For Lee, the 'obsession with sex permitted a blind eye to be turned towards the social scars that disfigured the face of Ireland' (1989:159). If the university had upheld the kind of conflict between philosophy and theology that Kant privileges almost two hundred years earlier in the university, then it might have produced a very different framing of 'immorality'.

However, Derrida's reading of Kant's *Conflict* is also important for another reason; it demonstrates how the emergence of a university system that allowed institutional space for theology and philosophy alongside the other faculties created a critical heritage in which a reasoned approach to civic morality was fostered. There have been several movements in work in the humanities from within this tradition, but the most recent 'turn' that speaks for the potential and value of interdisciplinary work in the humanities between philosophy, religious investigation and hermeneutics was the 'theological turn' taken by philosophy over the last thirty years.[6] Because theology and religious investigation were not present in any meaningful way in the National University curriculum, Irish people often lacked such an arena for examining the relationship between reason and faith.

Derrida's reading explains how, for Kant, the department of philosophy has a 'singular place' (2004c:53) in the university; 'No power should have a right of inspection [*droit de regard*] over the Faculty of Philosophy, as long as it is satisfied with *saying*, not doing, with saying the truth without giving orders, with speaking *within* the university and *not* outside of it' (50). Kant's work on the university can also be regarded as prefiguring Newman's understanding of how theology and civic morality are integral to a humanities education. For Kant, the Faculties of Law, Medicine and Theology are the 'upper faculties', and the 'lower' faculties include philosophy, and many of the subjects that would be regarded as humanities disciplines today. The 'higher' faculties are higher because each has a 'specific interpretation of radical evil'. But 'all three fail to understand it, because they deny freedom by conceiving of this evil as simply "hereditary"'. There is 'hereditary disease for the Faculty of Medicine, inherited debt for the Faculty of Law, and inherited sin for the Faculty of Theology' (2004c:53). Derrida reminds us that Kant's analysis of the university in terms of the 'conflict' it always embodied between faculties (and in the age of the 'knowledge industry', this age-old 'conflict' now takes place between science and the humanities without the humanities having anything like the 'silent power' that philosophy once had) is undertaken by Kant because the 'task of the scholar' is 'by right' one that sees this scholar as a 'researcher in religious theory' who has the 'task of one who studies religion from a philosophical point of view' (Derrida, 2004c:53). It is with the perspective of this religious scholar in mind that Kant argues, for Derrida, that the study of religion, or revelation, can 'include within it a pure religion of reason' or a 'religion according to reason alone' (Derrida, 2004c:53–4). In other words, Kant is arguing, in a similar manner to Newman writing sixty years later, for how the university has a unique role in helping a society understand what it means to be religious. Kant argues, again for Derrida, that the 'harmony' between these 'two religions', between the 'rational and the historical' kinds that the university now fosters, can 'remain thinkable' in such a university (Derrida, 2004c:54).

It is therefore philosophy, as the 'teacher of pure reason' (Derrida, 2004c:54), to use Kant's phrase, that has a 'panoptical ubiquity' (Derrida, 2004c:55) in the university. Kant reminds us that the 'Faculty of Philosophy' 'extends to all parts of human knowledge' including, from 'a historical viewpoint, the teachings of the higher faculties'. It is also noteworthy that in Kant's day, this faculty consisted of 'two departments': a 'department of *historical knowledge* (including history, geography, philology and humanities, along with all the empirical knowledge contained in the natural sciences), and a department of *pure rational knowledge* (pure mathematics and pure philosophy, the metaphysics of nature and of morals)' (Kant, 1979:45). It also studies 'the relation of these two divisions of learning to each other' (Derrida, 2004c:54). Such a Faculty can even interrogate religion but it only does so 'for the benefit of the sciences'. The government can also not 'forbid it do this without acting against its own proper and essential purposes' (Derrida, 2004c:54).

However, what is important from the Irish university perspective is that Kant argues that it is this 'topology' that then 'defines the jurisdictional powers' of the university. The higher faculties must 'put up with the objections and doubts it [the Faculty of Philosophy] brings forward in public' (Kant, *Conflict*, 1979:45; Derrida, 2004c:55). Kant is here describing the important relation between philosophy as companion discipline to religious investigation and the government itself. A healthy, rational state presumes a healthy 'conflict of the faculties' in the university. Of course, such constructive debate and criticism in the service of reason between faculties and departments may never have existed in the Irish humanities context because of the absence of a department of religion and because philosophy has never occupied such a position of 'privilege'. Into this vacuum crept the historical and nationalistic narratives that the government proposed and that would be supported by scholars in the universities as well as by the more influential ethos advocated by the Church.

But Derrida's assessment of the Kantian university goes still further; he argues that the 'topological structure of this teaching institution [...] has an essential relation with the architectonics of pure reason' (Derrida, 2004c:55). This is a radical argument; it suggests that the place of reason in any society and in any government has an 'essential relation' with the place of reason in its universities. Derrida argues that Kant's essay on this point from the end of the *Critique of Pure Reason* is 'well known in French lycées', and in response, one might argue that one would be hard-pressed to find a university philosophy department in Ireland, not to mention a secondary school class, that has ever privileged this text from the *Critique* in its curriculum. Derrida explains in detail what he means by using the word 'architectonics' here; it describes the 'art of the system', the 'theory of the "scientificity" of our knowledge'. Kant explains that all of this takes place under the 'government of reason' (Derrida, 2004c:57). The government, the State and the university are inextricably connected in this model:

> [t]o speak of the regime, government, or regency of reason is important when considering all of the following concepts together, in their essential relation to one another: the university, the Faculty of Philosophy, and State power. This is also a system of regulated relationships. Royal power will (should) be inspired by reason, by the government of reason, in order to rule the university. It would be in its interest to adjust its political government of reason. This harmony, as regulative idea, as idea of reason, inspires all of the Kantian politics of the university. (Derrida, 2004c:57)

Whether sovereign power was ever 'regulated' by the 'government of reason' in Ireland in adjudicating for the universities is unclear; however, what is clear is that the government as 'State of Power' never had an 'essential relation' with the university as governed by the 'Faculty of Philosophy'.

Derrida's account of privilege in relation to the university affects all facets of university life. Universities can unconsciously play out themes of canonicity, what John Guillory refers to in terms of 'a social order, with all of its various inequities' (1993:ix). The privilege invested in philosophy and in access to the university takes the form of what Derrida refers to as 'distinct discursive procedures' or 'intralinguistic translations', and Kathleen Lynch has described similar practices in the Irish university. Derrida argues that these movements '*inside*' languages must be linked 'to what we call "philosophy"' 'according to eras, places, schools, social and socio-institutional circles' ('Privilege', 2002a:29). In other words, 'philosophy' must be linked to some internal linguistic movements that are divorced from natural language divisions. This would appear to be advocating for a connection between language and philosophy that promotes reason without any necessary appeals to nationalism. However, the means for linking 'philosophy' (and its inherent

privilege) with these non-'natural', internal linguistic displacements, something that brings 'schools' and the 'social' into play, also requires a 'training'
or a 'schooling' that once again seems invested with university privilege:

> To have access *effectively* in effect, to these discursive procedures and thus to
> have the right to the *philosophical such as it is spoken*, for philosophical democ-
> racy, democracy in philosophy, to be possible (and there is no democracy in
> general without that, and democracy, the democracy that remains still to come,
> is also a philosophical concept), one must be trained in these procedures. One
> must be trained to recognize connotations, so-called stylistic or rhetorical effects,
> semantic potentialities, virtual folds and bends, a whole economy at work in
> what is perhaps, under the name of philosophy, only the most economical prac-
> tice of natural language. ('Privilege', 2002a:29–30)

This recalls Bourdieu's argument about the 'cultural arbitrary' that the
university serves to perpetuate because the humanities is often bound up with
the transmission of a certain privileged 'style' of living. Access and transparency
are two important concerns here. The fact that university professions can very
easily end up unconsciously embodying the privilege they set out to question
from a philosophically democratic, and hence for Derrida a *de jure* democratic,
standpoint raises questions in relation to university transparency. Derrida's
understanding of university privilege as synonymous with philosophy, a
philosophy grounded in a 'relation to Kant' and its 'privileged inscription of an
absolute privilege' ('Privilege', 2002a:49), something inherited and embodied
as a 'teaching discourse' (2002a:51), itself seems to privilege an allegory of the
university, or a moment of self-foundation, that as we have seen, government
officials can then use to their own advantage. As with all of Derrida's essays,
the language is significant. Derrida employs a rhetoric that exploits the
impossibility of differentiating the university's inside from its outside.
However, when he writes that '[w]e must recognise the university site outside
the walls of the institution itself: in the allegory or metonymy of the University',
we must question whether this only takes us back inside since it is only there
that we learn about such topics as metonymy and allegory (2002a:61).

Bourdieu is also concerned with interrogating the privileges associated
with 'professorial language' (1977:110) and with a 'pedagogic communication' that can be 'maintained as such even when the information transmitted
tends towards zero' (1977:21). Even though Bourdieu's rather more prescriptive and all-encompassing model of pedagogical reproduction does not offer a
persuasive alternative to this reproduction, he does not describe whatever
space he allows for 'outside the walls of the institution' in terms of a 'university site', or an 'allegory' of the 'University', as Derrida does ('Privilege',
2002a:61). Bourdieu phrases his argument on the university's system of reproduction[7] in terms of its inauguration of a 'capacity to employ the *internal logic*

of its functioning in the service of its *external function* of social conservation', a truth that can only be understood by examining the 'complete system of relations prevailing' 'between the educational system and the structure of class relations' (1977:177). He refers to a system of human relations that comes to be 'routinized' when 'professorial language' is not made to accommodate the above relation. The difference between these former pupils of the French university system might therefore be summarized by noting that whereas Derrida employs a rhetoric derived from the philosophy implicit in the 'battle of the classes of the [University] faculties' ('Mochlos', 2004b:428), Bourdieu writes of the conflict in terms of 'the educational system and the structure of class relations'.

Derrida's privileging of faculty relations through its constant return to the 'right to philosophy' may be unwilling to give up age-old privileges the humanities subjects no longer enjoy. José Ortega y Gasset writes in 1946 that the 'university represents a privilege difficult to justify or defend' (1946:40) and that 'the process of making the university accessible to the working man is only in small part the concern of the university; it is almost wholly the business of the state' (1946:41). The privilege that has become synonymous with the university cannot be addressed on the university's own terms. However, Derrida's recognition of this fact takes us back to the unique 'training' gained at university: 'to have the right to the *philosophical such as it is spoken*, for philosophical democracy, democracy in philosophy, to be possible (and there is no democracy in general without that ...), one must be trained in these procedures [Derrida's emphasis]' ('Privilege', 2002a:29). To have the right to democracy, one must be trained in the procedures for accessing the *philosophical such as it is spoken*. However, since this training is only officially recognized in the university, democracy, and hence any justification of privilege, must start and finish then with the '*philosophical such as it is spoken*', and this is found, for Derrida, only in the university. Therefore, despite the rhetorical subversions, Derrida's attempt to link democracy in the French state with the philosophical in the university is evidence of a distinctly different university ethos to that found in Ireland.

Derrida does refer to the contemporary state of the university when he links the university explicitly with 'multinational military-industrial complexes' ('Principle', 1983a:11) – what would still be considered outside the university for many – in making his strongest case for why the question of university privilege must be reappraised. The university's close relationship with these 'complexes', he argues, has done away with the old academic distinction between 'basic' and 'end-oriented' research (1983a:12). New research is 'at the service of war, [and] of national and international security' (1983a:13). This means, Derrida argues, that a 'State power' no longer needs to 'censor discourse'; censorship has been censored. What the 'techno-economic situation of a society' (1983a:14) driving research now does is to 'limit the means' and place 'restrictions on support' for research it does not support (1983a:13). This 'new "censorship"' (1983a:13) achieves the same end, then, as the old censorship, but for Derrida, it is never called censorship. Once again, it is a question of language; the new 'censorship' does not make headlines, but the researcher doing research that does not meet market requirements finds funding bodies refusing or limiting resources. Because it has not been called censorship, no philosophical justification is given for the decision. A culture of silence, then, has descended on what Derrida has referred to as those 'evaluative actions' whose 'restrictions on support', while achieving the same end, no longer resort to such phrases as the 'unacceptability of a discourse' or the 'illegitimacy of a course offering' (1983a:13). Decisions on access to the means of support, to funding, even to self-evaluation itself, are therefore phrased in terms of the 'techno-economic situation of a society' (1983a:14); decisions that work to configure our universities now justify support explicitly by reference to the market, not through any philosophical justification or judicial language that responds to censorship. When Derrida writes that 'studying such evaluations is ... one of the tasks most indispensable to the exercise of academic responsibility' (1983a:13), this seems to imply that the university's language of evaluation, its representation to itself of the privilege it embodies and its representation of 'self-foundation' and 'self-knowledge' must be revised. The university, or the 'knowledge industry' as it is often called in Ireland, must acknowledge the debt it owes philosophy and employ its privileging of reason to transform the language of evaluation into a transparent and judicial language that is not only effective at responding to the language of market economics.

Derrida ultimately regards the university's unique place in society, its privilege, as synonymous with an inherited understanding of profession unique to philosophy, the faculty that, through a philosophical allegiance to Kant, is the 'reflection' of the 'absolute autonomy of the tribunal of reason' and one that 'remains absolutely independent of the power of the state as regards pronouncing the truth in judgments' ('Privilege', 2002a:56). For Derrida, the university profession in philosophy gains its status as a 'moment of right' and as 'the discourse of the law' in its mediation through 'the self-reflexive forms of self-representation' (2002a:59). The unique privilege that is accorded he or she who is employed to profess this philosophy by a university is therefore understood in terms of what Derrida has already referred to, through Kant, as the 'most difficult' of reason's tasks, namely, 'self-knowledge' (2002a:55). And we recall that J. J. Lee has noted that it is ironic that the institution responsible for fostering the Irish 'knowledge industry' has never aspired to gaining a great deal of 'self-knowledge'. However, Derrida's work has championed a very specific understanding of self-knowledge and an analysis of self-knowledge or 'inner-life'[8] through a renunciation of what he calls logocentrism, presence and the linguistic incarnation and it is an understanding of language and logos that would depart quite radically from the Church's understanding of identity in the Irish context.

In an address entitled '*Mochlos – or the conflict of the faculties*' made to the faculty of Columbia University in 1980 on the centenary of its graduate school, Derrida returns to the Kantian sense of conflict that the university embodies. *Mochlos*, Greek for lever, refers, for Derrida, to an inner conflict of the faculties, such as a disparity in strength between the left and right sides, that a person might employ to get ahead. It also refers to the wooden rod that Ulysses forces into the pupil of the Cyclops in *The Odyssey*. In Derrida's essay, he is personifying the university in order to suggest that it embodies a similar inner conflict. The theme appears again in the essay 'The Principle of Reason: The University in the Eyes of Its Pupils'. Derrida asks: 'What can the University's body see or not see of its own destination, of that in view of which it stands its ground?' ('Principle', 1983a:5). However, Derrida appears to recognize that too much concentration on this 'inner conflict' or *mochlos* can lead to institutionalized introspection that 'narrows vision'. He then links this observation to Heidegger's problem of how the 'grounded university' is to be rooted in 'the principle of grounding or reason' and to Peirce's argument that 'one cannot well demand a reason for reasonableness itself'. Derrida argues that all these issues have not been 'thought through, scrutinized, interrogated as to' their 'origin' (1983a:10). However, in an age of academic capitalism where academic inner conflict is unlikely to draw much sympathy or to privilege such philosophical language, one must wonder where such issues are likely to be 'scrutinized' or 'interrogated'. However, it must be acknowledged that the Irish university, for good or bad, was far behind the French university in terms of even raising such philosophical questions about the origin of the university.

Derrida does address the more topical issues of utility and critical thinking in the modern university. In reading through Kant, Nietzsche and Heidegger, he concludes that the 'decision of thought' that 'cannot be an academic moment' and that yet must be the goal of the university must invest pupils with 'reason' and with 'the capacity to teach'. Such a vision is often prominent in university literature that promotes what is called 'critical thinking'. However, Derrida wants to move beyond the 'principle of reason', to a 'thought' that requires both the 'principle of reason and what is beyond the principle of reason' ('Principle', 1983a:18–19). He argues that 'this artefact that is the university has *reflected* society only in giving it the chance for reflection, that is, also, for *dissociation*' (1983a:19). This recalls Kant's description of the humanities (*Humaniora*) in terms of a very different sense or spirit that promotes instead a simultaneous universal self-imparting and a 'taking-part'. For Derrida, the kind of reflection that the university can teach is synonymous with a kind of dissociation or sundering. In recalling his unwillingness to interrogate embodiment to any great degree in his earlier philosophy of language, one must question how this regard for reflection as dissociation would sit with a university tradition that was guided for so long by the moral influence of the Catholic Church.

However, in a later talk given on another American campus, Stanford, Derrida speaks of the kind of profession[9] that is unique to the university and that will explain and situate the 'ideal thought' and 'reflection' of what he describes as the university without condition. In *L'Université sans condition*, he questions whether the task of the university is to ensure the 'reproduction of professional competence by preparing professors for pedagogy and for research who have respect for a certain code' (Derrida, 2001:17). In this lengthy essay, Derrida examines the nature of this code. The profession of professor, or university teacher, must imply 'the commitment to a responsibility freely declared, almost under oath: in a word, professed' (*l'engagement d'une responsabilité librement déclarée, quasiment sous serment: en un mot profésée*) (2001:50). He writes that 'the declaration of the professee is a kind of performative declaration. He or she is bound by an act of sworn faith, an oath' (*la déclaration de qui professe est une déclaration performative en quelque sorte. Elle engage par un acte de foi jurée, un serment*) (2001:35). However, if the profession of university employee necessitates a profession, oath or the enacting of a profession of faith, then one might suggest that in an age when market economics and accountability have made such professions redundant, this unconditional university might also appear somewhat unprofessional, or even *sans profession*, unemployed.

Derrida's description of the future of the university in terms of the 'profession to come' (*l'avenir de la profession*) is all too similar to his description of 'the democracy that remains still to come' ('Privilege', 2002a:29). Both states are dependent on the 'right to philosophy'. However, a university without condition grounded on a 'profession to come' is hardly likely to restore much faith in education for those millions of unemployed, young graduates in today's 'Europe of knowledge'. Whereas, for Derrida, the 'idea of profession' of the university involves the professee in a quasi-religious 'oath' and looks beyond 'a knowledge' to 'a sworn faith' that asks the 'subject to take account of himself in a instance to be defined' (2001:50), there is a distinct lack of detail in regard to how any profession, university or otherwise, can maintain such ideals in an era defined by academic capitalism, assessment criteria and accountability; how is the student or professor to understand the responsibility incurred by an 'instance [yet] to be defined'? Invoking a messianic or transcendental profession, a profession in its academic guise that Derrida tells us must be 'symbolically protected by a sort of absolute immunity' (2001:45), may only leave us with a sense of privilege that resembles little more than academic immunity. And if this is what the university must pass on, how will it account for itself in a European education environment that advocates 'autonomy and entrepreneurship in education' as 'the building blocks upon which a truly knowledge-based society can develop'?[10]

Derrida does recognize that the university is evermore influenced by 'the technologies of informatization' ('Principle', 1983a:14) and that this, in turn, affects notions of 'right' and justice. However, in a footnote to his essay 'Faith and Knowledge', he writes that his understanding of justice, and therefore privilege, works to a particular dynamic:

> I propose to think the condition of justice in relation to a certain sundering <*déliaison*>, in relation to the always-safe, always-to-be-saved possibility of this secret of *disassociation* [my emphasis] rather than through the bringing-together (*Versammlung*) towards which Heidegger retraces it. ... (2002c:60)

This 'secret of disassociation', or ethos of *déliaison*, consistently motivates Derrida's reading of texts and institutions. However, in privileging the 'always-safe, always-to-be-saved possibility of this secret of disassociation', Derrida's university privileges 'sundering' and separation at the expense of the 'bringing-together' that Newman's universal knowledge and even Kant's universal 'self-imparting' seem to promote. Kiberd, Lee and Fitzgerald would also seem to invoke a sense of community and 'bringing-together' in writing on the humanities in the Irish university. For Derrida, even the teaching body must perform this 'sundering'. The 'teaching body' becomes a 'body that in turn produces itself by erasing itself as the barely visible'; its essential ingredient, *dissociation*, does not allow 'the contract between these two bodies', namely, that of the 'philosophical and the sociopolitical corpus' to be 'brought to the foreground' (2002b:90). Such a teaching body that promotes erasure and dissociation may only misrepresent what lies beyond, or outside, as 'menacing' and parasitic. Ultimately, it presents us with a somewhat isolationist picture of the university that would work against the sense of community, real or otherwise, that was always part of the romantic nationalism and Catholic ethos Irish society privileged.

However, Ireland's 'knowledge economy' has privileged the kind of business acumen that Derrida predicted the university would have to familiarize itself with. Derrida spoke at Cornell in the 1980s of how 'a military budget can invest in anything at all, in view of deferred profits: "basic" scientific theory, the humanities, literary theory and philosophy' ('Principle', 1983a:13). One of the main Irish government documents on education in recent years, the 'chief white paper' on education from 2004, published when Ireland was the second 'most globalized' nation in the world, describes the 'national aspirations to engage in more high-value and knowledge intensive industry ... from specific industry sectors, such as information technology, electronics, pharmaceutical/biotechnology and the human and social sciences' (Downey,

2003:16). The Irish government, then, in being less philosophical than the French government, has not shirked the responsibilities of the new market-place of ideas. Ultimately, it is European policy that will have to patch over these different national approaches to the university and the humanities. The 'Bologna Accord' is a set of documents which urges education institutions to overcome established conflicts (inner or otherwise) they envisage arising between educational forces and market forces:

> Putting knowledge into the heart of Europe, building a 'Europe of knowledge', is a goal that cannot be realised without reform in higher education. Students and employers are the primary customers and consumers of educational services. To be competitive, institutions will have to be market-oriented and broaden their dialogue with customers and other stakeholders.[11]

However, Derrida's description of the university's inner conflict in terms of self-knowledge and privilege may be regarded as another aspect of the human-ities' state of crisis. Derrida compares this inner conflict to Ulysses' use of his left side against his right in blinding the Cyclops and, through Kant, to the 'Russian infantryman['s]' training to lead from his left foot in order to 'give himself the momentum to attack with his right'. What is important to remem-ber in both cases is that the struggle to master this inner conflict is only a preparation for a greater conflict to follow, be it with a Cyclops or an invading foreign army. If we become preoccupied with the inner conflict, we may trip ourselves up in finding the language to face the new 'Europe of knowledge'.

Asian universities and the humanities

As Asian universities appear more regularly in the international university rankings and begin to displace more familiar American and British universi-ties from the higher positions,[12] it is important to recognize the implications this knowledge transfer will have for the humanities in general. Hong Kong, with three universities in the world top 100,[13] is one of the strongest academic regions in Asia. Hong Kong, like Ireland, is also a postcolonial region; however, it is changing its undergraduate programme quite dramatically in moving away from a British university model. In the last number of years, universities in Hong Kong have changed the titles of their teaching staff, the length of the undergraduate degree and academic structures in order to move closer to the American liberal arts model. The Chinese University of Hong Kong (CUHK) is introducing a 'strategic policy' modelled on the system in place at the University of Illinois Urbana–Champaign. The university is mov-ing to Broad-Based Admissions and a new four-year university cycle for undergraduates from 2012. The universities in Hong Kong also offer general education courses in the Arts subjects for Arts majors.

The CUHK also has productive and vibrant Religion, Theology and Divinity sections. Religious education and theological training have been an integral part of the academic programmes of the Chinese University since 1957. In 1968, the Department of Religion and Philosophy was established, and in 1978, the Department of Religion became an independent unit with a Theology Division attached. While these departments have a strong Christian ethos, a level of East–West religious interdisciplinarity is practised in conjunction with such departments as Philosophy and Chinese Studies that is not found in Irish universities. Hong Kong University, the oldest and most highly ranked university in Hong Kong, has a more non-denominational, 'civic' structure and does not have a religion or theology department. It was modelled on the University of Manchester, a university that is representative of a type that Stefan Collini regards as 'local, practical, aspirational' and 'not afraid to teach practical subjects such as "commerce" alongside the traditional curriculum' (2012:28).

Hong Kong's university system was, like Ireland's, established when the region was under British rule. Therefore, the research on the Hong Kong experience of implementing British education policy throws up many parallels with the Irish experience. Edward Vickers, Flora Kan and Paul Morris suggest that it cannot be argued that education policy in Hong Kong was simply the result of cultural imperialism where a colonial power imposed a colonialist agenda on the teaching of such subjects as history and literature. There was a great degree of co-operation from the Hong Kong community. They argue that '[f]ar from forcing curriculum developers to promote "colonial values", the British authorities created broad curricular parameters within which conservative scholars were able to promote their own ideological agenda. The outcome was an "invented tradition" of depoliticised, ethno-cultural nationalism whose colonial parentage was obscured or quickly forgotten' (2003:107). Vickers, Kan and Morris argue that the 'subject community [the Hong Kong community] assumed a collaborative role vis-a-vis the colonial government. They were allowed to assume the role of guardians of Chinese culture in exchange for producing a depoliticised and decontextualised curriculum' (2003:103). This suited the sociopolitical conditions and entrepreneurial spirit of Hong Kong in the 1950s and 1960s. However, it led to a focus in education on 'ancient periods' to 'the neglect of the local context'. The local community, who were in Hong Kong a largely refugee population, were made to identify with a 'monolithic, homogenous vision of China'. Depoliticized, colonial Hong Kong was then something of a 'sanctuary for conservative Chinese scholars' who wished to restore some sense of pride in ancient Chinese culture.

This account of Hong Kong's transition from British colony to China SAR[14] bears some similarities to the post-independence 'two culture' debate in Irish society I have examined earlier in Corkery, Ó Tuama and Kiberd. They argue that the Celtic Revival ideology inspired an understanding of history that was idealized and also removed from an engaged understanding of local history. However, this brief comparison also raises the question of whether Irish educational institutions in navigating a somewhat similar colonial and postcolonial context also learned to rest content with a 'depoliticized and decontextualized curriculum'. Were Irish educational institutions and successive governments more content to privilege reactionary historical interpretations that romanticized tradition instead of confronting head on the local realities of an educational context where curricula and policy were becoming stagnant? The language and religion questions were always bound up with the debates around Northern Ireland, and this made the colonial transition far more protracted in Ireland than it was in Hong Kong. Hong Kong's institutional efficiency and entrepreneurial spirit may also have enabled it to throw off, far more quickly, any signs of the 'pathology of dependence' that was for so long a hindrance to Irish modernization.

However, it can also not be presumed that the Asian humanities model that emerges in the years to come will be a carbon copy of programmes in the United States or the UK. Leo Ou-fan Lee has recently urged scholars in the humanities in Asia to contemplate how to make a new beginning in the humanities to challenge Western philosophical thought from an Asian humanistic point of view. He argues that this is a task made more urgent by the ubiquitous effects of globalization.[15] For Lee, 'the task of reexamining and redefining Western philosophical theory should be undertaken by Asian humanistic scholars'; however, the term 'Asian humanistic scholar', he argues, should not be taken to mean 'scholars of Asian descent, but rather all humanistic scholars interested in Asia'.[16] Lee notes that subaltern studies, a school of thought that focuses on the 'postcolonial societies of South Asia and the developing world', can be thought to be a 'challenge to traditional Western narratives', and he asks: 'could there be Chinese ways of subverting these narratives?' However, other Chinese educationalists have pointed to weaknesses in the Asian approach to the humanities. Anthony Cheung Bing-leung, the former president of the Hong Kong Institute of Education, has recently warned in *The South China Morning Post* that education in Hong Kong is in danger of becoming 'commodity' education. He warns against what Harry Lewis, a former dean of Harvard, called 'excellence without a soul'. Bing-leung suggests that Hong Kong must offer a system of education where the 'new generation' should 'be able to display imagination and creativity unbounded by conventional wisdom and mainstream thinking', what replays many of the arguments made on behalf of the humanities by American academics like Martha Nussbaum and Louis Menand.

In the end, one can only hope that the degree of interdisciplinarity and comparative work necessary to equip the humanities for the new 'Asian century' will transform the humanities into a richer and more heterogenous practice and voice in the university. Western scholars will need to exhibit the same degree of industriousness and dedication for the Asian humanities as Asian scholars have shown for so long for the older Western variety in order to make the project as fruitful as it will need to be to maintain Kant's notion of a living tradition of conflict between faculties in the university to come. The CUHK has already earmarked five important areas of research for the next five-year period. While one of these areas is Chinese Studies, none of the five areas include any other humanities discipline. Because the disciplinary parameters and the philosophy behind Chinese Studies are so unique and because it is an area of study that predates the humanities as it is understood in Western universities, it is important that presidents and educationalists in Irish universities grasp how Chinese Studies and other aspects of the Asian humanities are positioned in regard to other disciplines in a modern university.

Notes

1 Even though the 'humanities' does not have a French equivalent, Lamoure Rontopoulou and Lamoure employ the term in their examination of the French University system.

2 See http://stats.oecd.org/

3 Bourdieu describes the habitus as a 'system of schemes of thought' (1977:40).

4 Ireland's first minister for Agriculture Patrick Hogan claimed in 1924 that 'national development in Ireland, for our generation at least, is practically synonymous with agricultural development' (Lee, 1989:112). J. J. Lee argues that Ireland was still a 'primarily agricultural' (Lee, 1989:187) society in 1937, the year before Durkheim's *L'évolution pédagogique en France* was published.

5 See Roundtable Discussion with Jacques Derrida at Villanova University, 3 October 1994: http://hydra.humanities.uci.edu/derrida/vill1.html

6 See Dominique Janicaud's *Phenomenology and the 'Theological Turn'*. Michel Henry, a leading figure in this 'turn', describes 'the "theological turn" of contemporary phenomenology as not a "deviation" or distortion of phenomenology, but its fulfillment' (2005:154).

7 Derrida also speaks of the university as a potential system of reproduction but only in relation to 'certain Eastern countries' where he writes that the 'University is totally confined to an activity of information reproduction' (Derrida, 2004b:413).

8 Derrida's work consistently questions an understanding of self-presence, voice and self-awareness grounded on what he calls 'presence'. His deconstructive understanding of these categories leads to the sense of 'erasure' or 'dissociation' that he foregrounds in relation to education, pedagogy and the 'teaching body'. He writes in *Speech and Phenomena*: '[P]resent to the self in the life of a present that has not yet gone forth from itself into the world, space, or nature. All these "goings-forth" effectively exile this life of self-presence in indications' (1973:40).

9 Derrida's discussion of profession and performance here also connotes J. L. Austin's conception of the performative (Derrida, 2001:16).

10 See 'The future of graduate management education in the context of the Bologna Accord', p. 20 (www.gmacbolognaproject.com).

11 www.gmacbolognaproject.com, p.18.

12 See *The New York Times*, 20 Nov. 2009, 'A Crown Jewel of Education Struggles With Cuts' where it is reported that the University of California, Berkeley, dropped from a position as high as number two in the rankings in 2000 to a position of 39 in the 2009 *Times Higher Education* rankings. Meanwhile, many Asian universities have appeared in the top 50 for the first time.

13 *QS World University Rankings* 2011.

14 The new political arrangement between Hong Kong and China is described in terms of 'one country, two systems'.

15 Professor Lee was delivering the keynote speech for the Eighth Annual Meeting of the Asian New Humanities Net (ANHN) held on 15 and 16 October 2010 at CUHK.

16 See www.cuhk.edu.hk/english/features/professor-leo-lee.html.

6

The transformation of the humanities in Ireland

The Bologna Agreement and the 'Europeanization' of university education

Implicit in what humanities learning represents is a willingness to overcome disparate national interests so as to embody a civic, ethical and cultural ethos that can speak across boundaries and uncover a common regard for enquiry. It speaks for a common good, or *sensus communis*, which, as Hans-Georg Gadamer explains, 'founds community' and gives the 'human will its direction' not through the 'abstract universality of reason' but through the 'concrete universality represented by the community of a group, a people, a nation, or the whole human race' (1995:21). However, because a respect for difference is also implicit in what the humanities teaches, its disciplines will always suffer at the hands of overarching educational policies, such as Bologna, that promote what they refer to as 'convergence', 'comparability and compatibility' and that must be written into law and put into practice by forty-seven (and counting) distinct national education institutions over what was an initial ten-year period.

The Bologna Accord, commemorating 900 years of the University of Bologna, privileges 'convergence' across the various signatories to the Bologna Process. However, as recently as 1967, only eighteen years after Ireland had left the Commonwealth, another external political force that had long influenced Ireland's educational policy, J. J. Lee argued that the universities in Ireland had only 'begun to shake themselves into contemplation of the 20th century' (in Dineen, 1992:409). Therefore, Ireland's fledgling academic 'contemplation' and interiorization of the twentieth century first had to sluggishly divest itself of a colonialist philosophy of education so as to briefly tackle institutionally the role of national identity and sovereignty in education. However, having begun such a task, it then had to embrace an educational programme integral to European confederacy.

The historical context of educational policy is important for invoking any national educational system. Allan Bloom's *The Closing of the American*

Mind relates the best kind of education, in the American context, to an embodiment of the founding documents of the nation: 'Over the history of our republic, there have obviously been changes of opinion as to what kind of man is best for our regime [...] Above all he was to know the rights doctrine; the Constitution, which embodied it; and American history' (Bloom, 2008:26–7). John Guillory also calls on the different pedagogical traditions embodied by Jacksonian and Jeffersonian political agendas in examining what he calls the 'failure' of general education in the 'American University' (2006:41). This raises the question of how a European initiative that has not yet finalized its own constitution is to negotiate the competing national discourses on education that mediate distinct notions of identity.

The general education course, if ever implemented in a unified manner across Europe, is one example of a popular humanities initiative that could be revealing of distinct differences in terms of national agendas in education. Guillory argues, in looking at the American University, that general education courses were first taught there as early as the 1920s and sought to promote, rather as Newman does, the education of the 'whole man' for 'general' as opposed to 'special' knowledge (Guillory, 2006:28). However, general education, what generally served up a 'lite' version of the 'literature, philosophy and art of the West' (Guillory, 2006:42) ultimately came to be 'elided with the humanities disciplines' and, in turn, drew the wrath of such cultural elitists as Irving Babbitt who, Guillory argues, wished to install 'sophisticated cultural credentials in the educated elite as the qualification of its right to rule' (Guillory, 2006:31). Guillory therefore sees general education as creating a new 'mass elite'. However, any claims made on behalf of general education in terms of 'democratization' were challenged by the fact that a 'culture of professionalism' (Guillory, 2006:36) and a more consumerist status hierarchy had replaced old school cultural capital as requisites for entry into the higher professional ranks. Ultimately, for Guillory, general education failed in the American University because the secondary school did not impart adequate cultural awareness that would allow the general education courses at the university to be anything more than 'remedial'. If Irish and European universities are to promote the general education course as the most popular expression of its shared humanities tradition, they will have to learn to accommodate this vibrant 'culture of professionalism'.

Irish educational theory will always struggle to ground its strategies on political and pedagogical discourses as influential as those invoked in the writings of Guillory, Derrida and Bourdieu. Whereas Derrida can inaugurate a college of philosophy in the presence of three government ministers referencing Rousseau and Bourdieu and whereas Guillory can debate educational initiatives by calling on Jackson, Jefferson and the 'two Blooms', Irish thought on education, despite the rich heritage, has a relatively short tradition in the philosophy of education against which to measure the claims of Bologna. The

Irish Government's White Papers on education only ever seem to translate rather than interrogate the dictates of Bologna. However, if we look closely at how our writers and academics value language and education, we can discover an equally rich tradition.

It cannot be denied that in a university climate where education is often regarded in terms of a Knowledge Factory (Aronowitz, 2000), a 'port to pillow ratio' (Slaughter and Rhoades, 2004) or a 'knowledge industry' (Irish White Paper), traditional notions of education, often inspired by those working in the humanities, are changing dramatically. As the metaphors for education borrow more readily from science and technology, the university itself shifts in this direction. Strident declamations of University Inc. are all the rage. Mary Gallagher argues in *Academic Armageddon* that the 'simplistic managerialist structures and controls put in place in order to embed the corporate order within Higher Education are incompatible with the intrinsic educational value of enlightenment as protective of human complexities' (2012:101). Tom Garvin argues that a 'grey philistinism' has descended on the 'public culture of the college' and that 'third-level education in Ireland went, in half a century, from the belief that higher education had nothing to do with economic development to the equally absurd assumption that higher education was about nothing except economic development' (2012). However, the Irish university is more vulnerable to ideological cajolery – especially when it helps fund the institutional squirm up the rankings ladder – precisely because it lacks a coherent philosophy of university education grounded on tradition with which to counter such corporate speak. Garvin notes how the Irish–American academic J. V. Kelleher warned in 1957 that a 'lack of intellectualism among Irish political leaders' was 'killing the country'. Ironically, it may now be that a similar lack of intellectualism among our state-funded academic managers is killing our universities. However, when Garvin suggests that the solution is to reinstate academics as the managers of universities, in deference to the kind of courses that keep our institutions afloat, one must ask whether they have the qualifications to manage? The management of the future of online education by way of the Khan Academy, the various edX online global university programmes and MOOCs also requires technological savvy that traditional humanities scholars will have to embrace not merely as technological know-how, but as the political, philosophical and cultural development in knowledge transfer that it represents. Recent European government initiatives on university education such as the 'Browne Report' or the 'Independent Review of Higher Education Funding and Student Finance'[1] in England published in October 2010 look to further erode humanities privileges. The Report advises that the UK government 'envisages targeted investment in priority subjects'. These priority subjects are clinical training subjects such as 'medicine and veterinary science' and 'technology and healthcare courses'. It argues for 'more dynamic funding' and for the removal of the 'blanket subsidy' to all institutions regardless of the courses they teach. This is justified by claiming that these measures, measures all humanities commentators believe, if implemented, will remove all government funding for arts and humanities research, are about 'safeguarding students' investment in higher education' (2010:45). Students are, therefore, regarded as investors before they have become earners, and the irony is that they must be seen as more committed investors because the other chief recommendations of the Browne Report involve the removal of the cap on university fees. The economic model applied to the universities is therefore a self-fulfilling prophecy. Universities will be forced to self-fund research programmes in the humanities. As Martin McQuillan, the co-founder of the London Graduate School, advises, 'Humanities departments in "elite universities" will only survive by piling students high and servicing them at low costs. The Browne Report does not set them free to compete with the world's best universities; it impoverishes them and turns all of the arts, humanities and social sciences in England into teaching-focused universities'.[2]

There is a precedent for how this privileging of teaching affects research. Alain Bienayme has argued that the French university's 'massive recruitment of teaching staff' in the 1970s and 1980s had a negative impact on research; the 'newly employed' staff became 'reluctant to devote much activity to doctoral research because it became clear that career prospects and opportunities for promotion in the grade of *Maître Assistant* and full Professor were very limited' (Bienayme, 1984:157). Irish universities, feeling the bite of austerity, will be forced to follow suit and may have pre-empted Browne's proposals on many fronts. Graham Allen writes in 2006 in relation to the Irish context that the National University of Ireland (NUI) has inherited an American rhetoric of scholarship and teaching. Even though he admits that the NUI has experienced an 'incredibly rapid process of modernization' since 1997, he argues that this modernization has also brought with it 'familiar features such as an exponentially expanding bureaucracy, a rhetoric and culture of Quality and Excellence, the establishment of performance-based criteria for funding and internal assessment, and the emergence of a pervasive logic I would figure in terms of the trope of transparency' (2006:12). This is compounded by the Irish university's increased dependence on staff on non-renewable and one-year contracts. Since a great many of the 1,293 PhD enrolments in Arts and Humanities for 2011/12 (an increase of 78% from 2005) – students who pay over €5,000 a year for library access and for the privilege to meet, however rarely, equally stressed academic supervisors – harbour thoughts of an academic career, it is perhaps no surprise that the university – to avoid another 'gentle revolution' – is eager to employ the very small number that it can on the shortest possible teaching contracts (Higher

Education Authority (HEA)). Many are also employed on a course-by-course or adjunct basis. Allen also argues that the resulting 'portfolio culture' in university teaching ends up '[p]rivileging a narrative and archivising (evidential) accounting of teaching over the scene of teaching itself, portfolio culture loses sight of the very thing it would prioritize' (Allen, 2006:5).

However, Europeanization has replaced the US and the UK educational models as perhaps the most influential force on the Irish university in recent years. It seems that the fluctuating gravitational pulls of these distinct power-houses of university governance rarely keep Irish university policy on a stable orbit. Donal Dineen's 1992 article on the Europeanization of the Irish universities argues that the 'old insular, inward looking approach' in Irish education can only be replaced through EU collaboration with a more 'outward dynamic and international outlook'. However, Dineen notes that Europeanization was often a 'drive' that was regarded as a threat to burgeoning 'national education systems' (Dineen, 1992:393). Dermot Scott also points out that '[e]ducation is felt to be close to the core of national identity and is sometimes a bastion of a particular language, culture or community' (in Dineen, 1992:393) and this was felt nowhere more strongly than in Ireland.

The Bologna Declaration of 1999 promotes a degree of public/private co-operation: it asks signatories to 'pursue the ways of intergovernmental co-operation together with those of non-governmental European organisations with competence in higher education', and it expects 'universities to contribute actively to the success of our endeavor'. Recent research on international education policy also notes that three scales of governance in education policy have emerged – subnational, national and supranational (Dale, 2005). The Bologna Process works on the supranational level, and yet despite this, Antonio Kupfer argues that national governments have 'retain[ed] power while operating in international settings' (2008:299). Kupfer argues that this is achieved despite great variations across the member states in terms of government budgetary allocations for education in the period since the 1960s through the implementation of new supranational and national practices such as 'soft law' and government delegation. Soft law describes an 'open method of co-ordination' accompanied by a 'target development and implementation' that is not legally binding (2008:287). Kupfer also argues that national governments working under such supranational guidelines and objectives 'tend to avoid responsibility for change by seemingly delegating their power' (2008:290). One might argue that elements of such thinking on delegation were evident in the Irish context in the 1997 Universities Act that granted greater autonomy to the constituent universities and in the creation of funding bodies such as the Irish Research Council for the Humanities and Social Sciences (IRCHSS) that essentially sustain research in the humanities in Irish universities.

However, the Irish public's sense of national identity was rarely aligned with those subjects in the university, namely, the humanities, that are seen by many, including Dineen, as grounding and fostering a society's self-understanding. Dineen argues in relation to Europeanization that '[u]niversities should be the conscience of society and are in danger of losing their role as the "esprit critique" of the social systems in which they reside' (1992:391). Whether the Irish universities, and in particular the humanities professors of these institutions, ever embodied what Irish society perceived as an 'esprit critique' is doubtful; however, the situation has changed somewhat since Irish universities began to keep students at university longer and increased the number of research positions. Séamas Ó Buachalla writes in 1992, in discussing the Irish state's move since the 1960s to adopt a 'more utilitarian' approach to education at both second and third levels, that '[a]lmost 30 years later it has not succeeded in shifting the curricular emphasis significantly towards subject areas which have greater relevance and employment poten-tial' (1992:76). In the 1990/91 academic year, 30.6% of all undergraduates were studying Arts. However, twenty years later, the HEA statistics on grad-uates would seem to show a slight shift towards the Social Sciences, Busi-ness and Law sector. The figures for 'degrees obtained' in Arts and Humanities in 2004 and 2005 were 27% and 28%, respectively, of total degrees obtained. However, this had fallen to 23% by 2010 with the figure for degrees obtained in Business, Social Sciences and Law rising to 28%. It seems that the 'ration-alization' measures have begun to take effect (Ó Buachalla, 1992:76). Irish society might be slow to accept directives with the Europeanization tag; however, when one is unemployed, 'rationalization' can appear far more beneficial than further romanticization.

Jeroen Huisman and Marijk Van der Wende paint a much less benevolent picture of the motivations for internationalization and Europeanization in educational policy. They read between the lines of the 1992 Maastricht Treaty in arguing that 'whereas higher education was previously accredited a national and cultural role, the economic rationale became more and more important'. They argue that it was recognized that 'national views on the role of higher education gradually grew closer – not necessarily intentionally – to the European Community (EC)'s perspective'. The reason for this was not always grounded on the founding humanistic principles of Bologna University or on anything approaching Newman's vision for the university. Huisman and Van der Wende argue that 'the economic rationale became even more dominant in the context of globalization where the mar-ket for transnational supply [in education] was estimated to have an annual value of 30 billion US dollars in 1999 and expected to be a growth market' (2004:22). They argue that even though 'large amounts of financial support were given for research and development projects', the 'supranational support was negligible compared to the national support for research'. It was at the level of 'individual higher education institutions' that EC support was often 'quite substantial' (2004:352). This might explain the greater degree of freedom evident in arts and humanities programmes in the Irish universities since the 1990s with more course choices being offered than ever before. They also argue that the 'relative vagueness' of the wording of the Bologna documents also gives national governments a great deal of latitude in terms of interpretation and implementation. However, there are areas of concern. The most pressing of these is related to the 'cultural rationale for internationalisation' (2004:353). This debate becomes particularly heated in countries with a minority language such as Ireland; such countries 'question the pressure to use a majority language' such as English. Despite the fact that in Ireland, there is a core group that questions this cultural rationale, it is no longer viable to claim that this is because education should be in Irish. Huisman and Van der Wende argue that the language question is of particular importance in Germany where critics fear that too much of a concentration on English will lead to a 'loss of cultural heritage' (2004:355) and, once again, this may still be valid in Ireland. However, Huisman and Van der Wende are perhaps right when they claim that more 'political turmoil' can be expected when it comes to implementing supranational 'quality assurance mechanisms' and 'accreditation' (2004:356). The supranational ideology that strives to harmonize educational polices so as to enhance collaboration between institutions is also not dissimilar to the 'league table' perspective on universities. The fundamental criteria for the 'league table' approach can only be met once there is a certain degree of harmonization. However, it is likely that national government autonomy and university autonomy will come to exert themselves should these quality assurance and accreditation initiatives prove too invasive.

If we see these accreditation models as typically driven by methodologies more applicable to the natural sciences, then Kwame Anthony Appiah's recent argument on cosmopolitanism and value is relevant. He argues that 'the methods of the natural sciences have not led to the kind of progress in our understanding of values that they have led to in our grasp of the facts. So we might be able to learn about values from societies where science is less deeply implanted than in ours: if scientific method has not advanced our understanding of values, then its superiority offers no reason to suppose that our understanding of values is superior' (2007:43). It is an argument that Irish university presidents should keep in mind when European initiatives impose supranational educational policies that describe the educational community, and the educational 'conversation', to borrow a term from Appiah, in terms of metaphors such as the 'knowledge industry' borrowed from scientific models. In following Appiah's logic, it is in those national educational environments where the scientific model is not wholly pervasive and where the humanities are somewhat independent that an education in values can truly be found.

The Irish government's most recent policy document on education in Ireland, the 'National Strategy for Higher Education to 2030', or the 'Hunt Report', is perhaps less scientific in its treatment of education than were previous White Papers. However, it still stresses the need for education to be perceived in terms of its economic potential; it speaks of the need to rebuild through education 'an innovate knowledge-based economy that will provide sustainable employment opportunities and good standards of living for all our citizens' (Higher Education Authority 2011:9). It goes further than other policy documents in arguing that '[h]igher education is central to the economic renewal we need to support individual well-being and social development' (Higher Education Authority 2011:9). Economic well-being has become perhaps the most important factor for 'individual well-being' in Irish government documents on education. Of course, this in itself presumes a distinct philosophical perspective; however, the Irish government is hardly alone in promoting such a view of identity in an age of consumerism. Nevertheless, when the policy document asserts that Ireland's economic 'recovery' relies on the creation and enhancement of 'human capital by expanding participation in higher education' (Higher Education Authority 2011:10), the philosophy of education begins to assume a more reductive tone. The document specifies that the phrase 'Human Capital' (Higher Education Authority 2011:69) is being used in line with a discourse on education that is promoted by the US Council of Graduate Schools, a Council that takes a distinctly utilitarian stance on education where 'the ultimate product of graduate education is a knowledgeable, productive, and innovative worker' (Higher Education Authority 2011:69). That such a corporate perspective on higher education would ultimately privilege the production of the 'worker' suggests that the education industry has ensured that capitalist forms of reification now unashamedly deploy even Marxist language to further market-driven ends. However, the National Strategy document continues by arguing that Ireland's 'knowledge economy' must ensure the reproduction of a new 'Irish PhD brand' (Higher Education Authority 2011:72) of high-skilled workers in order to compete and survive. Whether this 'high-skilled' worker of Ireland's twenty-first-century knowledge economy is any different to Marx's nineteenth-century manufacturing 'worker' in terms of access to the means of production, high-skilled or otherwise, remains unclear.

Thomas Docherty has also related this utilitarian vision of the university with its, in his opinion, Protestant capitalist underpinnings, back to the vision of the university put forward by Newman. Docherty aligns Alain Badiou's recent account of universality in Paul with the scope and vision of the university as outlined by Newman, a vision of the university that successive 'national governments' of 'every political hue' have, in Docherty's opinion, failed to honour. Docherty argues that Newman's Catholic University is one that wishes to 'circumvent the economics of business and to place before us the possibility of a different kind of social order, one based on a *universalism* that he equates with Catholicism' (2004:92). He goes on to argue that

> In the end, we would have to say that we have failed to fulfill Newman's idea of a University. The University, in most contemporary instances, is 'Protestant' through and through, in that its universalizing idea, its capacity for a globalization based on the diseconomy of grace, has been entirely and thoroughly betrayed by national governments of every political hue. Those governments see the University simply as an arm of national capital and thus use the institution precisely as a weapon in the further Americanization of the world's economy. In this state of affairs, the only possible outcome is further global inequality, both political and economic. Perhaps it is time to reconsider the possibility of an ethical globalization, such as that called for by Mary Robinson, in terms of the establishment of a University whose scope and ambit will be, genuinely, universal. (2004:92)

While it might seem foolhardy today to ground the university on anything like a 'diseconomy of grace', the unquestioned justification of higher education in terms of models of human capital and in terms of the economic trajectory of national governments should not lead us to forget that this is, at least historically, only one version of the role of the university. If it is to be debated anywhere in contemporary society, then it is the humanities that should take the lead in examining how political and sociological values can influence education policy.

The National Strategy document does acknowledge that there have been significant developments in regard to the funding and government assessment of the Arts and Humanities subjects in Ireland. The Humanities Serving Irish Society (HSIS) and the arts, humanities and social sciences (AHSS) are two recent bodies the National Strategy document commends in arguing that 'we embrace the arts, humanities and social sciences as well as science, technology, engineering and mathematics'. These disciplines should be embraced because, the document argues, the AHSS subjects are of 'fundamental importance to society – areas that impact on enterprise, job creation and public policy. In the Irish context, these disciplines study values and practices that are central to our national identity, our sense of self, and to how we progress as a society' (Higher Education Authority 2011:72). However, once again the economic perspective is privileged; these subjects are seen as 'important drivers of economic and social innovation, [they] promote ways in which the economy is managed and developed, and [they] suggest how individuals can engage and participate in civil society' (Higher Education Authority 2011:67). In looking for the positives in the Report from a humanities perspective, the

Report does acknowledge that the humanities subjects help promote 'civil society'; however, any guiding philosophy in the Report for such a civil society only takes us back to the economy.

The IRCHSS[3] and the future of the humanities in Ireland

The IRCHSS revolutionized graduate work in the humanities in the Irish universities. In 2002, when this writer was completing PhD studies at the University College Cork (UCC) English department, only approximately eighteen records for completed English PhD dissertations spanning the entire history of the department could be found in the library archives. However, between 2000, when the IRCHSS was established, and 2012, there have been thirty-five PhDs completed at the same department, and the majority of these were funded by the IRCHSS. The IRCHSS created a culture and community of research in Irish universities that did not exist prior to its establishment.[4] It arose partially because, as the initial submission for the Council states, it had been 'difficult to develop comprehensive and effective institutional policies on research' prior to 1999. Therefore, the Report to the Minister of 1999 recommends breaking up the government block grant for universities into 'two component parts: research and teaching' (8). It funds 'cutting-edge research in the humanities, social sciences, business and law with the objective of creating new knowledge and expertise beneficial to Ireland's economic, social and cultural development'. It also embodies the objectives of the Bologna Accord in creating a unified 'Europe of knowledge'; the IRCHSS is a member of the European Science Foundation, and it is a coordinator and partner in four of the European Commission's FP7 (Seventh Framework Programme) research initiatives. The mission of the IRCHSS includes encouraging 'excellence and the highest standards in the humanities and social sciences', encouraging 'co-operation between the humanities and social sciences' and supporting 'research and promo[ting] interdisciplinary collaboration'. It must also be acknowledged that the establishment of such a body was long overdue especially given the amount of funding bodies for the Arts and Humanities in the United States and the UK.[5]

The IRCHSS defines the humanities 'for the purposes of the Bilateral agreement between the IRCHSS and the AHRC' [...] in relation to 'research and practice-based research, in the subjects: Archaeology, Art History, Celtic Studies, Classics, Cultural Studies, English Language and Literature, Film Studies, Gender Studies, History, Languages, Law, Linguistics, Literature, Media Studies, Musicology, Philosophy, Theatre Studies, and Theology'.[6] However, there has been a significant decrease in IRCHSS support for postgraduate (doctoral) support in recent years. In 2001, 175 postgraduate fellowships were awarded for doctoral-level research. For the 2006/7, 2010/11 and 2011/12 academic years, this figure had fallen to 94, 92 and 101, respectively. The percentage of awards made out of total applications has also fallen dramatically in recent years. For the academic years 2007/8 and 2008/9, the ratios of applications to awards made were 365:124 (34%) and 461:153 (33%), respectively. The figures for 2010/11 and 2011/12 were 625:92 (15%) and 537:101 (19%). While some of this decrease in support can undoubtedly be put down to Ireland's economic downturn, it is important that the success rates do not fall further.

Two other significant developments in the humanities in recent years in the Irish university have been new directions in gender studies and feminism and in the digital humanities. Gerardine Meaney and Eibhear Walshe have been central to the development of gender studies as one of the most vibrant subjects in the humanities and social sciences in Irish universities in recent years. Meaney returns to neglected writers in the Irish tradition, typically women writers like Rosamond Jacob and Kate O'Brien, in arguing that there is 'evidence of a social and cultural context, far from the centre of power in Irish political and social life' that 'even at the height of social and sexual repression in Ireland bred dissident fictions', but that this context 'has never featured in political, social or cultural histories of the period' (2004:72). The digital humanities is also a field that Irish universities have embraced. Even though its form is diverse, it is generally regarded as a kind of 'scholarship and pedagogy' that is 'publicly visible', dependent on 'networks of people' and 'bound up with infrastructure in ways that are deeper and more explicit than we are generally accustomed to' (Kirschenbaum, 2012:9). An embrace of such research aims and initiatives is vital if the humanities subjects are to realize the full potential of the recent developments in information technology and knowledge transfer.

Despite a marked shift towards the sciences in recent years, even in the IRCHSS partnerships and initiatives, the role of the humanities in fostering civic morality, social harmony and creative thinking cannot be overlooked. The IRCHSS would appear to recognize the need for the humanities to figure more in public life. In 2011, it launched its IRCHSS ten lecture series (to commemorate its tenth anniversary year) giving the series the title 'The Public Intellectual'. The second lecture in this series was given by Martha Nussbaum, and it was entitled 'Not for Profit: Why Democracy Needs the Humanities'.[7] Nussbaum's argument is one that this book shares to a degree. Humanities advocacy, as it is now called, should not only be based on a sense of injustice before research funding bodies; it should also not only be about reinvigorating, or establishing, interdisciplinarity between theology, religious studies, the sciences and philosophy in the curriculum. It should be about investing future generations of students with a sense of civic morality, a creative imagination and a critical regard for the disinterested, nonevaluative embrace of human potential in all its democratic, spiritual and ethical dimensions. While it is true that it is in the survey course or general education course that the majority of students encounter the shrill democratizing claims of the humanities professor and while also it is true, as John Guillory points out, that many of these courses 'tend to be exaggerated or misidentified by taking at face value the grand rationales that support these programs', the crisis debate in the humanities would not have run for so long if the humanities did not impart a kind of knowledge that spoke for values students care about. Guillory also notes that it is both 'egregious and desperate' for educationalists to ground 'exalted claims' for such courses about how they educate 'citizens for participation in democracy' on 'clumsy ideological moves' that read 'the tradition of Western culture' only through the lenses of 'American democracy' (2006:36). Such claims will only become more problematic as the humanities moves away from a focus on the American model. However, as Martha Nussbaum argues, sometimes exalted claims are necessary especially at a time when a 'new conception' has emerged in education, one that focuses on profit and that is 'sidelining the whole idea of imaginative and critical self-development' (2010:3).

However, it is when Nussbaum returns the discussion of the humanities to a concentration on the notion of 'soul' (2010:6) and when she argues that European and Asian universities do not share America's 'liberal arts system' and, therefore, have 'no secure place in the structure of undergraduate education' for 'new disciplines of particular importance for good democratic citizenship' (2010:126) that we detect perhaps a hint of the national education bias that Guillory alludes to above. Nussbaum argues that the word 'soul' has 'religious connotations' and that she 'neither insist[s] on these nor reject[s] them' (2010:6). She then takes 'soul', as a privileged term for understanding the humanities, to describe 'the faculties of thought and imagination that make us human and make our relationships rich human relationships, rather than relationships of mere use and manipulation' (2010:6). However, as the power dynamic in academic capitalism shifts towards the Asian university, there is also a shift in emphasis in terms of what constitutes humanistic enquiry. This shift is largely driven at the moment in many leading Asian universities by a Chinese perspective that incorporates Confucianism, Daoism and other important Asian philosophies and practices. This tradition has a very different understanding of the aspect of the person aligned with the 'soul' (not to mention 'manipulation'). Nussbaum's work has always taken its understanding of such concepts from Greek philosophy and in particular from Aristotle. One of the central concepts in ancient Chinese philosophy *te* (what is used interchangeably with *jen* in Confucius) is described by Xinzhong Yao as 'both the power of humanity and the seed that can grow into full humanity' (Yao, 1997:140). *Li* (propriety or moral codes) and *jen* (benevolence) are important concepts for the Chinese tradition. Confucius advises that 'to control oneself and return to *li* is the way to *jen*' (in Yao, 1997:141). Placed beside these virtues or naturalistic moral guides, 'soul' may seem a far too abstract notion on which to base a programme of education. At any rate, this is the reaction I get to such western philosophical notions as 'self' and 'soul' in my classes in Hong Kong. However, it must be acknowledged that the IRCHSS has transformed the humanities in the Irish university, and in conjunction with the Irish universities, most of which have now established centres for Chinese studies, it also seems to be conscious of the need to impart to Irish students a greater awareness of the Asian perspective. However, the need to impart a greater awareness of the Asian humanities to students of Irish universities should not be held up as an excuse for Irish universities' recent love affair with the Confucius Institute. As Mary Gallagher argues, other cultural institutes in Ireland such as the Goethe and Alliance Française institutes are 'entirely independent of universities' (2012:180). Irish universities should be mindful of the fact that none of the US Ivy League universities appear to have invited Confucius Institutes on campus and of the claims of the petition to the parliament of New South Wales in Australia that called on the government to remove the 'Confucius classroom' from its region because, it argued, the 'teaching of Chinese language and culture [...] should be available free from the influence of Chinese Communist Party doctrine' (Gallagher, 2012:183).

In concluding, one must recall, once again, that the Irish people have a rich tradition in education and learning. As we have seen, Douglas Hyde traces the tradition back to the monastic culture that illuminated Europe with a 'torch of learning' (1901:214), and Joyce reminds us through Leopold Bloom that the soul of a people perhaps like the soul of a person 'is wafted over regions of cycles of cycles of generations that have lived' (1992:541). The humanities is a discipline that despite any 'potentially misleading ideology' it has earned will most likely not get the 'new name' Jonathan Culler calls for (Culler, 2005:42); it has always examined human culture and human values, and students may still want to believe that the human it speaks for knows no division or disciplinary boundary. While the institutions charged with imparting these truths and values might drape them occasionally in the national colours, the humanities will always speak for the unlimited potential for the open exchange of ideas on spiritual, ethical and aesthetic states unique to human enquiry. The humanities will continue to inspire and enthuse precisely because when they are taught well, they embody humanity's gift of wonder as self-reflection, a gift that will always call us back in awe to ourselves and the human.

Notes

1 See www.bis.gov.uk/.../10-1208-securing-sustainable-higher-education.
2 www.thelondongraduateschool.co.uk/thoughtpiece/if-you-tolerate-this%E2%
   80%A6-lord-browne-and-the-privatisation-of-the-humanities/.

3 The IRCHSS merged with the IRCSET (Irish Research Council for Science, Engineering and Technology) to form the IRC (Irish Research Council) in March 2012. There is now no stand-alone Irish government research funding body for the humanities and social sciences. Competition for PhD and postdoctoral research funding will now be even more competitive. Since the government has privileged the creation of a 'knowledge industry', it is highly likely that many valuable research applications in the humanities and social sciences will lose out to applications in science, engineering and technology in the years ahead.

4 The Irish HEA's steering committees on research reported in 2007 that 'Ireland is still some way behind other developed nations competing and collaborating in international research programmes' (Higher Education Authority 2007:11).

5 In the United States, the university research funding bodies include the National Association of Scholars, the National Endowment for the Humanities (NEH), the National Humanities Center, The Andrew W. Mellon Foundation and the American Council of Learned Societies, while in the UK, there is the Leverhulme Trust, the Wellcome Trust and the Arts and Humanities Research Council, to name but a selection that support the humanities.

6 See www.irchss.ie/aboutus/irchss-subject-areas.

7 This lecture took place on 18 March 2011 in St. Anne's Church, Dawson Street, Dublin. This was also the title of a book Nussbaum published in 2010.

Bibliography

Official documents

Bologna Process. Joint declaration of the European Ministers of Education convened in Bologna on the 19 June 1999.

——. *The Bologna Declaration* on the European space for higher education: an explanation, 29 February 2000.

——. 'Realising the European Higher Education Area'. Communiqué of the Conference of Ministers Responsible for Higher Education, Berlin, 19 September 2003.

——. 'The European Higher Education Area – Achieving the Goals'. Communiqué of the Conference of Ministers Responsible for Higher Education, Bergen, 19–20 May 2005.

Downey, Liam. 'Creating Ireland's Innovation Society: The Next Strategic Step – Attracting and Retaining World Class Researchers'. Dublin: Higher Education Authority, 2003.

Higher Education Authority. 'The Humanities and the Social Sciences: A Case for a Research Council'. A Report to the Minister for Education and Science. Rapporteur: Dr. Maurice J. Bric, November 1999.

——. *Towards a National Strategy: Initial Review of HEA Targeted Initiatives to Widen Access to Higher Education*, 2004.

——. *Who Went to College in 2004? A National Survey of New Entrants to Higher Education*, 2006.

——. 'Research Infrastructure in Ireland: Building for Tomorrow'. Dublin: Higher Education Authority, 2007. www.forfas.ie/publications/forfas061221/forfas061221_research_infrastructure_final_dec_2006.pdf.

——. 'National Strategy for Higher Education to 2030'. Dublin: Higher Education Authority, 2011.

OECD. 'Reviews of National Policies for Education'. Higher Education in Ireland, 2006.

——. *Education at a Glance 2007: OECD Indicators*, 2007.

——. 'Tertiary Education Entry Rates'. *Education: Key Tables from OECD*, 2010. No. 3. doi: 10.1787/20755120-2010-table2.

'Securing a Sustainable Future for Higher Education: An Independent Review of Higher Education Funding and Student Finance', 12 October 2010. www.independent.gov.uk/browne-report.

The National University of Ireland. 'Act of Parliament, Charter and Statutes'. Dublin: Printed for the National University by Alex Thom & Co., 1920.

Universities Act, 1997. Conference of Heads of Irish Universities, 2003.

Books and articles

Agamben, Giorgio. *Homo Sacer: Sovereign Power and Bare Life*. Trans. Daniel Heller-Roazen (Stanford: Stanford University Press, 1998).

Allen, Graham. 'Transparent Universities, Foreign Bodies'. *Oxford Literary Review*, 28 (2006), 5–17.

Appiah, Kwame Anthony. *Cosmopolitanism* (London: Penguin, 2007).

Aronowitz, Stanley. *The Knowledge Factory: Dismantling the Corporate University and Creating True Higher Education* (Boston: Beacon Press, 2000).

Atkinson, Norman. 'The Educational Ideas of Patrick Pearse, 1879–1916'. *Comparative Education Review*, 11:1 (February 1967), 68–74.

Augusteijn, Joost. *Patrick Pearse: The Making of a Revolutionary* (London: Palgrave, 2010).

Austin, J. L. *How to Do Things with Words*. 2nd Rev. Ed. (Oxford: Clarendon Press, 1975).

Barr, Colin. *Paul Cullen, John Henry Newman, and the Catholic University of Ireland 1845–1865* (Notre Dame: University of Notre Dame Press, 2003).

Barrington, Ruth. 'Terrible Beauty or Celtic Mouse? The Research Agenda in Ireland'. *New Hibernia Review*, 6:3 (2002), 138–50.

Beckett, Samuel. *Complete Poems in English and French* (New York: Grove, 1977).

——. *Collected Poems 1930–1978* (London: John Calder, 1999).

Bell, David A. 'Reimagining the Humanities: Proposals for a New Century'. *Dissent*, 57:4 (Fall 2010), 69–75.

Bhabha, Homi K. *The Location of Culture* (London: Routledge, 1994).

Bienayme, Alain. 'The New Reform in French Higher Education'. *European Journal of Education*, 19:2 (1984), 151–64.

Bloom, Allan. *The Closing of the American Mind* (New York: Simon and Schuster, 2008).

Bok, Derek. *Universities in the Marketplace: The Commercialization of Higher Education* (Princeton: Princeton University Press, 2004).

Bourdieu, Pierre. *Homo Academicus* (Paris: Les Editions de Minuit, 1984).

——. *Homo Academicus*. Trans. Peter Collier (Stanford: Stanford University Press, 1988).

——. *Language and Symbolic Power* (London: Polity, 1992).

——. *The Rules of Art: Genesis and Structure of the Literary Field* (London: Polity, 1996).

Bourdieu, Pierre and Jean-Claude Passeron. *Reproduction: In Education, Society and Culture* (London: Sage, 1977).

Bousquet, Marc. *How the University Works: Higher Education and the Low-Wage Nation* (New York: New York University Press, 2008).

Brock, Colin and Withold Tulasiewicz. Eds. *Education in a Single Europe* (London: Routledge, 2000).

Carrol, Claire and Patricia King, Eds. *Ireland and Postcolonial Theory* (Notre Dame: University of Notre Dame Press, 2003).

Chodorow, Nancy. *The Reproduction of Mothering: Psychoanalysis and the Sociology of Gender*. Updated Ed. (Berkeley: University of California Press, 1999).

Clarke, Desmond M. *Church and State: Essays in Political Philosophy* (Cork: Cork University Press, 1985).

Collini, Stefan. *What Are Universities For?* (London: Penguin, 2012).

Connolly, Claire, Ed. *Theorizing Ireland* (London: Palgrave, 2003).

Coolahan, John. '75 Years of the NUI'. *The Irish Times*, Thursday, 28 July 1983, p. 8.

Corish, Patrick J. *Maynooth College 1795–1995* (Dublin: Gill & Macmillan, 1995).

Corkery, Daniel. *The Hidden Ireland: A Study of Gaelic Munster in the Eighteenth Century* (Dublin: Gill & Macmillan, 1984).

Culler, Jonathan D. '"In Need of a Name," A Response to Geoffrey Harpham on The Crisis of the Humanities'. *New Literary History*, 36:1 (Winter 2005), 37–42.

Dale, R. 'Globalisation, Knowledge Economy and Comparative Education'. *Comparative Education*, 41:2 (2005), 117–49.

Davie, Donald. 'Reflections of an English Writer in Ireland'. *Studies: An Irish Quarterly Review*, 44:176 (Winter 1955) 439–45.

De Man, Paul. *Allegories of Reading: Figural Language in Rousseau, Nietzsche, Rilke and Proust* (New Haven: Yale University Press, 1979a).

——. 'Shelley Disfigured'. *Deconstruction and Criticism*. Ed. Harold Bloom, Paul de Man, Jacques Derrida, J. Hillis Miller and Geoffrey Hartman (New York: Continuum, 1979b), 39–73.

De Saussure, Ferdinand. *Cours de linguistique générale*. Pour les notes et commentaires de Tullio de Mauro, Laterza (Paris: Éditions Payot & Rivages, 1931 & 1967).

Deane, Seamus. 'Education, Freedom and the Teaching of Literature'. *The Black Book*. Ed. Richard Kearney and Barré Fitzpatrick (Dublin: Talbot Press, 1975).

——. 'General Introduction'. *The Field Day Anthology of Irish Writing*. Vol. 1. Ed. Seamus Deane (Derry: Field Day Publications, 1991), xix–xxvi.

——. *Strange Country: Modernity and Nationhood in Irish Writing since 1790* (Oxford: Oxford University Press, 1999).

——. 'Heroic Styles: The Tradition of an Idea'. *Theorizing Ireland* (London: Palgrave, 2003), 14–26.

Deleuze, Gilles. *Nietzsche and Philosophy*. Trans. Hugh Tomlinson (New York: Columbia University Press, 2006).

Derrida, Jacques. *Speech and Phenomena: And Other Essays on Husserl's Theory of Signs*. Trans. and Introduction. David B. Allison (Evanston: Northwestern University Press, 1973).

——. 'The Principle of Reason: The University in the Eyes of Its Pupils'. Trans. Catherine Porter and Edward P. Morris. *Diacritics*, 13:3 (1983a), 3–21.

——. *Dissemination*. Trans. Barbara Johnson (Chicago: University of Chicago Press, 1983b).

——. *Of Grammatology*. Trans. Gayatri Chakravorty Spivak. Corrected Ed. (Baltimore: The Johns Hopkins University Press, 1998).

——. *L'Université sans condition* (Paris: Galilée, 2001).

——. 'Privilege: Justificatory Title and Introductory Remarks'. *Who's Afraid of Philosophy? Right to Philosophy 1*. Ed. Werner Hamacher and David E. Welbery (Stanford: Stanford University Press, 2002a), 1–66.

——. 'Where a Teaching Body Begins and How It Ends'. *Who's Afraid of Philosophy? Right to Philosophy 1*. Ed. Werner Hamacher and David E. Welbery (Stanford: Stanford University Press, 2002b), 67–98.

——. *Acts of Religion*. Ed. Gil Anidjar (London: Routledge, 2002c).

——. *Eyes of the University: Right to Philosophy 2*. Ed. Werner Hamacher and David E. Welbery (Stanford: Stanford University Press, 2004a).

——. 'Mochlos, or the Conflict of the Faculties'. *Eyes of the University: Right to Philosophy 2*. Ed. Werner Hamacher and David E. Welbery (Stanford: Stanford University Press, 2004b), 83–112.

——. 'Vacant Chair: Censorship, Mastery, Magisteriality'. *Eyes of the University: Right to Philosophy 2*. Ed. Werner Hamacher and David E. Welbery (Stanford: Stanford University Press, 2004c), 43–63.

Dewey, John. *Moral Principles in Education* (New York: Houghton Mifflin Company, 1909).

——. *Experience and Education* (New York: Collier, 1938).

——. *On Education: Selected Writings*. Ed. Reginald D. Archambault (Chicago: University of Chicago Press, 1974).

——. *How We Think* (New York: Dover Publications, 1997).

Dineen, Donal A. 'Europeanisation of Irish Universities'. *Higher Education*, 24:3 (October 1992), 391–411.

Docherty, Thomas. 'Newman, Ireland, and University'. *Boundary 2*, 31:1 (Spring 2004), 73–94.

Donoghue, Denis. 'Notes Toward a Critical Method: Language as Order'. *Studies: An Irish Quarterly Review*, 44:174 (Summer 1955), 181–92.

——. 'The English Dickens and *Dombey and Son*'. *Nineteenth-Century Fiction*, 24:4 (March 1970), 383–403 (The Charles Dickens Centennial).

——. 'The American Style of Failure'. *The Sewanee Review*, 82:3 (Summer 1974), 407–32.

——. *The Sovereign Ghost: Studies in Imagination* (Berkeley: University of California Press, 1976).

——. *Reading America: Essays on American Literature* (Berkeley: University of California Press, 1988).

——. 'Teaching Literature: The Force of Form'. *New Literary History*, 30:1 (1999), 5–24.

——. 'The S. T. Lee Lecture in the Humanities – Joyce, Leavis, and the Revolution of the Word'. *Bulletin of the American Academy of Arts and Sciences*, 57:2 (Winter 2004), 12–20.

——. *Irish Essays* (Cambridge, MA.: Cambridge University Press, 2011).

Duddy, Thomas. *A History of Irish Thought* (New York: Routledge, 2002).

Dunne, Tom and John Coolahan. *The National University of Ireland 1908–2008: Centenary Essays* (Dublin: University College Dublin Press, 2008).

Eco, Umberto. *The Search for the Perfect Language* (London: Fontana, 1997).

Edwards, Ruth Dudley Edwards. *Patrick Pearse: The Triumph of Failure* (Dublin: Irish Academic Press, 2006).

Eliot, T. S. 'Tradition and the Individual Talent'. *Selected Prose of T.S. Eliot* (London: Faber & Faber, 1975), 37–44.

Ellmann, Richard. *James Joyce* (Oxford: Oxford University Press, 1972).

Farren, Sean. *The Politics of Irish Education 1920–1965* (Belfast: Belfast Institute of Irish Studies, Queen's University of Belfast, 1995).

Finnis, John. *Aquinas: Moral, Political, and Legal Theory* (Oxford: Oxford University Press, 1998).

Fitzgerald, Garret. 'Concluding Commentary: Religion and Politics at the Turn of the Millennium'. *Religion and Politics in Ireland at the Turn of the Millennium*. Ed. James P. Mackey and Enda McDonagh (Dublin: The Columba Press, 2003).

——. 'Foreword'. *The National University of Ireland 1908–2008: Centenary Essays*. Ed. Tom Dunne and John Coolahan (Dublin: University College Dublin Press, 2008), i–xviii.

Flannery, Eóin. *Ireland and Postcolonial Studies: Theory, Discourse, Utopia* (London: Palgrave, 2009).

Fluck, Winfried. 'Resistance! Cultural Studies and the Question of Cultural Change'. *The Yearbook of Research in English and American Literature*. Vol. 20 (Tübingen: Verlag, 2005), 11–26.

Foster, R. F. *Modern Ireland 1600–1972* (London: Penguin, 1989).

——. *Luck and the Irish: A Brief History of Change, 1970–2000* (London: Penguin, 2008).

Gadamer, Hans-Georg. *Truth and Method*. Rev. Ed. (New York: Continuum, 1995).

Gallagher, Mary. *Academic Armageddon: An Irish Requiem for Higher Education* (Dublin: The Liffey Press, 2012).

Garvin, Tom. 'The Bleak Future of the Irish University'. *The Irish Times*, Tuesday, 1 May 2012.

Gibbons, Luke. 'From Celtic Twilight to Celtic Tiger'. Keynote Address at the Annual JASIL, Shinwa Women's University, Kobe, Japan, 26 October 2007.

Glendinning, Dympna. 'Recent Developments in Education in Ireland'. *European Journal for Education Law and Policy*, 2 (1998), 79–83.

Grafton, Anthony and Lisa Jardine. *From Humanism to the Humanities; Education and the Liberal Arts in Fifteenth and Sixteenth-Century Europe* (Cambridge, MA.: Harvard University Press, 1986).

Graham, Colin. 'Liminal Spaces: Post-Colonial Theory and Irish Culture'. *The Irish Review*, 8 (1994), 29–43.

——. '"...maybe that's just Blarney": Irish Culture and the Persistence of Authenticity'. *Ireland and Cultural Theory: The Mechanics of Authenticity*. Ed. Colin Graham and Richard Kirkland (London: Macmillan, 1999), 6–28.

Graham, Colin and Richard Kirkland. *Ireland and Cultural Theory: The Mechanics of Authenticity* (London: St. Martin's Press, 1998).

Guillory, John. *Cultural Capital: The Problem of Literary Canon Formation* (Chicago: University of Chicago Press, 1994).

——. 'Who's Afraid of Marcel Proust: The Failure of General Education in the American University'. *The Humanities and the Dynamics of Inclusion since World War II*. Ed. David A. Hollinger (Baltimore: The Johns Hopkins University Press, 2006).

Hardt, Michael and Antonio Negri. *Commonwealth* (Cambridge, MA.: The Belknap Press of Harvard University Press, 2009).

Harpham, Geoffrey Galt. 'Beneath and Beyond the "Crisis in the Humanities"'. *New Literary History*, 36 (2005), 21–36.

——. *The Humanities and the Dream of America* (Chicago: University of Chicago Press, 2011).

Hayden, John. 'Funding Research in Institutions of Higher Learning in Ireland'. *New Hibernia Review*, 6:1 (2002), 138–45.

Hayward, Katy. *Irish Nationalism and European Integration: The Official Redefinition of the Island of Ireland* (Manchester: Manchester University Press, 2009).

Heaney, Seamus. *Government of the Tongue* (New York: Farrar, Straus & Giroux, 1990).

Heller, Donald E. 'State Oversight of Academia'. *Governing Academia*. Ed. Ronald G. Ehrenberg (Ithaca: Cornell University Press, 2004), 49–64.

Henry, Michel. *Entretiens* (Arles: Sulliver, 2005).

Higgins, Michael D. *Causes for Concern: Irish Politics, Culture and Society* (Dublin: Liberties Press, 2006).

Hilliard, Christopher. *English as a Vocation: The Scrutiny Movement* (Oxford: Oxford University Press, 2012).

Holbrook, Clyde A. *Religion, a Humanistic Field* (Englewood Cliffs: Prentice-Hall, Inc., 1963).

Horgan, John. 'School of Ecumenics Founded'. *The Irish Times*, Friday, 29 May 1970, p. 10.

Huisman, Jeroen and Marijk Van Der Wende. 'The EU and Bologna: Are Supra- and International Initiatives Threatening Domestic Agendas?' *European Journal of Education*, 39:3 (2004), 349–57.

Hyde, Douglas. *A Literary History of Ireland* (New York: Charles Scribner's Sons, 1901).

Ingelbien, Raphaël. 'Irish Studies, the Postcolonial Paradigm and the Comparative Mandate'. *Affecting Irishness: Negotiating Cultural Identity Within and Beyond the Nation*. Ed. James P. Byrne, Pádraig Kirwan and Michael O'Sullivan (Oxford: Peter Lang, 2009).

Irigaray, Luce. *This Sex Which Is Not One*. Trans. Catherine Porter with Carolyn Bourke (Ithaca: Cornell University Press, 1985).

——. *An Ethics of Sexual Difference* (London: Continuum, 2004).

Janicaud, Dominique, Jean-François Courtine, Jean-Louis Chrétien, Jean-Luc Marion, Michel Henry and Paul Ricœur. *Phenomenology and the 'Theological Turn': The French Debate* (New York: Fordham University Press, 2000).

Joyce, James. *Ulysses* (London: Penguin, 1992).

——. *A Portrait of the Artist as a Young Man* (Oxford: Oxford University Press, 2000a).

——. *Occasional, Critical, and Political Writing*. Ed. and Introduction. Kevin Barry (Oxford: Oxford University Press, 2000b).

Kafka, Franz. *The Collected Short Stories of Franz Kafka*. Ed. Nahum N. Glatzer. Trans. Willa Muir and Edwin Muir (London: Penguin, 1988).

Kant, Immanuel. *The Conflict of the Faculties*. Trans. and Introduction. Mary J. Gregor (London: University of Nebraska Press, 1979).

——. *The Critique of the Power of Judgment*. Trans. Paul Guyer and Eric Matthews (Cambridge, MA.: Cambridge University Press, 2000).

Kearney, Richard, Ed. *The Irish Mind: Exploring Intellectual Traditions* (Dublin: Wolfhound Press, 1985).

——. 'Challenging the Guarantee of Inevitable Progress'. *The Irish Times*, Wednesday, 30 December 1987a, p. 8.

——. 'Creatively Rethinking the Break-Up of the Nation State'. *The Irish Times*, Friday, 25 December 1987b, p. 8.

——. 'Our Evolving Culture Without Frontiers'. *The Irish Times*, Tuesday, 29 December 1987c, p. 9.

——. 'The Need to Become Cultural Citizens of Europe'. *The Irish Times*, Thursday, 31 December 1987d, p. 14.

——. *Transitions: Narratives in Modern Irish Culture* (Dublin: Wolfhound Press; Manchester: Manchester University Press, 1987e).

——. *Postnationalist Ireland: Politics, Culture, Philosophy* (London: Routledge, 1997).

——. *Anatheism: Returning to God after God* (New York: Columbia University Press, 2009).

Kearney, Richard and Barré Fitzpatrick, Eds. *The Black Book: On Third Level Education* (Dublin: Denam Press, 1977).

Kellaghan, Thomas. 'The Interface of Research, Evaluation, and Policy in Irish Education'. *Irish Educational Policy: Process and Substance*. Ed. D. G. Mulcahy and Denis O'Sullivan (Dublin: Institute of Public Administration, 1989), 191–218.

Keogh, Olive. 'Milltown Sheds Its Clerical Vestments'. *The Irish Times*, Tuesday, 3 May 1994, p. 34.

Kiberd, Declan. *Inventing Ireland* (Cambridge, MA.: Harvard University Press, 1995).

——. 'Joyce's Ellmann, Ellmann's Joyce'. *The Irish Writer and the World* (Cambridge, MA.: Cambridge University Press, 2005a), 235–49.

——. 'Museums and Learning'. *The Irish Writer and the World* (Cambridge, MA.: Cambridge University Press, 2005b), 219–34.

——. *The Irish Writer and the World* (Cambridge, MA.: Cambridge University Press, 2005c).

——. 'The War Against the Past'. *The Irish Writer and the World* (Cambridge, MA.: Cambridge University Press, 2005d), 158–90.

——. *Ulysses and Us: The Art of Everyday Living* (London: Faber & Faber, 2009).

Kinsella, Thomas. 'The Divided Mind'. *Irish Poets in English: The Thomas Davis Lectures on Anglo-Irish Poetry*. Ed. Seán Lucy (Cork: Mercier Press, 1973), 208–18.

Kirkland, Richard. 'Questioning the Frame: Hybridity, Ireland and the Institution'. *Ireland and Cultural Theory: The Mechanics of Authenticity* (London: Macmillan, 1999), 210–28.

Kirschenbaum, Matthew. 'What Is Digital Humanities and What's It Doing in English Departments?' *Debates in the Digital Humanities*. Ed. Matthew K. Gold (London: University of Minneapolis Press, 2012), 3–11.

Knight, Christopher J. *Uncommon Readers: Denis Donoghue, Frank Fermode, George Steiner, and the Tradition of the Common Reader* (Toronto: University of Toronto Press, 2003).

Kupfer, Antonio. 'National Power in European Educational Policy'. *British Journal of Educational Studies*, 56:3 (September 2008), 286–303.

Lacan, Jacques. *Écrits*. Trans. Bruce Fink (London: W. W. Norton & Company, 2006).

Lamoure Rontopoulou, Jeanne and Jean Lamoure. 'French University Education: A Brief Overview, 1984–1987'. *European Journal of Education*, 23:1/2 (1988), 37–45.

Leavis, F. R. 'Joyce and the "Revolution of the Word"'. *Scrutiny*, 2:2 (September 1933), 193–201.

——. 'The Literary Discipline and Liberal Education'. *The Sewanee Review*, 55:4 (October–December 1947), 586–609.

——. *Education and The University: A Sketch for an 'English School'* (London: Chatto & Windus, 1965).

——. *English Literature in Our Time and The University: The Clark Lectures 1967* (London: Chatto & Windus, 1967).

——. 'T. S. Eliot and the Life of English Literature'. *The Massachusetts Review*, 10:1 (Winter 1969), 9–34.

——. '"Believing in" the University'. *The Critic as Anti-Philosopher: Essays and Papers*. Ed. G. Singh (London: Chatto & Windus, 1982a), 171–85.

——. 'The "Great Books" and a Liberal Education'. *The Critic as Anti-Philosopher: Essays and Papers*. Ed. G. Singh (London: Chatto & Windus, 1982b), 156–70.

Lee, J. J. *Ireland 1912–1985: Politics and Society* (Cambridge, MA.: Cambridge University Press, 1989).

——. *The Modernisation of Irish Society 1848–1918* (Dublin: Gill & Macmillan, 2008).

Lee, Leo Ou-Fan. Keynote Speech for the Eighth Annual Meeting of the Asian New Humanities Net (ANHN), The Chinese University of Hong Kong, 15–16 October 2010.

Lennox, P. J. *The National University of Ireland. Printed from The Catholic University Bulletin*, XVI: 2, 89–112 and XVI:3, 223–65 (Washington, D.C.: The Catholic University of America Press, 1910).

Lévi-Strauss, Claude. *Structural Anthropology*. Vol. 2. Trans. Monique Layton (Chicago: University of Chicago Press, 1976).

——. *The View from Afar*. Trans. Joachim Neugroschel and Phoebe Hoss (Chicago: University of Chicago Press, 1992).

Lloyd, David. *Nationalism and Minor Literature: James Clarence Mangan and the Emergence of Irish Cultural Nationalism* (Berkeley: University of California Press, 1987).

Lucy, Seán. Ed. *Irish Poets in English: The Thomas Davis Lectures on Anglo-Irish Poetry* (Cork: Mercier Press, 1973).

Lynch, Kathleen. 'Carelessness: A Hidden Doxa of Higher Education'. *Arts and Humanities in Higher Education*, 9 (2010), 54–67.

Lynch, Kathleen and John Baker. 'Equality in Education: An Equality of Condition Perspective'. *Theory and Research in Education*, 2 (2005), 131–64.

MacIntyre, Alasdair. *God, Philosophy, Universities: A History of the Catholic Philosophical Tradition* (London: Continuum, 2009).

Mackey, James P. and Enda McDonagh. Eds. *Religion and Politics in Ireland at the Turn of the Millennium: Essays in Honour of Garret FitzGerald on the Occasion of His Seventy-fifth Birthday* (Dublin: The Columba Press, 2003).

Masterson, Patrick. 'Theology in the Universities'. *The Irish Times*, Thursday, 6 January 1969, p. 11.

McCartney, Donal. *UCD – A National Idea: The History of University College, Dublin* (Dublin: Gill & Macmillan, 1999).

McDowell, R. B. and D. A. Webb. *Trinity College Dublin 1592–1952: An Academic History* (Cambridge, MA.: Cambridge University Press, 1982).

McElligott, T. J. *Secondary Education in Ireland, 1870–1921* (Dublin: Irish Academic Press, 1981).

McGarry, Patsy. 'Catholic Institute of Theology May Be Established at Trinity'. *The Irish Times*, Monday, 22 December 2008, p. 3.

McNamara, Robert J. 'Catholics and Academia'. *Review of Religious Research*, 8:2 (Winter 1967), 81–95.

Meaney, Gerardine. 'Regendering Modernism: The Woman Artist in Irish Women's Fiction'. *Women: A Cultural Review*, 15:1 (2004), 67–82.

Menand, Louis. *The Metaphysical Club: A Story of Ideas in America* (New York: Farrar, Straus & Giroux, 2002).

——. *The Marketplace of Ideas: Reform and Resistance in the American University* (New York: W. W. Norton & Company, 2010).

Mercier, Vivian. 'An Irish School of Criticism?' *Studies: An Irish Quarterly Review*, 45:177 (Spring 1956), 84–7.

Mulcahy, Dónal. *Curriculum and Policy in Irish Post-Primary Education* (Dublin: Institute of Public Administration, 1981).

Mulcahy, D. G. and Denis O'Sullivan, Eds. *Irish Educational Policy: Process and Substance* (Dublin: Institute of Public Administration, 1989).

Murphy, John A. *The College: A History of Queen's/University College Cork 1845–1995* (Cork: Cork University Press, 1995).

Newman, John Henry. *The Idea of a University*. Ed. and Introduction. I. T. Ker (Oxford: Oxford University Press, 1976).

——. *Discourses on the Scope and Nature of University Education: Addressed to the Catholics of Dublin*. Cambridge Library Collection (Cambridge, MA.: Cambridge University Press, 2010).

Nietzsche, Friedrich. *Ecco Homo: How One Becomes What One Is* (London: Penguin, 2004).

Nussbaum, Martha. *Not for Profit: Why Democracy Needs the Humanities* (Princeton: Princeton University Press, 2010).

Ó Buachalla, Séamas. *A Significant Irish Educationalist: The Educational Writings of P. H. Pearse* (Dublin: Mercier Press, 1980).

——. *Education Policy in Twentieth Century Ireland* (Dublin: Wolfhound Press, 1988).

——. 'Self-Regulation and the Emergence of the Evaluative State: Trends in Irish Higher Education Policy 1987–1992'. *European Journal of Education*, 27:1/2 (1992), 69–78.

O'Connell, Rory. 'Theories of Religious Education in Ireland'. *Journal of Law and Religion*, 14:2 (1999–2000), 433–523.

O'Faolain, Sean. *The Irish* (London: Penguin, 1947).

O'Sullivan, Michael J. *Ireland and the Global Question* (Cork: Cork University Press, 2006).

Ó Tuama, Seán. 'Daniel Corkery, Cultural Philosopher, Literary Critic: A Memoir'. *Repossessions: Selected Essays on the Irish Literary Heritage* (Cork: Cork University Press, 1995a), 234–47.

——. *Repossessions: Selected Essays on the Irish Literary Heritage* (Cork: Cork University Press, 1995b).

——. 'Synge and the Idea of a National Literature'. *Repossessions: Selected Essays on the Irish Literary Heritage* (Cork: Cork University Press, 1995c), 219–33.

Odin, Jaishree K. and Peter T. Manikas, Eds. *Globalization and Higher Education* (Honolulu: University of Hawaii Press, 2004).

Ortega y Gasset, José. *Mission of the University*. Trans. Howard Lee Nostrand (London: Kegan Paul, 1946).

Parkes, Susan M. 'Higher Education, 1793–1908'. *A New History of Ireland VI: Ireland Under the Union, II 1870–1921*. Ed. W. E. Vaughan, Royal Irish Academy (Oxford: Oxford University Press, 2010), 539–70.

Pearse, Pádraig H. *Political Writings and Speeches* (Dublin: Talbot Press, 1952a).

——. 'The Murder Machine'. *Political Writings and Speeches* (Dublin: Talbot Press, 1952b), 5–52.

Pedersen, Olaf. *The First Universities: Studium Generale and the Origins of University Education in Europe*. Trans. Richard North (Cambridge, MA.: Cambridge University Press, 1997).

Pelikan, Jaroslav. *The Idea of the University: A Reexamination* (Yale: Yale University Press, 1992).

Readings, Bill. *The University in Ruins* (Harvard: Harvard University Press, 1996).

Ryan, Alvan S. 'The Development of Newman's Political Thought'. *The Review of Politics*, 7:2 (April 1945), 210–24.

Said, Edward W. *The Edward Said Reader*. Ed. Moustafa Bayoumi and Andrew Rubin (New York: Vintage, 2000).

——. *Orientalism* (London: Penguin, 2003).

Shumway, David R. 'National Knowledges: The Humanities and Nationality'. *Poetics Today*, 19:3 (Autumn 1998), 357–73.

Sisson, Elaine. *Pearse's Patriots: St. Enda's and the Cult of Boyhood* (Cork: Cork University Press, 2004).

Slaughter, Sheila and Gary Rhoades. *Academic Capitalism and the New Economy: Markets, State, and Higher Education* (Baltimore: The Johns Hopkins University Press, 2004).

Smyth, Gerry. *Decolonisation and Criticism: The Construction of Irish Literature* (London: Pluto, 1998).

Tierney, Michael. 'UCD Has Greatest Concern in Agricultural Institute'. *The Irish Times*, Monday, 31 October 1955, p. 4.

Tight, Malcolm. 'Crisis, What Crisis: Rhetoric and Reality in Higher Education'. *British Journal of Educational Studies*, 42:4 (December 1994), 363–74.

Turner, Frank M. 'Newman's University and Ours'. *The Idea of a University (Rethinking the Western Tradition)*. Ed. Frank M. Turner (Yale: Yale University Press, 1996), 283–301.

Van der Velden, Rolf and Emer Smyth. 'Editorial'. Special Issue: Transitions Into and Out of Higher Education. *Irish Educational Studies*, 30:2 (June 2011), 135–39.

Vickers, Edward, Flora Kan and Paul Morris. 'Colonialism and the Politics of "Chinese History" in Hong Kong's Schools'. *Oxford Review of Education*, 29:1 (March 2003), 95–111.

Walsh, Brendan. *The Pedagogy of Protest: The Educational Thought and Work of Patrick H. Pearse* (London: Peter Lang, 2007).

Washburn, Jennifer. *University, Inc.: The Corporate Corruption of Higher Education* (New York: Basic Books, 2006).

Weber, Samuel. *Institution and Interpretation. Theory and History of Literature*. Vol. 31 (Minneapolis: University of Minnesota Press, 1987).

Whyte, J. H. *Church and State in Modern Ireland: 1923–79* (Dublin: Gill & Macmillan, 1984).

Williams, Kevin and Gerry McNamara. 'The Landscape of Curriculum Inquiry in the Republic of Ireland'. *International Handbook of Curriculum Research*. Studies in Curriculum Theory Series. Ed. William F. Pinar (Mahwah: Lawrence Erlbaum Associates, 2003), 367–78.

Yao, Xinzhong. *Confucianism and Christianity: A Comparative Study of Jen and Agape* (Brighton: Sussex Academic Press, 1997).

Index